Children in Care Revisited

THE LIBRARY

University of Ulster at MAGEE

Please return to or renew at the library from which this was
borrowed by the date stamped below.

Child Care Policy and Practice
Series Editor: Tony Hall
Director and Secretary
British Agencies for Adoption and Fostering

Published:
Adoption and Race
Black, Asian and mixed race children in white families
Owen Gill and Barbara Jackson

Specialist Fostering
Martin Shaw and Tony Hipgrave

Helping Children Cope with Separation and Loss
Claudia Jewett

Long-term Foster Care
Jane Rowe, Hilary Cain, Marion Hundleby and Anne Keane

Children in Care Revisited

PAMELA MANN

Batsford Academic and Educational

in association with

British Agencies for Adoption and Fostering

First published 1984

All rights reserved. No part of this publication may be reproduced, in any form or by any means, without permission from the Publisher

Typeset by Progress Filmsetting Ltd E.C.1.
and printed in Great Britain by
Biddles Ltd
Guildford and Kings Lynn.

for the publishers
Batsford Academic and Educational Ltd, an imprint of
B.T. Batsford Ltd,
4 Fitzhardinge Street
London W1H 0AH

British Library Cataloguing in Publication Data

Mann, Pamela
    Children in care revisited.—(Child care policy and practice)
    1. Children—Institutional care—England—Case studies
    I. Title   II. Series
    362.'7'32'0922   HV751.A6

ISBN 0 7134 0928 2
ISBN 0 7134 0929 0 (Pbk)

CONTENTS

ACKNOWLEDGMENTS

Social work research is pursued most often in teams. My project was of a more personal nature, and I undertook the journey of discovery on my own. However, the young people and care-givers who welcomed me back into their lives gave a real sense of teamwork as they talked so willingly in order 'that other children might benefit'. My warmest thanks go to them.

There are other people to whom I am much indebted. Jane Rowe, Professor Elisabeth Mapstone and Gill MacGregor read and commented helpfully on the MS in whole or part; Paula Melville helped in the planning stage. Juliet Berry has contributed ideas, practical help and unflagging support. The deep commitment of these and other friends (including Clare Winnicott and Dr Colin Woodmansey) to the welfare of children and families has been a particular source of encouragement; affectionate thanks go too to the many Sheffield students with whom I have learned more about work with and for children. John Lucas of Merton College, Oxford, has shared some of his wisdom and experience as an author, and Tony Seward at Batsford has been both prompt and patient in giving advice.

I am grateful too to Professor Eric Sainsbury and other colleagues who made it possible for me to have a term's study leave; to Joan Shaw and Sylvia Parkin who spent long hours listening to and transcribing the tapes, with help from Christine Bell, Sheila Fuller and Jeanette Leaman. I was also helped by a grant from the University of Sheffield Research Fund.

Pamela Mann
October, 1983

ACKNOWLEDGMENTS

1

Introduction

Setting the scene

> I think it's nice to keep in touch – do you? . . . I was in your care, and you've come today and you've seen John and I happy, and Sharon – do you feel nice?

I agreed that I did feel nice. The questioner, Michelle, was now 30. As I looked at her sitting there in her comfortable farm cottage, I remembered her at 14, a pregnant schoolgirl, sitting silently in tears at the kitchen table while her mother emphasised the need for her to come into care.

Michelle is one of a number of children and young people on my caseload (and some of their care-givers) who have been in touch with me in some way (large or small) since I left the children's department in a county I will call Ringshire in 1968. The amount of contact has varied, ranging from spasmodic requests for help or comfort in crises, or news about particular life events – an engagement, a wedding invitation or photographs, the arrival of a baby, the death of a parent or partner – to regular or occasional Christmas cards and letters. Most of the young people have been known to me now for nearly 20 years – for some that is all their lives, and for others a substantial part of it.

This may not be as unusual an occurrence in the life of a social worker (turned social work teacher) as may at first appear. Probably numerous members of the former child care service could claim that at least a handful of young people still seek them out. (Lomax-Simpson and Gwen James are perhaps rare in the degree to which they have shared their lives and homes with children in care and after.)[1] Those of us who are prepared to sustain such long-term contact are of course open to accusations of possessiveness, of 'unprofessional' holding on. I cannot speak for others, but certainly have myself enjoyed the continuing contact; however, apart from my sending Christmas and birthday cards initially, contact was initiated by the project people.

Perhaps because this kind of long-term 'passive availability'[2] can draw criticism, and is less fashionable than short-term contracts or task-centred work, virtually nothing has been written about it. Also,

1

recent mobility of social workers gives less opportunity to build up a long-term picture of the unfolding of a child's life for which there is public responsibility. Perhaps related to this, young social workers may find it hard to accept how important they can become to a child in care. Occasionally, however, when I have talked about on-going contact, some social work students have appeared relieved and mentioned, a bit shamefacedly, a child who is still in touch or who has been to their home (or indeed an old lady who still looks forward to the occasional visit).

Partly then to try to legitimise this willingness to keep in touch when needed, and taking advantage of a term's study leave, I undertook a small project of following up more systematically some of these young people who are still known to me. The study had two main purposes: *first*, to obtain the views of the young people on their experiences in care and after, and of the social work intervention, in the hope that this consumer opinion might help me and others in our teaching, and *second*, to examine the need of children and young people growing up in care to be known by at least one constant person throughout their childhood, and to have the opportunity during their subsequent young adulthood to discuss again difficult life events which were hard to understand at the time.

This was obviously going to be a different kind of project from one where a social work researcher is interviewing people previously unknown, and is sometimes worried at not being able to give help when this is sought or noticeably needed. I had some anxieties about going back as a researcher to people whom I had earlier tried to help, but I also hoped from the outset that there would be a therapeutic component in my meeting with the young people, and saw this as attendant on both the purposes outlined above.

In relation to the first objective, it has already been found in other social work studies which have elicited consumer opinion, that it is helpful to people 'on the receiving end' to be asked for their opinion about a service they received.[3] Kahan,[4] who as Children's Officer for Oxfordshire met with a small group of people who had grown up in the care of her authority, advocates a wider use of this potential source of information. There is more emphasis now, particularly since the work of the Who Cares? groups,[5] and NAYPIC (National Association for Young People in Care), on consulting young people about plans etc., though it is still easy for them to feel relatively impotent. I hoped that it might give these young people more sense of control over their lives to be asked even retrospectively how they might like things to have been different.

The exploration of my second concern about the need of children and young people in care to be known long term and to have opportunities for later discussion, had an even more explicit therapeutic potential. As a child care officer it had been important to me to try to preserve continuity for the children in my care and to help them keep their sense of identity. I had made considerable use of my camera in keeping them in touch with their parents, and made life-story books with or for some of them (a good many years before it became recommended practice).[6] In going back now I hoped to be able to enhance their sense of identity – in a sense this reunion might prove to be an extension of the life-story book, bringing it up to date and recapitulating and reflecting on earlier events.

Tom O'Neil,[7] brother of Dennis who was killed in his foster-home in 1945, describes how he wrestled with the hurt of his own past, particularly during his residential social work training; and how he helped his brother Terry revisit Bank Farm, the fateful foster home he had shared with Dennis. He shows how it is possible to be freed to live better with painful memories. Kahan[8] also showed how the adults with whom she talked valued the later opportunity to discuss reasons for their reception and separation from their families; and Berry[9] has recently suggested that this facility might well be made available more generally, to give young adults another chance to discuss events which earlier were too painful to absorb. As one of the group in Kahan's study said, 'Fear gives you a blind which you pull down and it's just impossible to pull it back again.'[10]

This could be seen to be helpful generally. It might be that my going back as someone who had known these young people when they were growing up or were troubled could have an added advantage. I hoped in meeting them again to help them to rediscover themselves in my eyes through feedback or reflection from someone who has known and been fond of them over a substantial period of their lives and has gone on caring about what happened to them. I was obviously influenced here by Winnicott's mirror reflection model.[11] He suggested that in terms of emotional development, what the baby sees when he or she looks into the mother's face is him or herself. 'In other words the mother is looking at the baby and *what she looks like is related to what she sees there.*'

Winnicott relates this metaphor of the reflecting face, and later the actual mirror, to the psychotherapeutic task. 'Psychotherapy is not making clever and apt interpretations; by and large it is a long-term giving the patient back what the patient brings. It is a complex derivative of the face that reflects what is there to be seen. I like to think of my work in this way, and to think that if I do this well enough the patient will find his or her own self, and will be able to exist and to feel real.'[12] He was writing about psychotherapy, but as Tonnesmann[13] suggests he would have been likely to agree that this metaphor could equally be applied to all human encounters in the caring professions. It seems to me that this long-term giving back is particularly relevant to work with children in care whose lives apart from their original parents can so often leave them uncertain about themselves.

Linked with Winnicott's idea, another obvious influence was Rogers and his recommendation that the worker needs to show warm regard (neither possessive nor earned) so that the client may come to accept himself because he sees himself as accepted by the worker.[14] The worker mirrors back to him her affectionate acceptance of what she sees and the client experiences himself as lovable.

Sometimes it seems that one of the hazards for a child or young person growing up in care can be that he or she lacks sufficient affectionate feedback about him or herself to be able to develop a comfortable sense of identity and well-being. Some of the young people in the study had been more fortunate in this respect than others, and I wanted to see which of these care (and after) experiences had been most helpful, and to contribute something to their belief in themselves by my own long-term interest and affection for them.

I was also naturally most interested to see how they were faring, what capacity they now had for relationships, for coping in the adult world, and what kind of parents they might be making.

As mentioned earlier, a number of the care-givers of these young people had also been in touch from time to time and I wanted to visit them as well. Here again there were two main purposes: *first*, to obtain their views of the experience of being foster/adoptive/house–parents to the young people, and of the social work input, and *second*, to value what they had done for the young people – that is in some way also enhancing their sense of themselves as parent-figures with a job to do.

Setting up the project

I first had to identify the young people and care-givers who came within

the scope of the project. I found I had a potential sample of 17 young people and nine care-giver couples or individuals. (There were a further two young people who had not been in touch themselves though their care-givers had.) This is a small group, but they form a cross section of the kind of family troubles which can lead to children needing substitute care – and some of the alternative responses to this need.

They included a large family of children who had grown up in residential care, long and short-stay foster-children, including two fostered by relatives and one who was mentally retarded, a young single parent whose baby was adopted, and four children who were adopted – in infancy and at one, three and 11 years respectively.

Before I approached them I wrote to the present Director of Social Services in Ringshire to ask for his co-operation, and permission to refer to the files if necessary. If the young people wanted to review past events and how these reflect upon their present identity, I thought I might need to refer to the files to refresh my memory of events, their parents' circumstances and the reasons for their entering care.

The Director could not agree to my having access to the files without the knowledge of the young people concerned. The whole question of clients' access to their files is of course a controversial one, and some social workers are pressing currently for 'open' files, designed for this purpose. These were past files, and under present departmental policy in Ringshire adults who had been in care would not have direct access to the information which is held on their files, but the information could be shared with them at their request. He therefore suggested that I discuss the matter with them by letter or telephone; and that subject to their agreement I could have access to the files, provided that 'the contents are not disclosed to any person other than the person to whom the file relates, and that any confidential information shared is done so in a professional manner with due regard for its significance and possible emotional impact on the current life situation of the person involved.'

I appreciated the caution of this response, and also the Director's concern for the current emotional well-being of the young people. His compromise suggestion seemed a fair one, but I did not want to ask all the young people in advance of meeting them if they would agree to my having access to their files, as this might have worried them unnecessarily. I decided to rely as far as I could on my memory, and we agreed that if when I saw the young people any of them wanted information which I could not recall, I would ask them if they would mind my referring to their file. If they wanted information or clarification about events which took place after I left Ringshire I suggested that it might be more appropriate to encourage them to seek this for themselves.

The delicacy of the task I was undertaking was further brought home to me when I came to design two interview schedules, one for the young people and one for the care-givers. Both schedules needed to allow space for reunion and our finding where we were with each other. The people I would be meeting might well have expectations of me or particular things they wanted to talk about, and any schedule would need to allow scope for this. Also my questions needed to be helpful for them to discuss as well as informative to me. I wanted them to feel that it *was* a discussion and that I was interested in them, not just in obtaining information for my own purposes.

I hoped to overcome some of these difficulties by my own preferred style of interviewing, which owes its development to two main influences. The first is Rogers's client-centred non-directive approach, with its emphasis on empathy and the use of comments where possible rather than questions.[15] The second (and related) influence has been in psychotherapeutic supervision from Dr Colin Woodmansey, who has helped me to feel at ease in being aware of and bringing out dissatisfactions or fears present in the interaction, and in trying to see which fears one is responding to in an alternating transference.[16] His belief that people need to be cared about and that this cures a lot of ills is obviously also relevant to this study.

The areas I hoped to discuss with the young people were, first, their *present circumstances*: how things were with them now in terms of general well-being, employment, education, resources in their local community, and in particular their capacity for relationships, how satisfying these were and whether they felt their own experiences influenced their approach to marriage or cohabitation, parenthood etc. Then, moving to the past and *recollections of care experiences*, I hoped they would be able to talk about relationships with care-givers, their contacts with natural parents, their understanding of why they were in care and whether they received enough help to talk about this, a sense of plans or otherwise; *recollections of social workers* and how we might have been more helpful, their *contacts with me since* and what they had hoped for from these. *Leaving care* was an important issue, their sense of preparedness or not and to whom they felt they could turn. I wanted to stress their *potential influence on my teaching* and to invite their views on what they thought was important to teach social work students. Then in rounding off the interview, I wanted to hear more about their *present feelings about themselves*, and finally the *experience of the interview*, how it had been for them, whether they had had mixed feelings on getting my letter, and whether there were any uncertainties that still needed clarifying.

The interview schedule I had in mind in talking with the care-givers mirrored the one for the young people, dealing with virtually the same range of topics applied to their own viewpoint; for example, how they were now, what sense of satisfaction they had in having 'fledged' the children they had cared for, together with their perception of them now.

There were many other people with whom I had worked in Ringshire that I would have liked to meet again but who did not come within the scope of the project. There were indeed two other mothers of families I had known who had also been in touch, one regularly at Christmas and one in a crisis. However, the children of the first mother had never been in care, and although the stepchildren of the second had, I think her desperate appeal to me had been unknown to them so it did not seem appropriate to include them in the study. Because I chose those who had in some way chosen to be in touch with me, it seemed more likely that they would be willing to take part. I considered approaching a control group of young people and care-givers who had not kept in touch, and it would have been interesting to examine the differences. Had they found me unhelpful, or had they other people to turn to? Although I would have had fairly easy access to a number of them, others would have needed tracing, and, as my first group was already quite scattered, in the end constraints of time and distance decided me against enlarging the study.

I wrote to the young people and care-givers I have described, and eventually 13 of the original 17 young people and eight of the nine care-giver couples or individuals agreed to see me. Of the two additional young people whose care-givers rather than themselves had been in touch, Ralph (chapter 4) was abroad, and Cherie (who was less than three when I left) did not want to see me. Mrs Knight (her foster-mother who adopted her and who figures in chapters 4 and 8) did not want Cherie to be upset and decided not to see me either. Elaine, the eldest of the Waldo family (chapter 2) whom the others see as having cut herself off, did not reply, and the youngest, Sally, agreed to see me and then retracted. Mark's elder sister (chapter 3) was (I understood from him) intending to reply but was preoccupied with a current crisis, and my letter did not reach his younger sister.

Of those who did return the reply form agreeing to take part in the project, quite a number also wrote a warm accompanying letter, often beginning, 'What a lovely surprise'. Some, according to their circumstances, invited me to a meal or to stay; they wanted me to see their children, meet their husbands etc. It was an encouraging response.

The interviews

This group of people had once all lived within a thirty-mile radius of the Paxton area office where I was based. Some were still in the same houses I used to visit, but others had moved away, a number of them to other parts of the country, and I myself had moved two hundred miles, so planning my visits now was something of a jigsaw. In the event I made a number of rounds of visits, each lasting about a week, travelling in all about three thousand miles.

I started my journeys in April when the blackthorn was in flower, so the wind was cold but there was a green haze in the woods and the hedgerows were full of primroses. I had often been back to Ringshire but this return felt as if it had a special significance. I was retracing some of my own life-story in setting out to meet a group of young adults whom I had known as children, and it occurred to me as I drove that I might be wanting to confirm my own identity as a social worker.

I was able to stay with or visit a number of friends who lived near the project people. My affection for all these friends and involvement in their joys and sorrows added an extra dimension to my reunion with the people in the project (and vice versa), as in all our interactions – personal or professional – we draw on resources within ourselves which are fed and nurtured by loving relationships. Returning to Winnicott's mirror image metaphor, perhaps the degree to which we are able to be a friendly mirror which reflects kindly what we see relates not only to what we see but to the reflections we have received ourselves from others – again either in our personal relationships or professionally in helpful supervision. It is another way of looking at the concept of care for the care-givers[17] and at the belief that giving and receiving are closely related. These were concepts which were also likely to have some bearing on the people in the project.

All the interviews lasted at least two hours, and where I was invited for a meal or to stay we were together for three to four hours or longer.

8

It was not easy to keep to my outline for the interviews, particularly when people had much to tell me. I did not use a questionnaire and did not want to formalise our meetings by producing a schedule, so memorised a list of headings and worked out before each interview the particular relevance or otherwise of the questions to the people I would be seeing.

I hoped to tape-record the interviews, with their agreement; no one objected though two or three were initially nervous of it. I had not used a tape-recorder myself before in interviews, because although this is an accepted mode of learning how to improve one's skills, and a respected research tool, I had always feared that someone I was there to help would feel that I was trying to get something out of the interview for my own purposes rather than concentrating on his or her needs, and that the machine would thus almost inevitably be counter-therapeutic. In these interviews I apologised if I seemed to be coming back because of the project rather than just to see them. As far as I could tell, it seemed as though I was able to carry out the therapeutic part of my project in spite of the tape-recorder, but on one occasion where one of the young people was in tears over a past hurt that still needed comforting, I turned off the machine for a while. And on another occasion one of them was so full of a pressing need to talk that it was some time before I felt able to ask if I could use it.

I was aware, as Lishman had been, of dangers of subjectivity in examining my own work. In a small exploratory study she returned to interview some of her own clients (in a Child Guidance setting) six months after closure, to investigate what factors in her work had contributed to their satisfaction or dissatisfaction and whether there had been a clash in perspective.[18] I would be looking back over a longer period, which I hoped might aid objectivity; but because work with children in care can involve responsibility for a wide span of their lives, I knew the young people – and their care-givers – might well have strong positive or negative feelings about how I or other social workers had served them as well as possible difficulties still in expressing these, of which I would need to be aware.

The historical and legal context of the project needs to be borne in mind. I was looking back to the child care service in the mid to late 1960s. The Children Act, 1948, which established local authority children's departments from the blueprint provided by the Curtis Committee,[19] was swallowed up by the consolidating Child Care Act, 1980, just as in 1971 children's departments themselves were absorbed into the large new generic social services departments. Therefore the legislation under which we worked then now has different section numbers and I have referred to current usage for clarity. A historical survey cannot be dealt with so summarily, but Pugh[20] gives a comprehensive picture of the work of children's departments and the values, policies and practice pertaining then, while Packman[21] traces developments in child care policy from the Curtis Report through into the 1980s.

All the young people in the project had by definition experienced separation from their own parents. For some this was ameliorated more than for others, and some lost other parent figures subsequently. 'Care' which sounds so safe and comforting is, alas, no guarantee against further disruptions. Separation has become theoretically controversial, not least because of its emotional undertones for researchers and practitioners as well. I must declare a debt to Bowlby (often misunderstood and misquoted) particularly in his later work on attachment and loss[22] and the roots of self-reliance;[23] also to the Robertsons[24] in their unflagging efforts to help people develop more understanding of the meaning of separation to small children and how the experience may be eased. The Clarkes[25] provide encouraging evidence of children's resilience when subsequent good experiences are maintained, though they seem more interested in cognitive than emotional development. Rutter[26] in his second edition of *Maternal Deprivation Reassessed* reaches the more cautious conclusion that humans are remarkably and gratifyingly resilient, but that early disadvantage may not be totally reversed by later experience. There does seem to be some agreement now that what happened *before* the separation (e.g. security, or parental conflict or hostility) and *after* it (in terms of better experience or further disadvantage) have more long-term effects on a child than the actual separation experience itself. However, as both Bowlby and the Robertsons maintain, separation remains hazardous and should be avoided wherever possible. This book illustrates the varied meanings of the experience for a group of young people.

As Gill and Jackson[27] write from their experience of interviews with black adolescents in the British Adoption Project, 'with all such fieldwork, there is ultimately no way of telling the extent to which respondents are allowing the researcher to enter their lives'. On the other hand, I share their confidence that the young people tried to answer the questions as honestly as possible, and I had the added

advantage of coming as a known person. In presenting them it will be obvious that apart from my earlier relationship with them, I know as much of them as they have told me in the time available and as I have observed. For some this could amount to a very partial picture of the complexity of their lives in the intervening years. So far as space allows I have let the young people and care-givers speak for themselves, but otherwise the perceptions of them are mine.

It is also necessary to make clear that I am writing about them mainly from the standpoint of personal relationships. Other valid perspectives of a more socio-political nature would also contribute to an understanding of their situations and life chances. If I had worn those spectacles it would be a different kind of book; only in chapter 11 does Liz insist on more weight being given to that kind of analysis.

This was obviously not the kind of large statistical study from which I could draw generalised findings which might influence policy. I hope its usefulness will lie more in the direction of presenting consumer accounts of the experiences of children and young people in care (bearing in mind all the influences on their perceptions), which could be an aid to empathy for practitioners working with children in care now. And because some consumer studies select themes for discussion and illustrate these with clusters of views from the people interviewed, it can be difficult to keep in mind the profiles of the individuals concerned. For these two reasons I have given each of these young people a chapter to themselves, either individually or in families, so that their stories can more easily be followed. Names and placenames have been changed to safeguard confidentiality, and most of the people concerned chose their own pseudonyms.

. . . too often it has been assumed that those who provided the services knew best, so that there was no need to ask the wearer of the shoe where it pinched. Yet only those going through any experience can know how it feels, and, after all, how it feels to them is how it *is* to them.

Eileen Younghusband[28]
Foreword to *Growing up in Care*

2

The Waldo family and their housemother

You can tell them there was a family . . .

Was Tolstoy right when he wrote, 'All happy families resemble one another, each unhappy family is unhappy in its own way'?[1] Certainly there seems no limit to the ways in which the unhappy families whom social workers meet can be hurt or hurt each other, though many of course also share a common vulnerability to economic pressures.

Money was not particularly short in the Waldo family, but Mrs Waldo seemed to lack the basic capacity for mothering and as her family expanded dealt with this by leaving them for a period after she had given birth to the next child. From the viewpoint of her seven children this unnatural behaviour was hard to understand or forgive. From hers it might be said that she was in the unenviable position of being expected to bear children whom she had no ability to nurture. Would some of my more radical students, particularly the feminists, have wanted to stimulate her capacity to assert herself rather than be trapped in a situation where she could not succeed?

Queen Victoria, that epitome of respectability, had no taste either for child-bearing. 'I think, dear Uncle,' she wrote to King Leopold of the Belgians, 'you cannot really wish me to be the *"Mama d'une nombreuse famille"* . . . Men never think what a hard task it is for us women to go through this very often.' If someone with all her advantages had no stomach (emotionally) for the task, how much harder must it be for mothers who are less cushioned against the exigencies of family life. Mrs Waldo married at a time when society still offered no really acceptable alternative role to working-class women who had no particular educational aspirations, and when the pill was not yet freely available.

Mrs Waldo always returned to her husband and he always wanted her back. However, their relationship was stormy and the pattern would repeat itself as Mrs Waldo deserted after the next baby was born. At times she also took flight before a court summons on a charge of larceny, or was absent in prison; but whatever the cause, each time the children came into care.

The family lived in another area and I have no direct knowledge of their early placements. It was often not possible for them to return to the same foster-parents, and this must have compounded their separation experiences and their sense of not being wanted and somehow to blame for what was happening. They were in voluntary care each time under what is now Section 2 of the Child Care Act, 1980[2] and were returned at the request of their parents. There were no legal powers then to prevent this repetitive 'yo-yo' movement in and out of care,[3] but when Elaine the eldest was twelve, and Sally the youngest was two, the need for a longer-term plan was evident. A decision was made to bring the seven children, who had usually been scattered in different foster-homes and children's homes, together as a family and to try to give them some stability.

It so happened that five places in a small family group home in Paxton became free at the same time – a rare event – and Elaine (aged 12), Kathleen (11), Charlie (8), Wally (7) and Maxine (6) came to live at 7, Mulberry Close, while Paula (aged 3) and Sally (2) were found a foster home in the neighbourhood. Shortly after, an anonymous allegation was made that there were bruises on Paula. This was just before the general professional realisation about child abuse[4] and over a decade before the series of child deaths (starting with Maria Colwell's in 1974) resulting in public inquiries which have made social services departments so nervous of the possibility that injuries may be non-accidental. However, although there were doubts as to whether the foster-father was responsible, the memory of Dennis O'Neil's death at the hands of his foster-father was still influential and the risk was not taken. So to the foster-mother's distress, Paula and Sally were moved to complete the family at Mulberry Close. By that time these two small children had had 12–13 moves.

A number of child care officers had tried to help Mr and Mrs Waldo and because of Mr Waldo's eagerness to hold his wife and family together for years there had always seemed some ground for hope. This was the decade before the Children and Young Persons Act, 1963 gave local authorities their main preventive powers, but the department had anticipated the Act and was in the forefront of family casework.[5] Perhaps they persevered in trying to keep the Waldo family intact longer than was in the children's interests. Certainly Mrs Waldo's emotional handicap and lack of affect became increasingly obvious and more than one child care officer said that it seemed dangerous to encourage her beyond her capabilities. So once the children were together in Mulberry Close they grew up there, cared for throughout by the same housemother, Mrs Meg Plover.

With the help of her husband (who had employment outside the Home) and assistant staff, Meg Plover tried to provide for the Waldo children the security and consistent affection which they had lacked. She is a warm, caring, ebullient woman, strongly partial to the children who claimed her as 'Auntie'. She worked hard to create a lively affectionate unit and achieved something very close to the Curtis Committee's ideal model of a homely family base for a small group of children.[6] She had no illusions that she could fully compensate the children for the loss of their own parents or that it was possible in residential care to provide a real sense of family. But she did establish a caring base for them, which they called 'home', and to which they continued to look after they had grown up.

I took over the supervision of the children from our Area Officer, M.R.V., when they had been at Mulberry Close about two and a half years. There were no Homes Advisers then – middle-management staff with special responsibility for particular residential units. Instead, field staff who were linked with Children's Homes had statutory responsibility for the children and also tried to work as supportive colleagues to the residential staff. This had its disadvantages. It is much easier to concentrate on the viewpoint of a care-giver if you know another social worker will be listening to the child, and Berry[7] has provided evidence of the effectiveness of care for the care-givers in residential work. In her study of 44 units she found that the quality of care provided for the children was closely linked with the quality of support received by the staff.

I dealt with the double responsibility by concentrating mainly on listening to Meg Plover on my visits and less frequently talked with the children when she was off duty, knowing that she was well able to talk with them about their troubles and had many more natural opportunities for this than I. Not surprisingly, after such disturbing beginnings, the Waldo children showed a range of behaviour problems. Meg Plover understood the cause of these as well as I and did not need explanations from me so much as my appreciation of the daily (and nightly) difficulties of enuresis, rocking and stealing, and the children's wariness about relationships. There were hurts to comfort too, and Meg Plover felt these with them – other children's thoughtless (or sometimes deliberate) teasing at school about their parents, and their mother's inability to appreciate their feelings on her spasmodic visits.

All the children had good looks – one gift at least from their parents. Elaine seemed the most bitter about the deficiencies of their family life and the multiple moves, and she had little sympathy to spare for her brothers and sisters; she perhaps resented that she would be the first to leave their newly found security. When I commented once that she perhaps felt angry with her mother for not looking after them, she said bleakly, 'I hate her.' Kathleen was gentler, soon became very attached to Meg Plover and feared having to leave her. Charlie was a 'loner' when I knew him, and showed his affections (I thought then) most openly to pet animals. His rabbit Hoppity earned certain notoriety by repeatedly burrowing under the fence to eat the neighbours' lettuces, and I had to placate an irate visitor to the area office. Both he and Wally were very loyal to Mr Waldo, looked forward to his visits and boasted to their schoolfriends about what he would do for them. They were also attached to 'Uncle' and Wally enjoyed accompanying him to the Plovers' cottage to help in the garden, and was proud of a piece of wall he had helped to build. Maxine had been the most disturbed when she came to Mulberry Close aged six, a very withdrawn child who did not speak to Meg Plover for several weeks and just rocked to comfort herself. Her last foster home had broken down because the foster parents' young son regressed when Maxine sought their affection, and this apparent rejection, compounding earlier separations, had turned her in on herself. The two little ones were natural companions, though Paula had that rather frightening eagerness of some children in residential care and related shallowly to every visitor, while Sally was a nervous, shy little girl with many fears.

Meg Plover had a great gift of fun and laughter and was able to make ordinary routine events enjoyable, as well as showing her exasperation at times – and was then remorseful. The children knew her weakness for having her toes tickled and would happily sit in front of the fire in the evening attending to this. (When I reminded her recently she said that this pleasure is now called Reflexology![8]) The Plovers' two daughters became close to the Waldos and grew up with them.

Elaine left school and moved from Mulberry Close into a residential domestic job at a nearby girls' boarding school. I was soon to move, too, to become a tutor in child care. Just as I was leaving Ringshire (and perhaps because I was) Elaine was more able to talk about her fears that she must have been very bad for her mother to have left home so often – an extra burden she had carried too long. It was hard to leave children who had known so many changes. I introduced my successor, R.G.,

15

and took photographs of the Waldos in the garden. I sent them each one of themselves to keep, and as a token that I was taking a reminder of them with me.

Three years later I received a letter from R.G. – Charlie had been killed in a motorcycle accident. I grieved to think of him and of the family at Mulberry Close and knew I must be with them for his funeral the next morning. (R.G., who was leaving, could not be there.) I drove the 200 miles overnight and arrived to find them all gathered in the house, except the two youngest. They were dazed and shocked by Charlie's sudden and untimely death; Meg Plover, who had mothered him, was stricken too, as were her husband and daughters. Mrs Waldo was in prison, but Mr Waldo was there and his unhappy silent presence added to the general sense of strangeness.

I was amazed and moved to find the church full of young people. I remembered Charlie as a gentle, vulnerable, 14-year-old who was still a 'loner'. However, when he left school he had enjoyed a steady gardening job and at 17 had attracted quite a wide circle of friends – and here they were to mourn him. It was good, too, to see ex-colleagues, including the Director of Social Services. It is not easy for a local authority to be a parent and there is an extra sense of sadness when a boy or girl dies in care.

We went on to the cemetery on this gold September morning. As we made a circle Mr Waldo stood looking down into his eldest son's grave. He swayed perilously over its depths and for a nightmarish moment I thought he might fall in. One could only guess the content of his misery. He turned abruptly and strode off across the cemetery. As we watched, Wally ran after him and they disappeared together.

Afterwards at Mulberry Close Meg, in spite of her sadness, was as ever the warm, comforting hub of the house. There was time now to talk of Charlie and for me to hear all the events of the evening he died. R.G. had virtually left; her successor, though there, had barely started, and for a day I slipped back into my old role as their child care officer/social worker.

There is a growing body of knowledge, not exclusive to social work, about the needs of bereaved people and how one can try to help.[9] Anyone who has lost someone important knows the frequent awkwardness of other people who seem to lose their ability to be natural in the face of death. I have found there is a barrier, even between people who are normally close, until the actual name of the dead person is spoken. He or she is the sole preoccupation of a bereaved person or family as they desperately try to recover and recreate the image of the person who has died, so as to be able to hold it in their heart and mind's eye. Everyone at Mulberry Close that day was still stunned in the initial stage of shock and disbelief, but I knew they would be helped by talking about Charlie and remembering past anecdotes. So after I had heard about the accident itself, we also recalled earlier times and were even able to smile over Hoppity's escapades, and the burned poker marks which still decorated the kitchen floor (an experiment of Charlie's not popular at the time!). Mr Waldo arrived back with Wally when the pubs closed and I sat with him in the garden for a while.

Our sorrow brought us all close together that day. In times of crisis we are more open to feelings and it is possible that I helped the Waldos more in those few hours than in several years of routine visits.[10] They regretted they had no recent photograph of Charlie, so I later sent them each a copy of the one I had taken of him three years before and an enlargement for the mantlepiece.

They were more in touch with me after that day. Elaine wrote a dozen times or more in the next couple of years – about her boy friends, jobs etc. In her first letter she said, 'I think it was very brave of me to walk with Dad behind the coffin when I hadn't seen him for three years. I didn't know what to say, so just said "Hullo".' It is hard when feelings are too strong for words and must be harder still when there are no words. Maxine had more of an aptitude for expressing herself and kept up a spasmodic correspondence for about six years. Paula, too, wrote quite often, wanting a photo of me and immediate replies.

I heard periodically from Meg Plover about their escapades and troubles. In turn they had to leave Mulberry Close and make their way at the vulnerable age of 16 or 17 in lodgings or residential jobs. They were luckier than the many young people leaving residential care who are represented by the remark in *Who Cares?*[11], 'Even though you've lived in a children's home all your life you don't feel you belong there once you've left,' and who often find strange staff if they do return. The Waldos' beds were soon occupied by new children, but Meg Plover was still there and somehow found a corner for any of them when they needed refuge and the walls became elastic at Christmas time. People who have never been homeless, or lacked a secure base which can be taken for granted when trouble comes, may find it hard to imagine the loneliness of many young people leaving residential care. 'Well for the man on such a night,' wrote Turgenev, 'who sits under the shelter of home, who has a warm corner in safety.' And the poet Robert Frost has a definition, 'Home is the place where when you have to go they have to take you in.' It was not easy for Meg Plover to take them in, but she usually did and continued to make them feel they could come 'home'.

At the time of my project Elaine was 30, Sally was 20, and Meg Plover had been at Mulberry Close for 21 years. Meg, together with Kathleen, Wally, Maxine and Paula all agreed to see me, but there was no reply from Elaine, now married, who had virtually cut herself off from the family.

Sally agreed initially to see me but became so agitated at the prospect that it seemed wrong to continue. She was fearful that people in her residential job might discover she had been in care. More than any of her brothers and sisters she had felt the stigma which arises from the widespread misunderstanding that all children, whatever their route into care, are themselves to blame for their status.[12] Elaine had an internalised sense of badness; Sally was terrified that other people would despise her if they knew about her background. If the framework of your first 18 years casts a secret shadow which no one else must see, not much space is left to be yourself in daily living. I felt dissatisfied that I could do no more than write a letter to try to comfort her. More important was the fact that although she sometimes hides for a while even from Meg Plover, she does periodically get in touch. I remember watching Meg with Sally in hospital when, aged six, she had an appendix operation, and that kind of comforting over the years must have given her something to hold on to.

The four Waldos who were willing to see me were scattered well away from Ringshire and each other and it was a moving experience seeking them in turn and piecing together the composite family story. However, Kathleen (the second to eldest, whom I saw first) does not want her part of the chapter included. She talked freely of the painfulness of the past but does not want her feelings about it published, and I had to accept this loss to the chapter. She was very welcoming, appeared fortunate in her marriage and to be enjoying her two small children. Seeing her with her own family I felt hopeful for her.

Paula, the next Waldo I saw, was less happily placed and her plight was a cause of worry to her family and to Meg Plover. Her first baby had been adopted and now, eight months pregnant, she was in a Probation hostel. She had answered my letter by return and sounded depressed when I telephoned. She was looking out for me from her window, came down to greet me barefooted and took me up to her bed-sitting-room. I was struck by her height – Paula had been one of the two 'little ones' and here she was, 21, splendidly tall and pregnant. Paula was in a strange town a long way from Mulberry Close. She was very homesick for Meg Plover, glad of any link with her, and on tenterhooks about her reaction. She had not found it easy to tell Meg she was pregnant again just because she felt so close to her. 'She wasn't exactly over the moon.' Paula was more optimistic than Meg that she could cope with this baby and was wanting a chance to prove herself.

> *Paula:* I think what hurt me most was when I couldn't before, and that ten days in hospital – and then I had to leave it and that was it. I wouldn't do it again. Auntie was there all the time, she was seeing it every day . . . But I think she'll accept it given time.
> *P.M.* It's what she feels about you that you're worried about really, isn't it? You can see Auntie accepting any baby, can't you?
> *Paula:* Oh yes! I think she's upset that it was *me*. At first I thought she'd go against me, but – I think she'll sort of like take it in her stride. Every day, each letter that she gets from me, everything I say or everything I do, she just accepts it, me the way I am – I've made a few mistakes, and I've gone back to Auntie and had a little weep . . . Being up here has like broken up a parent relationship with a daughter. I don't see Auntie now, you see, and every night when the phone rings I think, 'That could be Auntie' – but it's not. Because what you write in a letter isn't always the same as what you can say over the phone . . .
> *P.M.* It's hard to put into words on paper.

She had written to Meg Plover asking her to come and see her. She kept reiterating that the Plovers would not reject her – possibly to reassure an underlying fear that their patience was not limitless.

> *P.M.* She was there and helped you when the first baby was born – it's hard to have to manage without her this time.
> *Paula:* She came to visit *every* day last time – that's what I'll miss I think.

Having minded very much losing her first baby to adoption, Paula was the more keen to manage this time and could not really envisage her long-term problems. There is now a range of research and consumer studies which illustrate the particular difficulties which beset single-parent families,[13] and further reference to these are made in chapter 6. Paula was more preoccupied with immediate practicalities and before I left showed me a shelf of baby clothes and various other preparations. She would be able to stay on in the hostel for a few months but was essentially homeless and without visible means of support, though she did think her Probation Officer might help to get her a Council flat. She had felt close to the baby's father: 'He'd take me shopping . . . I used to do his washing, and cook his tea and darn his socks.' However, they had drifted apart since she had to move and he had not replied to her letters.

I wondered how her own experiences affected her hopes for the coming baby.

Paula: The love and affection I had as a child I'm going to make sure *mine* has. It might not be from two but it'll get as much as it can . . . Whatever happens to me, I'll make sure that nothing ever happens to my child. I'd never hurt it, and that is one thing Auntie never did to us. She never hurt us. She gave us all love. She gave us everything – so I know what it's like – except that it wasn't from the beginning – only from the age of three.

P.M. A lot had happened to you before then, hadn't it?

Paula: Not that *I* know of, but from what I can gather it did.

Not surprisingly she could remember nothing of the constant moves before she was three, nor of living with her own parents. 'Auntie and Uncle are more Mum and Dad – like stepparents.'

Paula: I always wonder where my Mum is at the moment. Sophie (her room-mate) and I were talking about our parents and family and she was saying, 'Where is your Mum? Why did she leave you?' I tried to explain my background, some of the story, not all of it.

P.M. It takes a lot of explaining, doesn't it?

Paula: Mm. I don't know where she is. I can remember what she looks like. (She sketched an unflattering word picture.) I think I remember my Dad more 'cos I was like him, I think. It was me and Charlie who were more like our Dad than any of our family.

P.M. Well, you were very like Charlie to look at.

Paula: Yes . . . I don't think it's my Mum that bothers me, I think it's the fact now that my Dad's not here, and I've lost the brother that was closest to me – I've lost them both. But it's brought me and Sally and Maxine very close.

P.M. It was very sad for you to lose Charlie.

Paula: Being close – like if I got told off and was sent to bed, it was always Charlie who used to come and say, (Whispered) 'Are you all right?' The only picture I've got of him is the one that you sent us all. (Sighed.) I'd give anything for Charlie to be alive still. I can remember what he looks like. I've got that picture at home in the photo album.

P.M. You've got a picture of him in your mind too, have you?

Paula: Oh yes. If I'm reading a book, I sort of lose my words and am thinking of something else.

P.M. It's hard that the one you were closest to was the one that got killed . . .

You perhaps feel that he might have been able to help you now.

Paula: I think Charlie would do anything for anybody, but more for me because we were close.

P.M. Sitting here talking to you reminds me very much of him, because as you say you were alike.

She talked of Sally and Wally who were also close. It had seemed especially cruel that a few years after Charlie's death, Wally had a serious car accident which resulted in his left arm being amputated. Paula had found it painful visiting him in hospital but felt closer to him. She did not know where he lived now and I promised to let her have his address. She seemed to have very little understanding of her family background.

Paula: I think at the age of 17 I found out I had a Gran. But I don't know where she is, so I can't go and see her.

P.M. It sounds as though there are a lot of things you feel you didn't know about, or weren't actually told about.

Paula: I do actually. There's a lot more that I should know that I don't. Like what happened in our family, what happened really between my Mum and Dad and why she kept running off and doing the things she did.

P.M. Well, it might be hard for her to say why, even if you'd got her here.

Paula: (Forcefully) I wouldn't want to get her here . . . I'd ask Auntie, I'd ask anybody, but if she was sat here – I'd more likely try and plonk her one.

P.M. Because you're so fed up with her.

Paula: I used to get tired of seeing her – although we didn't see her that often. I think when a parent comes to see their child in a place where they're happy, that drags it all back down.

P.M. Perhaps you feel I'm bringing it all back now when we're talking about it . . . She just did seem to find it very hard to be a mother.

Paula: Yes, but when you say things like that it means that some of us, like Maxine, me and Sally – we weren't even supposed to be there! As though we were a mistake. If she found it so hard to be a mother why have so many children?

P.M. That's very hard to understand, isn't it?

Paula: But if I were to see her now – I just wouldn't want to know. She could sit there and cry – I don't think it would hurt me at all. That sounds rough, but –

P.M. *You* had it rough, didn't you? But you're feeling as though you were a mistake, as though that was your fault – as if there was something wrong about you, instead –

Paula: No, I think it's more if she found it so hard to be a mother, then why have seven kids? You can't blame it all on my Dad – takes two. (Pause.)

P.M. It just is very hurtful to think you were brought into the world by a

woman that didn't –
Paula: Didn't care.
P.M. That didn't have it in her to care perhaps. That's a hard thing to live with.
Paula: I don't know – I think we could have had someone a lot worse than Auntie and Uncle. I think they were really good – we could have had some old battle-axe like my Mum.
P.M. They made up for a lot, didn't they?
Paula: Yes. They made up the price of about four or five parents – they were *always* there. (Pause.)

She thought Elaine and Kathleen knew more what had happened between her parents and complained of unfairness – that some of the family knew and others didn't. It seemed that she had not asked about her circumstances as she was growing up, and only began to wonder more when she was older. 'Maybe we were told so much but not enough to know what was going on in our family.' It is possible to be *told* something painful without fully hearing it. I encouraged her to ask Meg Plover more. It seemed likely that there would have been some discussion with Paula, and she would have heard talk about their parents. The fact remains that she did seem to know almost nothing about her family history and we should be careful not to assume that younger family members have also understood.

P.M. Perhaps you're feeling that I didn't talk with you enough about it.
Paula: (Laughed.) I can't remember when I last saw you – I was 9 or 10. (Pause.) I think I'd like to go right back and start all over again.
P.M. Would you, Paula? And what would be different?
Paula: I'd go back – knock out bits. It upsets me because I don't see Auntie and Uncle. I just lie on my bed and all the tears flow.
P.M. Ah. Because you miss them so –
Paula: I really feel I was quite close to them – and not having them here knocks me down a bit.
P.M. Well, you and Sally had the longest stay with them . . . What things would you like to change?
Paula: I couldn't think anything bad about Auntie and Uncle – it's after I left them that I'd want to change.
P.M. Things that went wrong for you.
Paula: Yes – and other things like with Dad dying, and Charlie being killed.

Her sadness at the loss of these particular two members of her family interwove with the theme of her lack of knowledge about why she was in care, which in its way seemed like another form of loss. I was concerned at her sense of ignorance about her family history at the moment when she was waiting for her own child (and perhaps we did not talk enough about her first baby who was adopted). Her predicament was already serious, and it is hard to look forward if the past is uncertain. Also Pincus and others [14] suggest that a daughter can assume her mother's identity, and Paula was half-prepared to accept the family myth that she might become a second Mrs Waldo.

She did not find it easy to identify what social workers need to do or know, and her picture of me was more 'received' through Meg Plover than her own impression. She saw me as 'doing the job properly', and 'all you can teach them is what you know, what you learned when *you* started'.

Paula: You didn't cut yourself off from us anyway.

P.M. Well, you wrote to me quite a bit – what do you suppose you were hoping for?

Paula: I think it's just that someone that's done a lot for your family, I think it's nice that just one or two of that family should keep in touch with that person . . . I think Auntie and you, put yourselves together, do a lot for our one family . . . You never kept anything away unless you thought at that time it was going to hurt us by telling us. (Pause.) But I hope your students get on well, I really do!

P.M. I don't know whether you feel it spoils it that I should come back partly in order to help my students?

Paula: No, I don't. I think what you can find out and what we think that you've done for *us* – I think it'll help your students a lot.

P.M. But I'm also interested in you and in what's happened to you.

Paula: In me! I don't think I've changed – I think I always look the same.

P.M. You're a good-looking girl, Paula.

Paula: I don't think so – not all the time. Bad tempered I am at the moment.

P.M. You're feeling miserable.

Paula: I think it's just depression. The last month or so it really gets you down; it gets heavy and you could take it off and fling it somewhere. But you can't.

P.M. Something heavy sitting on you.

Paula: Yes.

She described her present sense of moodiness and how her flat-mate helped her. I suggested that the sort of love she had from the Plovers gave her confidence to respond to people and expect them to care for her.

Paula: . . . I think you can see for yourself what I'm like . . . it's up to you if you think I've changed – gone for the worse, or –

P.M. You've grown up into a fine tall girl. You're wondering very much about yourself and about your family . . . You perhaps wondered when you had my letter what I would think of you now.
Paula: I did actually.

We talked again about how she was going to cope on her own with the baby.

Paula: I'm going to give it as good a childhood as I can. I'll just have to see how it goes – take each day as it comes . . . Every mother's bound to find it really hard, but some find it harder than others. And I just think that if you're on your own all you can do is give it as much as you can, and give it a life that you think you've had. Me – well, I can't be Auntie and Uncle again, but what they gave me I can give to somebody else.
P.M. Well, there was a lot of love there to pass on, wasn't there?
Paula: I think quite honestly that they treated us just as their own – except there was seven and not two.
P.M. You must have felt at times that there were a lot of you to share their love.
Paula: Mm. But I think at that stage in our lives there was a lot of love between *all* my family. But it just got to the stage that I knew everything was going to break down when the family grew up, married, had children and that was it.
P.M. I think you're feeling cut off from them, Paula, and it sounds to me as if a lot of them are thinking about you and concerned for you. Maybe as a family you're not very good at getting it over to each other that you're really very fond of each other.
Paula: I think it's since Charlie and my Dad died that the family has just drifted so far apart that it's going to be hard for us to come back together.

Paula told me she would let me know when the baby was born – 'when my work is done!' In spite of her isolation and natural depression she was facing the future courageously, and with some hope. Her devotion to the Plovers and their care for her obviously outweighed in her own mind the hazards and multiple moves of her first three years, which she could not remember. Whatever objective assessment might be made of the effect on her capacity for relationships of those constant disruptions and failed parenting at such a vulnerable age, from her own point of view she had experienced closeness, particularly to Charlie and to the Plovers, but also to S.lly, and more recently to Maxine – whom I was to see next.

Maxine comes between the elder quartet of two sisters and two brothers and the two youngest sisters. From this position she seemed able to empathise with the others' experiences. She would have been nearly 15 when I last saw her ten years before at Charlie's funeral. She wrote spasmodically in the first years of leaving Mulberry Close when she was lonely, missing Meg Plover (and counting the days till she could go 'home' on holiday) but seeming to manage well in her residential jobs in an animal sanctuary and as a mental nurse. More recently I had had news each Christmas of her marriage and the birth of two children. Earlier there had been a stormy, rather precarious time, which included a court appearance, a suicide attempt and a stay in a psychiatric hospital from which she was gathered up by Meg Plover.

However, this and her childhood unhappiness seemed well behind her now. She and her husband Paul (from Mauritius) lived in a staff flat in the hospital where they both worked with mentally handicapped people. Maxine prepared lunch in a quick, competent way which reminded me of Meg Plover, and coped simultaneously with the demands of Daniel, aged three. He and the baby, Jo, were dark skinned like their father, both lively and attractive. Maxine was a capable hostess, and over lunch I met Paul who was friendly and shy. He appeared to share the care of the children and put Jo to bed after lunch, leaving Maxine and me to talk.

Maxine: I'm very happy, *now* – but I think it's been very hard, coming out (of Mulberry Close) and having a lot of problems anyway. But now I couldn't wish for it better – I've two little children –

P.M. You feel you've come through a lot.

Maxine: Oh yes . . . I don't think it affects me now – it might do without my knowing . . . I feel sorry for Daniel sometimes because he hasn't got grandparents on my side – he's going to miss out. I think you tend to spoil the children in some ways – you don't want anything to happen to them what you've been through.

P.M. You want it to be better for them.

Maxine: Oh yes. I think that way you bring out what you haven't had yourself.

P.M. You talk about spoiling as though it's something wrong – and yet it's nice to be indulgent, isn't it?

Maxine: Oh yes, but he gets his own way too much sometimes when he shouldn't really. You know, spoiling, not material things.

An interruption from Daniel was only partly responsible for my not pursuing this topic. It is sad that many parents are afraid of being too nice to their children. Woodmansey, writing about the 'myth of spoiling' makes the point that you cannot spoil or mar a child by

25

kindness. Parents who lavish material presents often do so in compensation for their inability to give the child the affection he or she needs and craves. The whining, over-demanding, so called 'spoiled child' who clamours miserably for whatever comfort he can get, suffers not from excessive kindness but from a permanent feeling of insecurity.[15] This was obviously not the case with Daniel, whom Maxine dressed to go and play on the grass outside the room where we were sitting. He returned frequently through the sliding glass doors more in mischief than anxiously, and he was reasonably able to share his mother's attention with me. Maxine seemed to respond intuitively with Bowlby's maxim of 'firm but friendly intervention' when he needed checking.[16]

> *P.M.* You say the children haven't got grandparents on your side, but you've still got Auntie in the background.
> *Maxine:* Yes. But she doesn't act like a grandparent. She's very good – if I want advice or anything I always phone her, but it's not the same. I love Auntie very much and I know she's always there if I want to speak to her, or if I've got any problem, but I could never look upon her as a mother for myself or a grandparent for the children. I know some people you talk to might think that, but I don't.
> *P.M.* You were always conscious she wasn't your mother?
> *Maxine:* She could never replace a mother. If she was my mother she would come and see me or see the children, but Auntie doesn't do that . . . At Christmas I go down, or some other time, but it's not the same.

Paula had perceived Meg Plover as a step-mother, but Maxine was more acutely aware of the reality constraints on the relationship. It is, of course, one of the paradoxes of residential social work that staff have to provide the daily physical and emotional nurturing care that is part of parenting and yet are not in a position to act as complete substitute parents.

Maxine also appeared to dwell less on the past, only occasionally thinking back. She had no real sense of having had parents and thought that Elaine, who could remember more of the dislocation of their family life, and who had also felt pushed out of Mulberry Close, was more affected.

> *Maxine:* She was there for a very short time and then she had to go and find digs.
> *P.M.* So she didn't have the longer time of Auntie that you and the younger ones had.

Maxine: Yes. I think that made me more stable – until I was 15 and I went to work.

P.M. And did you feel close as a family, do you think?

Maxine: No. It's a shame, because I always thought that we would.

P.M. Because that was the idea, your all being together there in one small Home.

Maxine: I think it was a good idea that we were all together – I can't really remember if we were close when we were there or not – but I know *now* we're not a close family, by a long way. Because I know what Paul's family's like and they're very close and I can see that we're not. (She described her various efforts to be in touch with the others.) Sometimes you'd think because of what we went through when we were smaller – you'd think we'd grow up more close.

P.M. It would bring you together.

Maxine: Yes. But it didn't. Because we all left at different times.

P.M. You all had to make your own way.

Maxine: That was it, yes – sort of '15, that's it'. (Laughed.) 'Get out and earn your living!' (She had been 16.)

P.M. That was hard, I imagine, having to leave.

Maxine: Yes . . . I think you get mixed up – you're young and you just do stupid things . . . and then you've suddenly got to settle down. When you've got a family you've got to go and make yourself think.

P.M. And can you remember your mother coming?

Maxine: I can remember when they used to come to tea. For some reason my father hated me anyway. He always used to give me a clip round the ear – for things not necessary. I can always remember this.

She recalled that one day Meg Plover had told her that Mr Waldo had said he was not her father. It had come as a shock but had not upset her unduly.

Maxine: If I was with my father and we lived together . . . or even if we were in a Children's Home and he was very good to me, or we were close, then it would upset me, but because he was nothing to me anyway it didn't bother me.

I could not recall this doubt and she preferred to believe that his denial of paternity was a fabrication, particularly as his name was on her birth certificate. Uncertainty about parentage can erode a firm sense of identity but Maxine seemed satisfied by other people's comments that she resembled her father physically. She used to escape when her parents visited.

Maxine: I remember when she used to bring stupid things, but now I can see

27

it was in a way guilt.

P.M. Trying to make it up to you?

Maxine: But when you're young you don't think like that. And I can remember when I was in hospital for appendix she sent me a postcard and some crayon books.

This was almost the first hint of empathy for Mrs Waldo that I had heard from her children, or recollection that she had made any small gesture. However, Maxine was firm that her mother was no longer part of her life.

Maxine: I can remember things like that, but I can't remember what she looks like. And I would never go to see her – if I could find her. My husband always says, 'Go and see her,' because he's close, he can't understand really. But I would never go because I know what she did to Wally – she slammed the door in his face. I just wouldn't – it would be like lowering myself. She's never done anything for me.

P.M. Except bring you into the world.

Maxine: I know! But she didn't do anything after that, did she. She doesn't want us. I think if I went to see her it would cause upset – I don't want that.

P.M. I think you feel she really hasn't got anything to give you, perhaps, and that it would only be hurtful to you.

Maxine: I think if she had us all, she should look after us all and give us love whatever. And I think now – obviously she's got to have some love inside her, she must have, she must think of us sometimes. But I think if she wants to see us, any of us, she would do so – it's not that difficult to find somebody.

P.M. It does seem that some women do find it extra hard to be mothers, as though they haven't got it in them. It doesn't always come naturally.

Maxine: But then why did she have all of us? Why did she have seven if it was that difficult to be a mother? I don't know what my reaction would be if she did come to the front door. I don't think I'd want to know her. I think there would be trouble – either I or the children would be hurt – because what sort of mother? Her son goes to see her and she slams the door in his face. If I hadn't heard of that maybe I would wonder whether to go, but after Wally – and then Elaine as well, 'Who's your girl friend?' She thought Elaine was Wally's girl friend!

P.M. It sounds as if the rebuff they each had affects you all – you feel it on their behalf.

Maxine: Yes. I suppose you just think about what she's done to the others. We have grown up and they've wanted to go and see her and made that effort and she still doesn't want to know. So I'm sure now if I went she wouldn't want to know *me* – so –

P.M. Well, I suppose she's part of your history, but she doesn't come into your life at all now.

Maxine: No. Sometimes I think, I wonder where she is, but that's as far as it goes.

P.M. Do you think she affects how you see yourself as a mother?

Maxine: No. I don't worry about what sort of mother I am.

P.M. You must feel you're making a better job of it!

Maxine: Oh yes. (Laughed.) I don't think, 'I don't want to do what she's done' – I just get on with it. It's not an effort of any sort.

P.M. So it sounds as though it does come more naturally to you.

Maxine: Mm. But then she shouldn't have had seven. If it didn't come that naturally, why did she have seven?

P.M. I suppose actually conceiving children – and bearing them – comes naturally, but the daily looking after them, that's the hard part, and the loving.

Maxine: Yes, but I don't think there's any excuse. Anyway I don't think of her really as a mother – she's a person – somebody I might have known a few years ago.

Maxine was concerned that Paula might follow her mother's pattern, but was also sympathetic towards her.

Maxine: I've phoned Paula and told her the baby is hers and I just hope it works out for her. We know Paula's going to keep it so we might as well face it and help as much as we can . . . Maybe she'll find the same difficulty as our mother – she has it but after a few months the novelty of the whole thing wears off.

P.M. Well, it's going to be hard without a husband to help her.

Maxine: Yes. But I don't think she realises this. At times I feel myself, 'Oh, I've had enough' – I can quite easily see how a child is battered – I'd never do it myself – I *say* I wouldn't – I know when the children are both awake and you've just had enough for that day, and they won't sleep. And usually I shut the door, because once before I slammed the door, and I've gone out and got the washing in and sort of took it out on the washing at midnight! Just to get it out of yourself. I can see how it can happen. I hope I don't do it myself. I can see sometimes if you've got trouble with your husband and the kids are screaming – I hope nothing happens like this to Paula.

Daniel interrupted us as Maxine was talking so frankly of a common fear and pitch of pressure which many mothers, of all social classes, feel but do not easily acknowledge. She found the double pressure of going to work (in order to supplement Paul's low nurse's pay) and being a mother very hard. Her own lack of an accessible mother had hit hard when she left Mulberry Close.

Maxine: I think the worst time is when you're coming out of care – or rather when you've got to leave the Children's Home. Then you've got to find your own way – that's the most difficult part. And if anything goes wrong – all right, Auntie's there, you're lucky to have somebody like Auntie anyway because you might have been in a bigger place. But even then, when you're out at 15 or 16 you've got to find your own accommodation.

P.M. It's very young to be on your own, isn't it?

Maxine: Mm. You've got nobody to fall back on. Auntie's there, but it's not the same as if it was your mother, 'Oh, it isn't working out, Mum, can I come home?' If anything goes wrong, you can't just go back home, because there's no home to go to, is there?

P.M. Do you think you would have been better off if you'd been in a family then, rather than in a Children's Home?

Maxine: Ummm. If the family worked out well – if you got on well, I think so. Auntie had got a lot of ties, there's different children in and out – you can't just go home when you feel like going home.

P.M. You can't always be sure there'd be a bed.

Maxine: But not just that – many a time before I was married I'd think, 'If only I could go home to a mother' sort of thing. And you'd know you'd be secure in that house with your mother. Auntie's always there if you've got any problem, but it's not the same.

P.M. You can't take it for granted in quite the same way.

Meg Plover had salvaged Maxine more than once in her troubles, but to mention this would have seemed like arguing with her, rather than understanding her sense of loneliness in that wasteland beyond care which many young people can inhabit. When I commented that she used to write to me occasionally, she said, 'Well, if somebody – I suppose you just think, "I wonder if that person wants to know what you are doing."'

Maxine's profile of a helpful social worker was someone who was confident in themselves, whom she could trust, and who *stayed*.

Maxine: A lot of them used to come and ask you – you'd tell them everything, the history of your life sort of thing, and then they'd just go. You'd never get to know one person well enough to trust them – and you have to have a lot of trust to talk to anybody in the beginning. I think you and Miss V. were the only ones really that I felt confident of – to talk to or to go out – other people, they'd just come and go and in the end you can't be bothered, you feel they're not really trying to help you – they just want to know what's happened and they don't do anything.

P.M. And what would you have liked them to have done?

Maxine: Well, I don't know – I think you have to have confidence that they're listening, and interested, or they're trusting you, or they're not just going to listen that day and not come back.

P.M. Perhaps you're feeling that about me today, that I'm coming and asking
you to talk and –

Maxine: No, because it's past now. When you're in a Children's Home, that's
all you think of really, 'Why has it got to be me?' Now it's not the same, is
it?

P.M. You can't remember times when there were things you wanted to talk
about and it wasn't made possible? Or maybe you always had Auntie.

Maxine: I think Auntie was good, and it was good in a Children's Home that
size – if we had any worries, we would go to Auntie, not to the social
worker.

A social worker had been helpful when she was pregnant with Daniel.

Maxine: I was mixed up and I didn't know what to do, and I had to find
somewhere to live. Miss C. was very concerned – she didn't say to me, 'Oh
well, you've got to go to the mother and baby home,' she said, 'Would you
rather go to the –!' She sort of –

P.M. She gave you a choice.

Maxine: Yes. Do you remember anything when you were a social worker for
us?

P.M. Well, I can remember being there and talking with you. I suppose what
I can remember most clearly, because it's nearest in time, is that day
coming down to Charlie's funeral. (Pause.) And you were all so shaken and
shocked.

Maxine: I always think – Charlie always wanted his father, and then of course
Dad died, and they're together now – they might not be, but I just hope
they are.

P.M. You comfort yourself thinking that.

Maxine: Yes. At the time you think you're never going to live with the
thought of Charlie being killed, but you do in time. When I'm home I go
up to the cemetery – I still think of Charlie a lot actually.

She wished she was closer to Wally and that he would come and see the
children. She had visited him in hospital after his accident and had
hoped he would be in contact more. She talked too of her plans to go
and see Paula.

P.M. It seems to me that you're the one who's wanting to get the family in
touch.

Maxine: . . . We could help each other a lot more than we do – but we don't!

Daniel was tired now and our time to talk was running out. Maxine
needed encouragement to think about her own sense of well-being or
otherwise.

Maxine: I'm happy I've got my own family. But I'm still very young to formulate a whole – it's not very long ago that I was in a psychiatric hospital. But obviously I'm pleased now because I can see that I'm not going to break down. I'm strong now and I think that really made me the way I am now. I always think of what I would like and I suppose that's why I work, because I know if I keep working I will get it. I'm happy now, and I've got two lovely children, but I haven't got what I want.

P.M. In a sense you *are* telling me how you see yourself – as strong and having come through a lot and – determined really – that you've got hopes for yourself and that you believe you've got the ability to –

Maxine: Oh yes – I will, I will get what I want.

She also expressed contentment that she and Paul shared employment and the care of the children. She was lucky in having a reliable baby-sitter so that she could get out if she was feeling depressed. In contrast to some of the other young people I saw, where there was a measure of unfinished business – old hurts or uncertainties that needed comforting or clarifying – Maxine seemed to have put the hurts of her past firmly behind her.

Maxine: You've got to grow up for your children's sake. Obviously I think about the past sometimes but it doesn't hurt me. I live for now – for every day, I don't live in the past.

P.M. I'm glad for you that it doesn't hang over you.

Maxine: It *might* do, without me knowing. Obviously there've been hurtful times – even now you get hurt, you're bound to, life is full of hurt, isn't it? But I don't think about the past and think, 'Oh I was hurt then.' You've just got to get on and face life as it is.

Maxine was due to go on duty soon and I nursed the baby while she prepared tea. Looking at Jo on my lap I felt there were good grounds for hope that she and Daniel would have a more settled childhood than their mother. Maxine had come into care at six months until her first birthday. (Had this anniversary prompted Mrs Waldo's return?) She had 13 moves in all before she arrived at Mulberry Close just before her sixth birthday. She must have received warmer mothering in some of her six foster homes, but each of these experiences was short-lived and the last one broke down. Meg Plover later describes how Maxine had seemed walled up in her misery when she first came to her and how she had to wait to gain her trust. Maxine had been vehement now that Meg could not replace the mother she felt she had not had. This did not imply a lack of love for Meg; she was just painfully aware of reality. As a small girl she used to write dozens of little letters to Meg, each a declaration of affection. She was in touch then with her unhappiness and confusion, and able to express both this and her growing attachment to Meg, with whom she lived for 11 years. She felt those years gave her a stability which she lost in her late adolescent struggle on her own. She had now found a new strength and equilibrium in response to her children's needs.

I wondered if Maxine needed to defend herself against hurtful memories, but had to respect her conviction (particularly on a one-off visit) that these no longer affected her. And indeed her openness to the hurts at the time perhaps meant that the sorrows worked themselves out then – it is the hidden sorrows that go on smouldering. 'If the feeling is not expressed, it cannot be left behind.'[17]

Wally, whom I saw next, is the only surviving brother in this family. On his suggestion we met at a pub where he helped (unpaid) for two hours a day. He was waiting outside and despite his beard I knew him at once before I noticed the empty left sleeve of his denim shirt. It was lunch time and he insisted on buying me a drink and a salad, which I tried to prevent as he was unemployed, but it seemed important to him.

He plunged straight in and said that he had not seen me since Charlie's funeral. As we sat in the corner of the saloon bar, partly screened by the intermittent blare of music from the loud-speaker over our heads, he talked with such urgency that I felt unable at first to ask if I might use the tape recorder. The boy I remembered had not seemed particularly keen to talk to social workers, but at 26 he undoubtedly wanted me to know how angry, frustrated and hurt he was. 'We've all been hurt,' he said, 'but I feel it's been me that's been hit the hardest.' He listed the hammer blows which he felt life had dealt him, over and above the family background of rejection and having to grow up largely in public care. Charlie had been of extra importance to him as his elder brother (and they had usually been placed together in foster care as small boys), so he had felt his death acutely. There followed the death of his father, his mother's renewed rejection of him when, dressed for the occasion in a suit, he had gone to find her in London and she had shut the door in his face, and then the crippling accident which led to the loss of his arm. He included Maxine's suicide attempt in his own catalogue of misadventure.

His main urge, however, was to talk about his present predicament. He was still waiting to be paid compensation three years after the accident and was having to survive on invalidity benefit with a small supplement. He was handicapped not just by the actual loss of his arm

33

and all that that implied physically in terms of pain, discomfort and awkwardness, but also financially in his reduced chances of employment, and emotionally in his impaired self-image which complicated his relationships, particularly with women. Apart from death itself there is a whole range of other events which can be experienced as loss and which set in motion a pattern of bereavement. Parkes[18] examines some of the similarities in grief reactions between the loss of a loved person and the amputation of a limb. Caplan[19] defines the latter experience as a loss of integrity, of bodily wholeness, and Wally was now expressing the anger that is a natural part of mourning. He had felt baulked at every turn.

> *Wally:* When I was in hospital, the specialist came up to me and said 'Mr Waldo, we've got a one per cent chance of your being able to use your arm again,' and I just looked up and said to him, 'Cut it off.'

The surgeon had apparently refused (because of the one per cent chance) and waited a year during which time Wally's arm withered and the muscles shrank, so that it is now not possible for him to use his artificial limb. He was also bitter about the careless way in which cuts to his face had been stitched after a more recent accident when as a passenger he had been thrown through a car windscreen. He showed me the scars which were not very obvious or disfiguring, but they were further evidence to him of medical disregard.

He described the frustrations of life on the edge of poverty: the demoralising effect of unemployment, the poor lodgings, the long waits in a queue of 50 in Social Security.

> *Wally:* And now they want to tax us. How can you! How can a person survive? They reckon an average person's wage is £120 now . . . I'm on a quarter of that – I'm getting £32. A jacket would cost me £35; or you go to Social Security and ask for a new pair of shoes and they'll give you £8 – you can't buy a pair of shoes for £8.
>
> *P.M.* You were saying you'd tried to get something for new shirts – I would have thought with your shoulder wearing them out you could ask for more.
>
> *Wally:* I did. And I got nothing.
>
> *P.M.* You could take it to a Tribunal.
>
> *Wally:* I've never done anything like that. If they thought I'd beg for it – no way.
>
> *P.M.* It's not begging for it – it's saying 'I've got a right to it,' and trying to prove your own case.

I asked if he had approached an Advice Centre for assistance.

Wally: I went to a Citizens' Advice Bureau when I wanted a place to live. They could do nothing. I'm not getting anywhere. All I'm doing is standing still – or moving backwards. You can't fight the system.

P.M. No, but you can sometimes put a case and get what's due to you.

Wally: That's a joke in itself. They don't care.

P.M. Well, it just feels like a battle you're never going to win.

Wally: I ain't going to win. The only way I can become the winner is when everything is sorted out (with his compensation). And then I'm still the loser – no matter how much they give me – I won't have my arm back.

P.M. That's what hurts, isn't it?

Wally: I think what annoys me more than anything is the way the Government can turn round and put a price on a limb of yours. How do they know what it's worth? How do they know what you've been through?

P.M. Well, it's priceless – to you, isn't it? And as you say, it's not just your body – it's what you've been through.

Wally: This is it. The way it's acted on your mind, your ups and downs, your sleepless nights, your pain. What do they know? People say, 'We understand.' They *don't* understand. The only person that knows how you feel is yourself.

Carl Rogers might almost have written that last sentence. On the basis of his tenet that the only person who can fully know his field of experience is the individual himself, Rogers recommends that a helper can best understand behaviour (which is a person's response to what he perceives) by trying to see the world as nearly as possible through the other person's eyes, by wearing his emotional spectacles.[20] So I just commented: 'Other people can *try* to understand – they can't presume that they do.' I might also have acknowledged a possible underlying message that he was not sure that *I* could understand. It seemed important to recognise his bitterness and sense of failure, though I was also trying to reduce his sense of powerlessness.

When we were talking about the difficulties of managing with one arm, I added 'and only one arm to put round a girl'. He said it had been his biggest fear that he would be less good at making love, and that it did in fact hurt his shoulder and chest and his repertoire of love-making was reduced. He had a moment's embarrassment at telling me this but recovered himself quickly. He did not appear less virile but no doubt felt himself to be.

With his good looks and extrovert personality, Wally had not lacked girl friends, but it sounded as though his relationships with them had often ended abruptly because of his sensitivity about his arm, when he perhaps took offence or felt some slight was intended. One girl with whom he had lived for a couple of years left him when he lost his arm. Another relationship had been spoiled because his girl was working and he was sitting at home unemployed with no money to take her out. Impulsively he left her in the flat with most of his possessions. He had quite a happy relationship with an unmarried mother, but this too ended because of feelings about his arm. He was fiercely independent, constantly testing himself to prove that he could manage, and resented his girl friends' attempts to do too much for him. Most of us take two arms for granted and need not stop to think how to light a match or tie laces with only one hand. It is hard to watch someone struggle, but each handicapped person has his or her own particular tolerance level that has to be discovered.

Wally's handicap was uppermost in his mind in his relations with women, but it perhaps also compounded his fear of committing himself to any one person. His parents' failure, both as parents and as partners, made him wary of marriage. He would like to have children – though no more than two – and did not want their childhood to be a repetition of his. He could envisage a yearning to give them all the things he himself had lacked, but had a nagging fear that he too might fail. He asked if I had seen his sisters and was impressed that Kathleen and Maxine were enjoying being mothers. He felt Paula was fighting her own battles. I told him that these three had all wished that they could see more of him. He agreed but said he could not afford the fares.

As with his sisters, in retrospect Wally felt that his time of leaving Mulberry Close had been the hardest. His social worker at that time, on his recollection, had not been very helpful.

Wally: When I left school I went up to see him, and all I got was 'Wish you all the best. Anything you need up to 18 years old, come and see me.'
P.M. And he didn't visit you?
Wally: Oh no.

If Wally's recollection was accurate, this casual attitude was hard to credit. However, it was 1971 when social workers were submerged in a bewildering range of unfamiliar duties in the big new social services departments.[21]

Leaving care at 18 had therefore not seemed a particular milestone to Wally as he had already felt on his own at 16. His loneliness was painfully increased when he lost Charlie two months after he left school. The police had gone to his lodgings to tell him Charlie had been killed. 'I thought, "Is it true? Is it really true?" To be the first to know,

I think is the worst.' He had wandered the streets, dazed and disbelieving, till he met Paula, who in turn had repeated, 'I don't believe it.' Wally had sworn, 'It's true,' then burst into tears and ran off. Having to tell another person that someone has died often forces us to face the reality, as if something is not true until it is spoken and silence keeps it at bay.

Wally did not keep in touch with me after the funeral (I wrote to him after his own accident) and apart from the Plovers he had no further dealings with social services on leaving care. He was angry to realise that his social worker had not told him about the discretionary provision which allows social services to give certain financial and social work help to young people who have been in their care, up to the age of 21.[22] He was currently facing eviction because his alcoholic landlady was in arrears with her rent, and he could have done with some help.

Wally was seasoned in this aspect of adversity and would have benefited most ten years before (as would his sisters in their turn) from the kind of 'leaving care' schemes which some social services departments now provide, and which Stewart and Stewart[23] regard as a positive way of preventing homelessness in this group of young people. One pattern has three stages, starting with survival skills being taught in the Children's Home, followed by a move into a semi-independent unit still within the confines of the Home, culminating in the allocation of a tenancy from the Housing Department, with continued support from a social worker.[24] Young people are thus eased towards independent living in a planned way.

Wally prided himself on his solitary independence, painfully learned.

Wally: The only person who can help me now is me. I can't rely on anybody, in all honesty. Because either people don't want to know, because they are not interested –
P.M. And what about Uncle and Auntie? They're still there in the background.
Wally: Yes, I know they're there. But they've got enough problems – why should I go to them, moaning?

He seemed to want to emphasise his aloneness. Earlier he had said that what he had most lacked primarily was love, and secondly a good education. His parents had given him nothing and he interpreted the Plovers' affection for him as a sense of responsibility.

Wally: When we were there as a family, they done the best for us . . . Uncle wasn't getting paid for it – he was coming home and helping out. If you've

37

got to be paid to give somebody love, is it love?

P.M. It is different – but I think it can still be love.

Wally: Yes, but there's love – and there's love. I go out with a girl, and I say, 'I love you' – it could be lust. You just think you do. Because it's something new. But I've been in love and I've got kicked in the face. I knew it was love and I got kicked down. Now I just say, 'You're all right. I like you.'

P.M. You're not going to risk – saying that you love.

Wally: It's going to take me a long time to say it. There's a difference and I realise that. When Auntie and Uncle say they love us, they love us out of a sense of responsibility – not the same sort of love as a parent to a child. Auntie couldn't turn round and say that she loves everybody like she loves her husband. It's not the same.

P.M. Are you saying there's not enough love to go round?

Wally: No. There's three different kinds of love. There's love for her husband; there's love for her children, which is a different type of love; and there's love for other people.

P.M. For her other children.

Wally: For her other children. Right . . . the rest she loves, but in a different way.

P.M. I thought there was a lot of love there, but it isn't as much as you want or the kind that you want.

Wally: No. I respect Auntie and Uncle. I do respect them. Because if it wasn't for people like them, where would people like me be? Would I be able to talk to you, like this, and mean it – would I? . . . If I was living with my parents, would I be as wise now?

P.M. You think you've learned wisdom out of all your hardship?

Wally: I've learned to face life. It's like, when I had my accident Auntie wanted me to go there and stay with them, and I said, 'No.'

We were joined at this point by one of Wally's fellow lodgers, an ex-prisoner called Vin who was mildly inebriated. He asked who I was and Wally introduced me without embarrassment.

Wally: She used to be my social worker – when I was in a Children's Home. The last time I saw her was in 1971 – at my brother's funeral.

I explained my project briefly and Vin was eager to join in, mumbling and pontificating.

Vin: You must have been very good if they've kept in touch with you. Social workers are very underpaid. Very good people.

Wally: They take a lot of stick – it's a hard job.

Vin insisted that Wally would make a good social worker.

Vin: They'd listen to you, more than they probably would to the lady there.

You know yourself, you can talk to people. You've got the right to tell other people about it.

Wally had earlier been keen on my playing the tape to my students.

Wally: I would have thought it was a good thing, if you tell them – If they know before they go out, the problems that people have got to face.

The landlord ended our conversation as it was closing time. Wally walked back to the car with me and I gave him a lift. He wanted to know what I had thought of Vin's suggestion. I said he was perhaps wondering what I thought about him generally – that I could see he had been through a great deal and was still bitter about it, but that he had also grown through it and had potential and a way with people. He asked more about his sisters; he was hurt that Elaine had lost touch with him after the accident as they had been close, and was almost shocked that Sally had not wanted to see me. He asked if I was going to write about it all. 'You can tell them there was a family,' he said, 'and say that the eldest didn't want to know, and the youngest was still minding about having been in care, although she was nearly 20.' (He reminded me that Sally's birthday was the next day.)

Wally felt he had learned wisdom, but to some extent he knew his unwise tendency to drink too much. He also feared that once his compensation was paid he might spend it rashly and we discussed ways of preventing this. I could see how tempting it might be for him to compensate (*sic*) his bruised self-image in prodigality.

My discussions with Meg Plover were not confined to one discrete interview as their cottage was my base for the Ringshire rounds of visits. Living on the job is one of the obvious strains of residential social work and increasingly staff have become non-resident. Meg continued to believe in the value of actually living with the children but this warm and comfortable cottage in a village ten miles away was also important to her. So she came when she was off duty and we spent several long evenings talking by the fire.

After 21 years at Mulberry Close Meg was due to retire soon and was naturally preoccupied with the outcome of her work, so my interest met hers. The care of the Waldo children had constituted a substantial core of this period of her working life and for a time we had shared different aspects of responsibility for them. A working party chaired by Professor Parker[25] has pointed out that once children are in public care no one person has complete and comprehensive responsibility for their present care and future welfare in the way that is usually expected of a

39

parent. This adds to their vulnerability as they are 'dependent on adults whose responsibilities are ambiguous and who are themselves liable to be replaced'. Sawbridge even talks of a 'hydra-headed parent' and claims[26] that if a fundamental component of good parenting is consistency then a body and especially a changing body of people can never really be a parent. The Waldo children had certainly suffered from changes of field social workers, as Maxine had described, but for nearly 20 years the Plovers had been a constant factor in their lives, and Meg welcomed my continuing interest.

My visits to the young Waldos who were scattered followed the first Ringshire interviews, but it seemed proper to present their viewpoint first rather than introduce them through Meg Plover's eyes. So in the following account the reader will know more than I did at the time I talked with Meg.

She was (as ever) wise, witty and warm, and it was agreeably reminiscent to listen to her talk. Uppermost in her mind was concern for Paula's predicament, balanced by her pleasure that Kathleen and Maxine were managing so well as mothers. She felt sad for Wally and all his hurts, and for Sally's vulnerabilities, and was disappointed that Elaine had turned her back on the family.

Meg felt a sense of failure over Paula to whom she had tried to give consistent care from the age of three to 17. Although all the children had experienced repeated disruptions of attachments, for Paula and Sally the discontinuities of care had been concentrated in their first two to three years, when in Erikson's view children are learning the sense of basic trust in others, leading on to a sense of autonomy and trust in themselves.[27] It seemed as if Meg had been able to modify the damage of Paula's 13 moves less than she had hoped. Paula always responded to talks with Meg and expressed affection – 'She is the one that says, "Auntie, I'll look after you when you're old and grey"' – but she was thoughtless and impulsive. She had been secretive at first about her second pregnancy, fearful of pressure on her to have a termination, and Meg felt pity both for her and for the child's future.

> *Meg:* Paula has literally nothing; no home, not a penny, not a garment, no rent, nothing. And it's a pretty poor sort of life, isn't it, on social security. So I'm very concerned that she'll just take off.

There was a possibility that Paula might be able to come back to Paxton to live in some accommodation provided by a young Christian couple who had befriended her before. She had at that time experienced a 'born again' conversion and wrote to tell me she was living with a Christian family. Meg had been given little lectures:

Meg: She'd say, 'Are you a Christian, Auntie?' and I'd say, 'Well, I expect so, I try to be. Perhaps not a very good one.' 'Well, it's no good just saying that, you have to do this and you have to do that.' She was really putting me right.

This had been a relatively stable period for Paula. Earlier she had been evicted from her lodgings and had telephoned Meg who found her sitting on her suitcase on the pavement and had taken her back temporarily to Mulberry Close. She frequently returned 'home' and was there when she went into labour with her first baby.

Meg: I was by myself with all the children and one of the boys ran round to Phyllis (assistant) – they knew all that was going on, part of their education, wasn't it. And, oh dear, they were really getting worse these pains, and I found myself in the most peculiar gear in the ambulance with Paula going to hospital. The nurse said, 'Thank goodness, it'll be here in half an hour.' Meanwhile Paula was moaning and the nurse put her on a trolley and was taking her to the labour ward and I thought, 'Well, this is where I go, thank goodness I can leave her in their capable hands,' but she said, 'No, don't go, I need you.' So before I knew what was happening, I'd got my overshoes on and my mask and gown and was running down – and I had to laugh in spite of it all. Paula had gone on before and I could hear her shouting, 'Auntie!' and I was running up saying, 'Auntie's here, everything's going to be all right, Paulie, Auntie's here,' and she gave a hysterical giggle. You see I was peeping at her over this mask!

The labour lasted another two hours and Paula gripped Meg's neck as she mopped her brow.

Meg: I thought she was pulling my head off! Then the baby was born. I felt choked and I thought, 'It's a miracle. Whenever it happens it's a miracle. There's a little human being.' My emotions were see-sawing all over the place.

She visited Paula each day and tried to comfort her after the adoptions worker had visited.

Meg: 'It's probably for the best, Paula, she'll be loved and wanted,' and she just said, 'But I want her,' and she turned her head towards her and tears ran down her face and I pitied her. It was a primitive feeling; she didn't want to give her away but she'd no means of keeping her. So this time she's determined, against all the odds, she's not going to give that baby away.

As we talked late into the night we sometimes strayed laterally into poetry, philosophy and religion and arrived at Mother Theresa of Calcutta.

> *Meg:* She is what she is and destined to do this special job – so good and so happy in doing such horrible chores for the most abject, sad creatures –
> *P.M.* And yet she can somehow make it beautiful.
> *Meg:* It does make it beautiful, doesn't it. The moment Paula's baby was born was beautiful. You sort of get a glimpse of God, don't you, I find at the most unexpected times – I'm not thinking religious thoughts at all and suddenly the Lord gives me a nudge and you see a little miracle there in the midst of all sorts of things that are driving you mad. I had my happy moment amidst all my sorrows the moment that baby was born.
> *P.M.* It was marvellous that you were there with Paula. So often they have relied on you, they've wanted you and there you've been.
> *Meg:* Ultimately, I can't really judge Paula; I'm just sorry it's all gone wrong and she's messing up her life. I can't see what more I can do to help her – probably this is why I'm frustrated – except just keep in touch, which is useless now.

I encouraged her to think it would help; Paula had sounded so depressed on the telephone and anxious lest Meg had rejected her at last.

> *Meg:* And then I did write and she said, 'I thought you'd finished with me and were ashamed of me.' So to some extent she must have feelings for me.
> *P.M.* Well, there do seem to be feelings there. She cares more than you think. You always used to say they were so shallow towards you and yet every now and again you see signs of hurt or longing which show.
> *Meg:* I do really, I suppose, so I seem to be contradicting myself. I frequently contradict myself. It's just life still teaching me, I think.

Paula had at times accused herself of being like her mother, but Meg saw her as having more capacity to care, and in a moment of optimism speculated that she might, against all the odds, make a reasonable job of bringing up a child, although her need to have a baby to love her was not a good predictor for success.

However, Maxine, too had seemed to have the odds heavily weighted against her, and her development as a good mother seemed a special triumph in view of her earlier disturbances. Meg was happy to admit she had been wrong in her predictions.

> *P.M.* But that's a reward really, Meg, to think she manages so well as a mother.

Meg: Yes it is.

P.M. You know she was very attached to you.

Meg: I know. It wasn't that we thought she would neglect the baby, I felt she would keep it clean and warm and feed it. But she had such a short fuse – so quick-tempered, this was how I'd seen it with the baby, that she would get really out of control. In actual fact she's quite different and seems a very good little mother.

As an example Meg described how well Maxine had dealt with Daniel's jealousy after Jo was born.

Meg: They are beautiful children – Daniel and Jo. It's been interesting to me to see how she's changed since she had them. I thought she wouldn't cope, and yet not only does she cope but you can see now that she's happier – all right, she loved me in a way as a mother-figure, but now she is loved and is so necessary to those children, that's her fulfilment. And words of wisdom – she's so anxious about Paula, saying, 'She doesn't realise how demanding babies are and you've got to protect and care for them and you've got to be patient' and oh, she really knows the lot, and I'm constantly amazed that this disturbed, suicidal, hysterical young girl has now become a loving sensible mother!

Meg recalled Maxine's arrival at Mulberry Close, a withdrawn six year old whose last foster home had broken down.

Meg: I have never seen such a hurt child – she looked up under her eyebrows, no tears – like a little fortress, a little soul walled up in her misery. There was a barrier around her I'll never forget, you could almost see a black cloud, an aura around her, caused by this deep sorrow and hurt.

She did not speak to Meg for several weeks, just rocked and rocked. Meg longed to comfort her but could not penetrate the dark cloud and knew she must wait for a natural moment. The first breakthrough came when she took Maxine into town to buy some shoes.

Meg: And suddenly I felt her hand come into mine, like a little bird. I wanted to squeeze it but thought, 'No, let it come gradually.'

There were echoes here for me from the words used by Maria Colwell's teacher who had been shocked to realise how thin Maria was when she took her on to her knee to comfort her. 'She likened the sensation to holding a bird in one's hand and being frightened to hold it too tight in case one squeezed the life out of it.'[28] Maxine had not been physically ill-treated, but was starved and bruised emotionally by her sense of unwantedness. Meg had eased her gently into daily life at

Mulberry Close, and Pick[29] describes helpfully how at 'Treetops' they tried to shape messages of personal care to fit an incoming child, balancing their desire to show their intentions with their belief that they had time to let her go at her own pace and discover them. An emotionally frozen child needs time to dare to do more than go through the rudimentary motions of living, and needs help to develop and experience her senses. Meg responded naturally in a therapeutic way, wherever possible making the daily routines more manageable for her.[30] Children who have known repeated changes of care-givers are on tenterhooks to discover which transgressions of routine or ordinary behaviour in this new place are 'the bad things that make them send you away'.[31]

Maxine had not been able to manage the intensity of her feelings when her mother visited.

Meg: I remember her standing with her face to the wall, tears running down her face, when her mother came, not wanting to look at her even. She just used to go to pieces, would pull away and stand by the outside wall, her eyes running and her nose running and rocking and wailing. Her wailing was most pitiful.

P.M. And was it fear or longing?

Meg: Everything. She was completely mixed up. Her mother hadn't a clue how unhappy she was – this child she'd brought into the world. And of course she had the additional heartache that Mr Waldo didn't accept her.

It had never been clarified whether or not he was Maxine's father, but his lack of acceptance had been more hurtful than the question mark over his paternity.

Years later, struggling to live independently, Maxine's response to tangled emotions was a suicide attempt. Meg had been called to the hospital and found her silent and withdrawn, her eyes lifeless, and rocking as she had in childhood. Meg visited again when she was moved to a psychiatric hospital.

Meg: She looked so ill and so lost – such a bleak forlorn little thing. The Gideons had left a Bible and she said, 'Auntie,' in this slow and sleepy voice as if she'd been drugged to make her stay, 'I've been reading the 23rd Psalm, the one that Peter sang at Charlie's funeral. Wish I'd died and not Charlie.' She sat hunched up and the tears came and she made me cry, so we put our arms around one another and cried together. Then (after a week) she looked to be going downhill to me, and she said, 'Auntie, I want to come home, I can't stay any longer, I shall run away.'

Meg was aware that Maxine was receiving no treatment apart from drugs; she took the responsibility of discharging her, drove her back to Mulberry Close and tucked her up in a fortuitously empty bed.

Meg's warmhearted impulse to take back her young people when they faced crises of eviction, illness or personal trauma, did not always find favour with senior staff who perhaps interpreted their gate-keeping role somewhat narrowly.[32] Residential care is certainly a costly resource, for which there is public accountability. However, one could argue that for lack of a safe base to turn to in distress, many young people enmesh themselves more deeply in tangles which eventually prove costlier in terms both of public money and personal suffering. There is also available the discretionary legal provision, referred to earlier, by which local authorities may give financial assistance towards the expenses of accommodation, maintenance, education or training of young people over 17 who have been in their care. Holden points out that when it is suitable to a young person's needs, accommodation can be offered if necessary in an appropriate community home.[33] Meg was understandably indignant that she had been left unaware of this provision, and I recognised that I must seem rather tardy in telling her now. Equally she resented being made to feel possessive if she did provide refuge.

Meg: They don't suddenly get to a magic number and then are able to stand on their own feet. During those teenage years you try to help them to cope, but when it falls down, you've got to be there, haven't you, for a while. Eventually most of them do stand on their own two feet. But I still think you should take them back again and again, at least under 21, if anything goes wrong, because many of them are much younger than their actual years, and they've been rejected and hurt and have no stable parents to look after them . . . But you're made to feel as if you must almost apologise and keep saying, 'I've never been possessive, but this one needs help.' As though you're doing it for your own gratification or satisfaction, when you darn well know that particular kid's in need of a shoulder to cry on and a bed and somewhere to put their belongings.

P.M. It's hard that you should be criticised when you're giving them what they need.

Meg: They probably think that if you'd done a better job – there's the implication – that they would be standing on their own feet by then. Well, some do, but there are others, especially my Maxine, who take a lot longer, but now seem to be coping.

Social workers often fear that they will be blamed if they allow people to become dependent on them for longer than a respectably short period. Irrespective of whether this is a realistic anxiety in their particular context, they may themselves either disapprove of or fear such dependency. To counter this I and others have written of the helpful contribution which Bowlby's theory of a secure base can make to field and residential social work supervision and to social work training.[34] Bowlby draws on accumulated evidence to support his view that:

> not only children, but human beings of all ages are found to be at their happiest and to be able to deploy their talents to best advantage when they are confident that, standing behind them, there are one or more trusted persons who will come to their aid should difficulties arise. The person trusted provides a secure base from which his (or her) companion can operate.[35]

In contrast to the pejorative flavour of dependency, Bowlby sees it as healthy to be able to trust and rely on others, and asserts that self-reliance actually grows out of the knowledge that there is a secure base to turn to when needed and out of the capacity to use it.

The kind of secure base which Meg provided in crises would have increased in effectiveness had she felt sanctioned by the Department to offer it, and if the young people had felt they could turn to her as of right. Maxine's self-reliance for instance might have grown more comfortably if she had felt able to ask for help before she reached a point where she was rescued *in extremis* by a somewhat defiant Meg. Gutteridge[36] holds that teenagers need to know that there is a bolt-hole and that they are not cut off.

Allowing for the natural ambivalence of adolescence and the mixture of hope and dread that accompanies a transition from residential care into independent living, it is also important to check whether continuing social work help is desired. Many young people would not want this voluntary support but they should know it is available.[37] Meg became involved in another of Maxine's predicaments when she was summonsed for forging cheques (to help her boy friend) and, because there was no field social worker, Meg wrote to the police making a strong plea in Maxine's defence. A frightened Maxine telephoned, 'Auntie, I'm outside the court-room, and it's in half an hour.' Meg had raced to the court 12 miles away, but the hearing was over when she arrived. Fortunately her letter had been passed to the magistrates who made a Probation Order.

Meg said that she heard from Wally about twice a year. She and her husband had visited him in hospital and she grieved for him and his dashed hopes over the use of an artificial arm. She saw him as resilient (he had learned to write with his right hand) and very brave when he was in hospital, but thought he was lonely under his bravado.

Meg: He missed Charlie very much . . . I remember a couple of years after Charlie was killed, my husband and I went to the cemetery to take some flowers to his grave, and we saw Wally sitting there with his great Alsation dog lying beside him. He's always full of bravado and would never let one know that he really cared about anything and we just caught him in an off moment. We said, 'What are you sitting up here for all by yourself?' and he said with tears in his eyes, 'I often come and sit up here with Charlie.'

She felt Wally now seemed unable to make lasting relationships and moved from one girl friend to another. 'He pulls my leg and says, "Oh Auntie, you want to see me safely married, don't you?"' And yet it was Wally who had gone to London to find their mother after his father's death.

Meg: He said she opened the door and said 'What do you want?' and he answered, 'I've just come to see you, mother.' 'I don't want you,' and she shut the door in his face. He told me with great bravado but obviously very hurt.

Wally was perhaps more bitter about the past because his present difficulties were so unresolved, and he seemed almost closer to his memory of Charlie than in any current relationship. I felt that in a sense I had almost seen Charlie too, he was so markedly present in all the interviews because of their continuing sorrow for him. Meg had been moved that his motor-cycling friends had come to the funeral. She had not wanted him to have a motor-bike and felt compassion in retrospect for R.G. who had let him have one when he moved into digs. To R.G. had also fallen the grim duty of identifying Charlie's body in the mortuary – a harrowing end to her time in Ringshire.

P.M. When I came down that day I felt I'd just slipped back into being their social worker again.
Meg: That was absolutely wonderful. That was the greatest comfort to all of us . . . you'll never know what a good job you did there, Pam, coming all the way down . . .
P.M. It seemed a natural reaction – I just wanted to be there with you all.

Mrs Waldo was in prison when Charlie was buried. Meg's puzzlement over her failure to parent the children was a recurring theme. She described her as quite an attractive, big, well-built woman, very smartly dressed and clothes conscious, needing reassurance about her appearance. It was often clothes that she stole, and Meg felt able to accept her stealing, her disappearances and imprisonments, but not her apparent lack of feeling or understanding of the children's needs, and she found it hard to forgive the numberless hurts to them. These continued into their young adulthood, as instanced with Wally. Earlier he had persuaded Elaine to go with him to see their father when he was dying. Mrs Waldo had met their train and in a taxi to the hospital had said, 'Well, Wally, you haven't introduced me to your girl friend.' Elaine replied, 'Mother, I'm your firstborn, I'm your eldest daughter, I'm Elaine.'

> *Meg:* In a way she's robbed them of something no one can ever give them back.
>
> *P.M.* That's what makes them angry, that they've been robbed of what they feel they've a right to.
>
> *Meg:* She probably can't help it, but isn't it awful not to be able to love your own children?

Social workers (and other professional helpers and volunteers) often need help to feel friendly towards parents who have hurt their children, physically or emotionally,[38] and obviously it is particularly hard for residential staff, who live with the hurts of children, to be accepting of their parents. Meg talked of the contrast of her own secure childhood – in her memories it was always summertime – and her hard-working mother whose highlight of the week was wash-day when a friend came to help her, with dolly pegs and an old wash tub and no hot running water.

> *Meg:* But we always knew that (my parents) cared and they loved us, and no one can give them that. We can give it in a small measure, or try to, but it's second-best, they're always life's losers. So when they do marry happily and they make good parents – I keep on about it because it's something specially wonderful, isn't it . . . when you see someone like Maxine showing such love and care to those two children . . .
>
> *P.M.* Yes, but you can feel there's quite a lot of you in her, can't you, that she's able to do it.
>
> *Meg:* Well, I suppose other people can see that more than yourself.

Wally had tried to distinguish the different ways in which Meg was able to love and his share, perceived as a sense of responsibility, had left him less than satisfied. For Paula it was all she could remember of being parented. Maxine had not loved her less, but her vehemence that Meg could not be the complete substitute parent she wanted perhaps reflected the intensity of her earlier wish that she were. For her Meg had perhaps kept alive the capacity to be parented, and although she could not fully satisfy Maxine's needs, she did transmit to her the capacity eventually to be a parent herself.

Meg's parenting and the constraints on it had thus been differently experienced. Berry[39] has wrestled with the paradoxical position of supplementary parent figures, discussing Righton's view[40] of residential workers as 'stand-in' parents, and Beedell's[41] concept of 'stand-by' parents or even having a 'share in parenting'. But in examining the alleged danger of possessiveness which may beset substitute parents, she asserts that a kind of possessiveness is a positive aspect of parenthood, and quotes E. Newson's classic argument that 'the crucial characteristic of the parental role is its partiality for the individual child', whereas the best we can offer children in care is impartiality.[42] The young people whom Meg cared for must I think have known that she at least 'would go to *un*reasonable lengths, not just reasonable ones for (their) sake'.

Residential care has been described as a process which has an end product,[43] and the process will be influenced by the functions, overt and latent, of a particular unit. At Mulberry Close there was more acceptance of the prospect that children might grow up in residential care than there is now, so the function was long-term nurturing care. There has been scepticism for some time that group care can ever simulate family care, and the hope that these seven brothers and sisters, cared for by a constant housemother and her husband, would be helped to develop a sense of themselves as a family was only partially realised. The ones I saw, however, had developed individually into affectionate young people, with the capacity to talk about their feelings, though with varying degrees of success in their relationships.

As a postscript it can be said that Paula had another daughter, and returned with her to Paxton. She visited Mulberry Close every weekend and, with Meg in the background, was managing to be a rough and ready 'good-enough' mother.[44] Wally received his compensation, bought a well-appointed flat in Paxton, allowed his friends to exploit him, and then took off on his travels alone, sending Meg a trail of postcards from Amsterdam, Hamburg and points east to Delhi and Nepal.

Maxine and family moved into a house of their own with a garden. She telephoned Meg to share her pleasure when Daniel ran in excitedly holding a potato he had dug up which had magically grown leaves and roots. It was good to be able to set that distant first moment of trust in which Maxine's hand slipped timidly into Meg's, alongside her enjoyment now of her small son, firmly clutching a sprouting potato, entranced by this miracle of growth he wanted her to see. In these small ways, slowly, tenderly, healing comes.

> The point is seeing. Manifold, the world
> dawns on unrecognising, realising eyes.
> Amazement is the thing,
> Not love, but the astonishment of loving.
>
> A. Reid[45]

3

Mark

You get this feeling of unwantedness . . . It seems like they weren't bothered
– it seems like they were parking their responsibility on to somebody else and
not really caring for a while . . . I think at times I thought I would like to be
adopted so I could have a mother and father more quickly . . . But maybe
you'd be wandering around now trying to find out who your real parents are.

These mixed feelings were expressed by Mark, recalling the eight years
he waited in care for his parents to sort out their relationship. His
particular story may seem suspended in a void because I am omitting
virtually all the background details, as I doubt whether his parents
would give their agreement, even if it were possible to ask. Apart from
its expediency, this lack of explanation may in fact reflect Mark's own
uncertainty about why he was in care.

The stark reason was the desertion by one parent and the inability of
the other to care for Gillian, Mark and Kate Drummond, aged six,
three and two. They were received into care for three months, and
shortly after long-term. At the second point of departure Mark ran
down the road crying hysterically and the social worker had to pick him
up and carry him to the car.

They went to a special foster-home which acted as an assessment base
for younger children,[1] and I took over their supervision just as the
foster-mother, now pregnant, decided she could not continue, and we
had to move them to Milestones, our reception centre. The previous
social worker and I visited their father. Mr Drummond saw no hope of
any future with his wife and asked that the children be adopted.
Adoption of 'older' children was much rarer then – convincing evidence
of its success was to come later[2] – and at the time it seemed a strange
request. With hindsight it might have been in the best interests,
certainly of Mark, to have been adopted. A childless woman in the
village who cleaned for the foster-mother, did in fact ask if she and her
husband could adopt Mark, but at the time it seemed more important
to keep the three children together.

The foster-mother came with us to Milestones and I have a haunting
memory of Kate that day, standing rigid on the lawn a few feet from the

51

edge where we sat, her head straining over her shoulder, an arm half-raised, immobile, as though there were a blinding light between her and the foster-mother. Gillian was subdued, but friendly and eager to please. Mark wept as we drove away, seeing his world threaten to disintegrate yet again. It is important to say goodbye, rather than just slip away, but residential staff are usually glad if the field worker then leaves fairly quickly, as it is hard being left with unhappy children to settle in.

I visited again soon and found Mark sitting on the lawn in his bathing trunks, his head bowed on his arms. I have described elsewhere his air of waiting which can characterise children who are uncertain of their future.[3] I was reminded of words from *Dombey and Son*, quoted recently by a friend:

> And with fear in his young heart, and all outside so cold, and bare, and strange, Paul sat as if he had taken life unfurnished and the upholsterer were never coming.[4]

Linking these words and Mark's desolate figure, I later made a terracotta model, perhaps to express my own sadness. I showed this to the friend who had quoted Dickens and her very bright two-year-old son, running happily naked round *their* lawn, stopped suddenly and said with acute perception, 'But where's his Mummy?' Where indeed?

That afternoon Mark climbed into the back of my car and sat there refusing to get out, crying silently. He possibly had hopes that my car would reunite him with his mother, but I had no address for her. I talked to him about her and how sad I knew he was, and though he could not tell me what he was feeling, he showed me by the way he clutched every warm and woolly thing he could lay his hands on, how much he longed for his mother – and perhaps me – to comfort him.

I remember a happier visit. I went equipped with a photograph album and a collection of family photos (supplied by their father), ready to start what is now known as a life-story book. I had begun to work out this idea when leaving a group of children who had become attached to me in an inner-city parish in Sheffield, and had made them each a book of photographs of our times together. As a social work student I had extra time to spend in direct work with the Drummond children, and this seemed a potentially good way of helping them to hold on to their image of themselves as members of a family, albeit temporarily dispersed; it was a means of helping them to talk about their parents and to understand what was happening – what Clare Winnicott would call a 'third thing' between me and the children to help us communicate.[5]

We had barely settled on a rug on the lawn when Gillian, seeing the photographs, grasped them with a shriek of delight and ran indoors calling, 'Mrs Land! Mrs Land! I've got some photos of Mummy!' Mark, Kate and I trailed after her, and Mrs Land was helpful in settling us again indoors to look at the photos and begin to make the book. As other writers have since pointed out, it is important to involve residential staff and other care-givers in the enterprise as they have to live with the children's aroused feelings about their parents.[6] It was also an example of how quickly the person who is currently caring for a child can become important to him or her, alongside strongly held feelings for the natural parents.[7] As a social work teacher I have often asked supervisors if there might be an opportunity for students to make a life-story book with a child in care; having experienced how fruitful an exercise it can be, they are then more inclined to make time for it later.

The three children benefited from the warm and relaxed atmosphere at Milestones and were seen as needing another foster-home. We were glad when Mr and Mrs Pym (their first foster-parents) approached us and offered to foster them again (accepting that it might be short or long-term) and I planned to re-introduce them. It was agreed that the Pyms would initially come and take the children for a picnic. The nine months' gap since they had seen each other would have seemed longest to Kate, who had become very attached to Mr Land. I remember a difficult moment of decision when she clung tearfully to him as we were leaving. The foster-parents and two of their three children had travelled some distance and it was important that they and the three Drummonds should have time together; Gillian and Mark were also keyed up for the occasion. So I gave the key of my car to Mr Pym, took Kate from Mr Land and we drove off. Kate screamed most of the short ride while I held her on my lap and repeated in simple words that we *would* come back and see Mr Land that evening, we were just going for a picnic, we *would* come back. She recovered quickly and the foster-mother was then able to comfort and entertain her.[8] The actual move to the foster-home went smoothly and the children seemed to settle quite well. I continued working with them for the next four years.

There were more moves ahead, alas. Mr Pym's work took him to another part of the country and Mrs Pym found it difficult to care for the six children on her own, particularly as it appeared gradually that her marriage was breaking up. She decided she needed to go out to work, and after two years asked me to move the children. I took them on a re-introductory visit to Milestones, relieved that there was somewhere familiar for them.

There had been no direct word from their mother apart from birthday parcels with a distant postmark. However, with encouragement she visited the children that Christmas. She expressed a hope that she would be able to have them back eventually, but there was no room for them physically (and perhaps emotionally) in her present life. Because she still seemed so important to them, especially to Gillian (now aged nine) it seemed at the time worth working towards this hope, though with hindsight the decision is more debatable.[9] Again I looked for a foster-home for all three, and one which could accept contact between the children and their mother. Involvement with social workers, however, was distasteful to her.

Mark I remember as a solid little boy who would settle himself heavily on my lap and pull my arms around him (and in winter my coat too) and within that security could talk about things that bothered him. When I told them about some new foster-parents, Mr and Mrs Bluett, Gillian was impatient to go that day to meet them, but Mark (at seven) was more cautious and agreed that it would be better if I brought the foster-parents to meet them on familiar ground. 'After all,' he said practically, 'we've got to see what they're like if we're going to live with them.'

They did live with them – but only for six months as Mrs Bluettt developed a menopausal depression and became physically unable to care for the children. Once again I had to move them back to Milestones, this time on Kate's sixth birthday.

They were now at Milestones for the third time. We felt we could not risk foster-care again for them as a trio, and it was decided they should go to a small group Home where they were known to Miss Ash, the housemother in charge. Again Milestones provided some security and this time when I moved them it was Gillian who sat in tears beside me in the car, holding a photograph of her mother. 'Why is Gill crying?' Mark asked. I said she was unhappy, as they all were, to be saying goodbye again to the staff at Milestones and still not to be going back to their mother; also that she was perhaps worried their mother would not know where they were going, but that I had written to tell her their new address. They remained in the small group Home with the same housemother for another four years before returning at last to their parents, by then divorced and both remarried. At the hearing, custody of Gillian and Kate was given to their mother and of Mark to his father.

I left before then, sad to be leaving them with their future unresolved. When I said goodbye they each claimed a memento from my car. Mark wanted 'Candy Floss', his name for a fluffy orange duster. I was told that he dressed it with an apron round its stick and took it to bed with him for months – as a comforter, perhaps, or transitional object.[10] Mark also asked if they could each have a piece of elastoplast from a tin I kept in the car, 'In case' he said, 'we get hurt.' It was perhaps his way of saying that I had tried to comfort some of their hurts and he wanted some kind of symbolic assurance that I would go on minding in future.

I sent them birthday and Christmas cards and went back once. They all wrote a number of times and Gillian rang to tell me the plans for their going home. She later wrote to say she would like to come and see me one day.

Mark did not find letter-writing easy. Once he went to Scotland I heard nothing till a Christmas card came out of the blue five years later. Not long after he rang me one Saturday evening (and reversed the charges) to ask if I knew his mother's address – a request that echoed the past. I did not have it and he rang off before I was able to establish whether he was in difficulties. However, early the next morning he appeared on my doorstep with his suitcase. He had been turned out by his father and stepmother and had caught the overnight train from Scotland. He was by then 17. 'I thought I'd come to see the big world,' he said.

Mark spent the day with us and we made up a bed for him, while I went to some trouble to locate his mother. She sounded doubtful – they had just moved to a smaller cottage with no room to spare, she would need to ask her husband. Shortly after Gillian rang, warm and welcoming, to say that she had a room in her flat; Mark was her brother and she would have him.

He talked sensitively that day about his family and his recollections of care. I was disconcerted when he said one of the foster-fathers used to sit on his head when he wet the bed. I asked if he could not have told me this (and reminded him of how he was in tears once when I visited, and had said he did not like his Uncle Jock, but had not been able to tell my why) and he just said, 'Well, I might have got into trouble, mightn't I?' He used me as a bridge that day between the two sides of his family and I was able to help re-introduce him to his mother and sisters. In spite of his bravado of independence he looked rather small and lost when I put him on the train. I had a number of telephone conversations with Gillian at that time. She was glad to be in touch again and grateful that I had been there for Mark.

At the time of my project they had all moved house. Gillian had married but was preoccupied with separating from her husband, and my letter did not reach Kate who had also just married. Mark agreed to see me and we arranged a provisional time – in the evening as he was working. I had difficulty in confirming this with him and the 200 miles there and back seemed a long way to go without being sure of seeing him, but I set off in hope. When I eventually parked outside the flats where he lived a young man appeared and I recognised Mark. He was now 21, a tall, attractive boy with one gold earring. He offered to kiss me rather shyly and took me into the flat. He was vague about our arrangements but accepted my arrival with equanimity.

Mark was friendly and gentle, but uncertain at first. His memories of care included isolated details such as the big barn in one of the foster-homes and a raid on the larder at Milestones. He said they had been well looked after, but with encouragement admitted he had hated one couple they lived with. Milestones and the staff there were remembered affectionately and seemed to have provided some sense of continuity. I had to break it to him that Miss Ash had died. This was hard for him as he had thought of her still at the group Home. Some memories were muddled and we retraced the steps together and the reasons for their moves. He thought the last foster-mother became depressed through looking after them and I tried to take this feeling of responsibility from him as there had been other contributory causes.

One of the main issues that emerged, however, was his lack of understanding as to why they had been in care. This was sobering for me because although I realised they often found it difficult to take in painful facts, I knew we *had* often talked about their circumstances. But at least he was asking me now.

P.M. It's not easy being in care, is it, and wondering why you're not living with your parents.

Mark: I've always wondered why we did go into care. I don't think I've asked her (his mother). I don't think she'd want to talk about it.

P.M. But did we not talk about it? Did you feel you couldn't ask me?

Mark: I don't think I was really interested at that time.

P.M. When did you start to be interested?

Mark: I was talking to Kate – she used to say, 'I wonder why we went into care.' It just sort of caught on to me and I thought, 'Why did we?' It's not very nice when you see all your friends going home to their Mums and Dads at night, and you're just going home to some people who are being paid to look after you. And then being told by some of the children, 'Our Mums and Dads have to pay for children like you,' which I can't understand.

P.M. That was hurtful. And you didn't understand what they meant?

Mark: No. Don't the parents have to pay towards it?

P.M. Yes – they have to contribute.

Mark: Why did we have to go into care then? Was it just that she couldn't cope?

Here then was the direct question. I launched into an explanation which sounded rather lame on tape later. Even when one is familiar with all the circumstances (and I was struggling to recall as accurately as I could over a long period) it is not easy to present painful facts in a way that does justice both to the parents and to the feelings of the child, now grown up, who was not their first priority.

P.M. . . . But it felt to you that it took a very long time for them to sort things out.

Mark: It seemed it. It seems a long time when nowadays there are people getting divorced within a year – and we were stuck in some places we don't like and some places we do, not knowing what's going on.

P.M. And you felt you couldn't ask me?

Mark: I don't think I really went that far.

P.M. I used to think of you as being very able to talk about your feelings – it was always you who was able to ask the difficult questions.

Mark: (Laughed.) Things have changed. Gill does that rather better than me now. I rather shy away from people now.

He tried to recall his image of his mother then.

Mark: I think maybe I used to think about her as somebody who gave me presents when she came down.

P.M. Well, she was very glamorous, wasn't she. She used to turn up looking beautiful.

Mark: Like a sugar-plum fairy out of nowhere!

This last phrase was perhaps an apt description of what a small boy can feel about a mother who is an occasional visitor but who no longer has reality as someone who daily mothers him.

P.M. . . . But neither of them could look after you so other people were having to. Could it have been better – did you feel there was a plan for you?

Or did you wish something else could happen?

Mark: I think at times I thought I would like to be adopted so I could have a mother and father more quickly –

P.M. Yes.

Mark: – because it seemed to take a lot of time to me.

P.M. To get back to them?

Mark: Yes, because I think that was what worried me most, 'Will I ever leave here?'

I picked up his idea of adoption and told him I had often wondered whether our efforts to keep the three of them together were the right decision, particularly for him.

P.M. . . . . There was a couple in the second village you were in, who wanted to adopt you, when you were only four.

Mark: Maybe you'd be wandering around now trying to find out who your real parents are –

Mark's sense of having lacked consistent parents for eight years, and the length of that wait, came up several times as we talked. I gave him opportunities to reproach me which he did not seem able to take. When I asked him what he had thought I (and other social workers) had been about when we visited, he said: 'To see that we were all right, I suppose, and – to come as a sort of friend . . . You've got to be a friend to the children you're looking after – but maybe they give them too many to look after now.' He thought it was hard for an adult to talk to a child.

P.M. I used to think that you helped me to talk to you and other children. Somehow you made me feel as if I could talk with you, and that I had some idea of what you were feeling. (Pause.) You see, you could have an influence on my teaching if you wanted to!

Mark: I think the main thing they've got to learn is to find the source of the problem and try and get it sorted out as quickly as possible, so you don't get stuck in a Home for a long time.

P.M. And when you say 'the source of the problem', you mean the reason why parents can't look after their children?

Mark: Yes.

P.M. Well, you obviously feel you were left there far too long.

Mark: I think I was. Yes. I think eight years is too long. You go eight years without real parents, then somebody says, 'Hi! I'm your parent! I've come to look after you now.' Seems a bit odd. Whereas in Dad's case it was that – 'Hi! I'm your Dad!'

Mark had been 12 when he joined his father and stepmother. When he arrived on my doorstep at 17 he had already been turned out once before.

P.M. Where did you go?

Mark: I took this heavy suitcase; I walked up the road, up these steps, and just sat outside these houses on top of this case, putting my clothes on, my socks on, and the police came because they thought I was loitering. They took me home and talked to him and that's how I got back home. That was when I was 16.

P.M. And so this was the year after . . . It was very hurtful. (Pause.) And you came to me because you thought I might be able to find your mother.

Mark: Mm.

P.M. And you rang me up just to see if I was there?

Mark: I don't know what I really thought. I thought you probably would be able to find her as you always had done in the past. I got a taxi and got on the first train . . . I didn't think you'd recognise me when I came.

P.M. You'd grown such a lot – but I knew who you were.

Mark: Gill only just recognised me. I think it must have been the lost sheep look – looking to see if anyone knew me.

P.M. Well, she came up trumps, didn't she, that day.

Mark: (Pause.) She has been for the last few years – with my problems – sorting them out for me.

Mark's feeling of having a 'lost sheep look' and his phrase 'Looking to see if anyone knew me' at one level echoes the sense of anomie which any of us can feel on a railway station; but it was perhaps more acute for a boy of 17, turned out by his father and unsure of his welcome from his mother (with whom he now had not lived, apart from an occasional week, for 13 years). He had not been sure that I would recognise him, but must have had enough trust in me to risk just turning up. He had come hoping I would find his mother and this I managed to do. I think he also needed a sense of being known, a mirror image from someone who was fond of him, to give him courage to make his re-entry into the other half of his family.

These last four years, however, had not been easy, and his present state was a good deal less happy than I could have wished for him. He at least had a job, and had kept it, but it was not very satisfying. He had a number of friends, including girl friends, but did not seem particularly close to any of them. He was living near his family but rather on the fringe of it, and although he had written to his father three times since he left there had been no reply. His loneliness only gradually emerged.

P.M. So who are you really closest to now?

Mark: Well, no one really.
P.M. Aren't you?
Mark: It's a question of you and yourself.
P.M. That's what it feels like.
Mark: All part of growing up, I suppose. And Mum was always saying, 'You can't hold on to my apron strings all the time.' It was exactly the same in Scotland – 'You can't hold on to *our* apron strings all the time.'

Urged to grow up by both his parents, he still had not found comfort in a girl friend.

Mark: I don't want to get married yet – I don't even know if I will.
P.M. Is that because you've seen marriages go wrong?
Mark: I don't know. I think it is the worry that maybe that'll happen to me, and I don't want to go through that . . . If I got married I would want children. But then if I got divorced – I don't think I would want to get divorced until the children were grown up. It wouldn't be very nice for them, having a one-parent family.

He was upset that Gillian, who was his main support, was about to leave her husband, Dougal, who had also been friendly to him. He had lived with his mother and stepfather for about a year but had to leave when they moved, and his overriding feeling was of unwantedness.

P.M. Has it been pretty difficult then these last few years? You were saying you had to look after yourself now.
Mark: You get this feeling of unwantedness.
P.M. Unwantedness?
Mark: Yes. I was going to go and live there, and what Dougal told me was that she had phoned Gill and said that she couldn't really have me as there was no room, and could Gill have me?

Inevitably, there was ambivalence. Alongside the feeling of being unwanted, he wanted me to know that he and his mother 'got on fine together'. He recognised, however, that his close resemblance to his father was a barrier between them.

Mark: That's what upsets her, I suppose. She looks at me and looks at a younger version of him.
P.M. Yes. She wants to forget him, and you remind her of him.
Mark: Yes.
P.M. That's hard on you, isn't it – to have your Dad's shadow hanging over you.

When I asked him more directly how he felt in himself:

Mark: I think the only thing that's missing is probably the gap – the eight years not living with anyone – with one person – I suppose.

P.M. And that's affected how you feel about yourself now?

Mark: I suppose so, yes.

P.M. . . . And perhaps you used to feel I ought to be doing something more about getting you home to her.

Mark: I can't really remember. (Pause.) Maybe she could have sorted herself out a bit quicker. It was a long time to wait for a divorce. Did you have to wait that length of time then?

P.M. No – not as long as that.

Mark: It seems like they weren't too bothered – it seems like they were parking their responsibility on to somebody else and not really caring for a while. (Pause.)

P.M. Well, it's so hurtful when it's you that's left there. And it perhaps leaves you feeling again, 'What's wrong with me, that they didn't bother more?' You blame yourself rather than them. They were perhaps just thinking about themselves and you were having to make the best of it.

Mark: It seems that way in a lot of divorce cases – the parents don't want to know until it's 'Who gets custody?' Then they're really interested in you just to spite each other.

Because a large element in our self-esteem is the meaning other people give us in their reactions to us, Mark's sense of unwantedness not unnaturally left him lacking in self-confidence. He thought a job as a ship's steward, involving travel and meeting people 'might bring me out of my shell'.

P.M. Well, it's hard to force yourself to come out of your shell.

Mark: Mm. I thought joining the TA (Territorial Army) I would probably end up coming out of it, but it doesn't seem to have worked! Though I've made a few friends and I got on with people a bit easier because we were all in the same ditch, all having to do the same job.

P.M. I suppose it's finding the confidence that people are going to like you – and why shouldn't they?

Mark: I don't know. (Laughed.)

P.M. You know, you're very nice-looking –

Mark: Well, that's what everyone tells me, but I've not got enough confidence in myself to belive it! (Pause.)

P.M. – and you're gentle with people. (Pause.) I suppose I'm old-fashioned and would like to think of your finding someone you could really love.

Mark: Well, I hope to one day – I expect she'll come along!

He agreed that he seemed able to talk to me, but had been uncertain to begin with. My letter had put him in something of a quandary as he was uncertain what the rest of the family (particularly his mother) would think if he did see me, though his stepfather had said the decision was his. He concluded, 'At least now I know why we originally did go in (to care).' When I gave him a goodbye hug he said he would come and see me next time.

Driving home late that night I felt sad about this good-looking, gentle but unsure young man. It could be said that he is not unemployed or delinquent or seriously depressed; he is responsible and sensitive about other people's feelings. But his feeling of unwantedness and of not being close to anyone raises questions as to whether the best decisions were made for him.

Mark himself had wondered about adoption and this might have given him a more secure emotional base. It is, of course, much easier to assess with hindsight and it would not have been an easy decision at the time, as the children always seemed on tenterhooks for their mother who held a kind of magnetism for them. In addition, she might well not have agreed to adoption, and in those days a court would have been less inclined to consider her unreasonable in withholding her consent.[11] The prevailing ethos then was geared to prevention and rehabilitation and to respecting the role of natural parents. The move to give greater weight to the welfare of the child when his or her interests and those of the parents no longer coincide was subsequently embodied in the Children Act, 1975.[12] Looking back it seems to me that we *were* too passive in waiting for their mother to make room in her life again for the children, and were not geographically close enough to attempt to give her any help on her own account.

The children waited for another four years after I left Ringshire, but this does not exonerate me, as current opinion such as that argued by Rowe and Lambert,[13] Adcock,[14] Parker[15] or Mackay[16] would recommend a much earlier decision. They advocate taking hold of a situation once a child has come into care, and working intensively towards rehabilitation, or failing that, towards making a permanent family placement. Margaret Mackay's Scottish Authority has accepted a programme in which no child under ten is in public care for more than two years without a plan being made for the future. As a result of this policy a third of the children returned home and the rest were placed in permanent substitute care. The London Borough of Lambeth has adopted a similar policy to prevent children slipping into long-term care.[17]

The 'permanence movement' has come under fire from the lobby of opinion which points out that the separation of children from their parents often stems directly from a lack of income, housing or day care and that the rights of such parents should not be further eroded.[18] In this connection the BAAF evidence to the House of Commons Select Committee on children in care[19] recognises that

> Difficulties are created by an imbalance of financial and other provision in different parts of the child care service: for example, a policy of finding new families for children unable to return home is only justifiable when the failure of the original family to survive was not due to shortage of the resources needed to support it in the community.

The evidence further stresses that the philosophy of permanence for children in care is at least as much to do with prevention and rehabilitation as it is to do with adoption. Only when the first priority of enabling children to remain with their own families, or the second one of restoring them as quickly as possible after separation, have both failed, should the emphasis in local authority planning be 'whenever possible, to provide children with an alternative permanent family'.

Having campaigned in my teaching for some years for more purposive planning for children, influenced particularly by Rowe and Lambert's findings in *Children Who Wait*,[20] it was salutary to find that there had also been children on my own caseload who experienced themselves as waiting.

> In the third-class seat sat the journeying
> boy
> And the roof-lamp's oily flame
> Played on his listless form and face,
> Bewrapt past knowing to what he was
> going,
> Or whence he came.
>
> Thomas Hardy[21]

4

Ralph, his mother and his foster-mother

I knew you and what you did and how you did it. I trusted you and relied on you absolutely.

In contrast to Mark's long wait in care, I was fortunate in being able to plan a short-term placement for Ralph which almost perfectly suited his needs, although initially his future looked as uncertain as Mark's. His mother, Mrs Jane Ryder, specialised in fostering young pregnant girls, but when Ralph was nearly five she developed cancer of the uterus after the birth of her fourth child, and Ralph and the new baby came into care.

I had not envisaged this stark turn of events when I worked with Mrs Ryder the previous summer. She was then a young teacher-turned-foster-mother, expecting another baby herself, but coping serenely with Lily who was pregnant at 14, as well as her own three children, Ralph, Bridget and John, all under five. Mr Ryder worked as a public employee and as a gardener, and they lived fairly impecuniously but contentedly in a thatched stone cottage with thick mullioned windows and a long garden running up to the fields and the church.

Lily's baby was placed for adoption and two months later Jane Ryder also had a son, Justin. When we heard that she had cancer we offered help with the children. Her mother (who lived six counties away) was able to have Bridget aged nearly three and John, 18 months. Mrs Knight, who specialised in fostering babies (p.7) and who had just had Lily's baby prior to adoption, was fortunately free and able to take Justin, barely three months old. By what seemed another most happy chance I was able to place Ralph with Mr and Mrs Stone, new foster-parents in the next village a mile along the ridge. This meant he was still close to his father and could also start school as planned in company with Rupert Stone who was the same age.[1] I had done the home study when the Stones applied to foster that autumn and knew that Celia Stone, who was a sculptress, would be specially well equipped to respond to Ralph's lively temperament and enquiring mind. The placement seemed tailor-made for him. I took her to meet him at his own home – now sadly empty except for Ralph and his father

– and the next day Mr Ryder came with me when I took Ralph to his foster home.

I kept in touch with Jane Ryder by letter as she was now in a special sterile ward at Fulham Hospital in London. This remarkable unit had been built five years earlier to treat young women who have a rare malignant growth called chorionepithelioma which develops in the womb following pregnancy, and from which nine out of ten patients had previously died. A new and highly successful treatment had been evolved, which depended on the one hand on the response of the tumour to certain drugs, and on the other to intensive and sterile nursing, designed to reduce to a minimum the risk of infection for the patients, as the drugs drastically lowered their immunity to simple everyday germs.[2] Jane Ryder spent several months in a room virtually sealed off from the outside world, and could talk to her husband and Ralph, when they visited, only through a plastic panel in the door.

I saw her on my way through London at Christmas and was struck by the courage and serenity which she seemed to maintain even in the face of illness and separation from her family. I tried to help keep the lines of communication open between Ralph and his mother, and Celia Stone was imaginative in devising ways of doing this. She encouraged him to paint and these pictures would be pinned (sterilised) by his mother's bed. Celia also made tapes to send, for example of Ralph and Rupert singing and talking in the bath, and Jane Ryder returned 'letter' tapes.

That winter the future seemed precarious. Mr Ryder trudged faithfully between the dispersed members of his family, and one afternoon as I sat with him in the darkening cottage he faced the possibility that his wife might die.

However, Jane Ryder did gradually recover and came home. She waited a little while before having Justin back, to give herself time to settle the three elder children and to regain her strength, but visited him in his foster-home to get to know him again. Then one glad July day we drove over to collect him and the family was complete again.

After that there was a visit to a farm when they moved, a photograph of all four children perched triumphantly on a five-bar gate, an exchange of Christmas cards for some years and then a glimpse of Jane looking wonderfully well on a visit to her sister near Sheffield. At the time of my project I was sad to hear that her marriage had ended, and I found her eventually in a town where she was teaching, well away from Ringshire. She asked me to stay the night on my way to see Celia and Felix Stone.

The sedate exterior of Jane's nineteenth-century stone terraced house hid a warm, glowing interior, which in turn led into an enchanting small garden enclosed by high walls rampant with clematis, passion flower and vines actually bearing grapes – it was late summer. Indoors there was also a profusion of plants cascading from hanging baskets and trained over arches. We caught up with each others' news over dinner and then settled down to talk. The children were now grown up and scattered and I was not able to see Ralph who was working abroad, or Justin who was away at an art school.

Not surprisingly, Jane's memories of her hospital experience and having her own children in care were much more vivid than her recollections of being a foster-mother. She saw herself as very young and immature in those days before her illness. She had enjoyed fostering but had found it more difficult to deal with the girls' feelings than I had realised. She had not asked me for help on this, partly because she had not altogether identified it as a problem.

P.M. I remember admiring how calm you were.

Jane: I felt very calm. I think I just took it all in my stride. It just sort of flowed along, just seemed to happen, surmounting the difficulties as they came – hopefully we did. Looking back I wonder now how I managed. It seems an incredible thing to have taken on with three children and being pregnant as well. It does seem very strange that I even contemplated it. I don't remember having any such doubts *then* . . . it was a very enriching time.

P.M. That was what I was going to ask – did you get a lot of satisfaction from doing it?

Jane: Yes – not only satisfaction – enjoyment – although because they were in a dire situation one can't really say one enjoyed it, but I did enjoy the experience of having them to stay with me. I think it was another dimension of family life that I hadn't come across before.

P.M. And what about their mothers?

Jane: I felt very sorry for them because I felt they were missing out such a lot. I couldn't understand then – I think I could understand *now* how they felt. I couldn't understand, though, how they could put the neighbours before their children.

She had been a little in awe at first of my colleague, J.B. – 'a lack of confidence probably, feeling you don't stand as yourself, you stand as what other people see around you . . . maybe a need to impress.' But she relaxed and saw us both as colleagues after a bit and stopped worrying whether she was going to be what we wanted.

Jane: And then you were both so supportive and so helpful to me –
P.M. You mean in the next stage? It was curious the change of role, wasn't it?
Jane: Yes. And there you were, waiting to step into that terrible void that occurred – you just took over and sorted out all the problems. One by one they all sort of disappeared – they were terrible problems – I just couldn't see how to cope.
P.M. But did you feel consulted?
Jane: Yes and no. Yes, because you came and talked with me about it when I was in hospital, but no, because there was nothing else I could do anyway. So in a way, just by taking all the problems away from me you took away all the decisions as well.

What is now Section 2 of the Child Care Act, 1980[3] was designed to provide 'shared care' between parents and the Local Authority when parents are prevented from caring for a child themselves and are thus in need of help. For Ralph and Justin, as with the Waldos and Mark, this was voluntary care; the difference lay in the much greater extent to which their parents were involved and committed to being reunited with the children if humanly possible. Most parents feel some ambivalence when their children are received into care, even though they have asked for this and legally retain their parental rights. This can partly stem from a sense of failure,[4] and partly as Mapstone suggests from 'feelings about being caught up with their children in a powerful, impersonal and mysterious local government machine'.[5] When illness necessitates care, however, there is likely to be less sense of self-blame than where a parent has deserted or is in prison. And we had the extra advantage that I and the Department were already known to the Ryders. I thought I had tried to give them a sense of participation in planning for the children,[6] but Jane's main memory seemed to be one of relief that the children were in good hands.

She recalled the fortuitous way in which Ralph's and Justin's placements had seemed to materialise.

Jane: It all slotted into place most beautifully. Strange when you think of the meshing together of the various factors – but from my point of view, the fact that you were there and you cared –
P.M. I can remember our distress when this happened to you.
Jane: It was really a success story for you because it all slotted together so easily and it was all so vital from my point of view that things were sorted out, because I wasn't capable of sorting anything myself.
P.M. Mm. You must have been very frightened.

67

Jane: Yes. And by that time I was getting quite ill, too, wasn't I? I couldn't think straight all the time.

The success in the story was certainly earned as much by her, as I told her, and by her husband who did his best to keep in touch with his scattered family.

P.M. He plodded between you all, didn't he?

Jane: He was marvellous actually, and I felt really sorry for him because I was getting all the attention. Nobody understood, I think, what he was going through. He couldn't talk to people about it. Nobody wanted to listen; his colleagues didn't want to know – they were frightened, cancer was a thing you didn't talk about then . . . So he must have felt totally helpless . . . we were all spread around and he –

P.M. He was playing an important part, being a link between you all. He used to go up and see Ralph . . . and he used to take him back to the house, which I think helped Ralph.

Jane: Ralph *and* Rupert.

P.M. Mm. But I can remember sitting talking with him – I don't think he'd mind my telling you – in the darkened house, it must have been mid-winter, when we didn't know how it was going with you, and he was facing what would happen if you didn't get better – how he would cope with the children.

Jane: How did he think?

P.M. Well, he thought that somehow he would try and make a home for them, somehow get the sort of job to try to keep them together.

Jane: It was a rough time for him. (Pause.) But really, we all came out of it very well, I think – apart from him and me.

She talked of how well Ralph had coped, and appreciatively of how much Celia Stone had helped him – and her also – by keeping them in touch. She pointed to the poised bronze head of Ralph which Celia had made to stand on the window shelf outside her hospital room.

Jane: And his lovely drawings. She was very imaginative – and, of course, he was too. She was his sort of person. He kept in touch with her for quite a long time . . . You couldn't have picked a better place for him, could you?

P.M. No. It was marvellous that it was there!

She talked of the illness itself.

P.M. Did you always go on hoping, or were there times –?

Jane: There were two times when I gave up hope. Most of the time I was terribly positive – I swanned through it really. I think knowing right from the beginning that I had cancer . . . was for *me* a great help. I'm glad that I knew. (A young doctor in Paxton Hospital had told her.) He came about 10 o'clock in the evening and took me out of bed, and I remember sitting on the dustbins in the kitchen leaning against the wall, and he said, 'I couldn't come and see you earlier because I knew you were going to ask questions . . . I knew I wasn't going to be able to fob you off with any old story. I knew I was going to have to tell you the truth and I didn't know how to.' But it all came out . . . and I asked questions and he answered. I think perhaps it was the first time for him.

She had despaired when she developed pleurisy after a heavy dose of the drugs. 'I couldn't breathe. There were ten days that were completely lost to me. I could feel myself going downhill . . . losing contact with everything. I could feel myself thinking it would be much easier to die.' Two months later, when she had been promised that Bridget could come and see her on her birthday, she had another set-back and was too ill for the visit and had wept bitterly with disappointment. She had also been terribly upset earlier, at Christmas time, when she was temporarily in Charing Cross Hospital. The wards were decorated and there were carols and everybody had a present – 'but all I could do was cry'. She was glad it had happened there before she went back to Fulham.

Jane: I suppose it's vanity really, keeping a good face on, not letting anybody else know . . . Maybe crying's a good thing, but . . .
P.M. It needs to come out, doesn't it?
Jane: I just cried and cried – there was nothing anyone could do for me.
P.M. Perhaps I started you off.
Jane: I don't know. I think you came before I got terribly upset. But I got it out of my system.

Most of the time she had been 'absolutely determined to get better', and philosophical about being isolated. 'It's a good thing you don't get uptight about something you can't do anything about. Things you can change you change, but those you can't you just accept.' She felt a certain remoteness from the children, perhaps to protect herself as she could do nothing about being separated from them, except write letters.

P.M. I was wondering whether you saw me differently at that point, because before you and I had shared the responsibility for someone else's child, and there I was responsible for yours.
Jane: No, I think it was absolutely marvellous that I knew you. I didn't worry about them . . . I passed my responsibility for them on to you, and you can only do that if you trust somebody and I trusted you implicitly to do the very best that you could. It never occurred to me that anything would go wrong or that it wouldn't be a success . . . or that you would let me down.

Such complete trust can be a little frightening, but of course a large part of my reliability was based on two excellent foster-homes. However, any social work service has to be mediated.

> *Jane:* I think knowing you and knowing that you cared was the thing that was probably more important and that you took all the worry out of it . . . You were the link, the go-between, and knowing you I didn't worry about what was happening to them.

I said that my students would often have to arrive as a stranger to make arrangements. What would make it easier?

> *Jane:* We were in a unique situation really, weren't we? It was like a jigsaw puzzle that went together – a horrific jigsaw puzzle, a horror story – but it all fitted together in a most remarkable way. If I hadn't known you, if you'd been a stranger to me at the time I was in hospital and you'd come to talk about looking after my children, I think the thing that would have put me at ease more than anything else was knowing that you cared – I don't think anything else matters.

However, she also said, 'It's having confidence, and I think the thing that must come across is a feeling that they're capable of coping.' Hospital based social workers know well how worries at home can prevent a patient from responding to treatment, so it was good that Jane was free to concentrate on fighting her illness. Spring came, death receded and she began a new kind of life.

We recalled a strange time when she still needed to be based in hospital but spent her days from 10 till 6.00 discovering London, Shakespeare's 'quick forge and working-house of thought'.[7] She visited art galleries and exhibitions, window-gazed, weak still but tasting freedom and, like Virginia Woolf delighted in 'life, London, this moment in June'.[8]

> *P.M.* I was thinking tonight when you were saying you'd suddenly got this freedom to be you again, with the children grown up and gone, and how you were enjoying it, I was remembering that time in London, because there you were without any responsibilities then, weren't you?
>
> *Jane:* That's true, yes it's true.
>
> *P.M.* You'd been through all that illness and worry and fear. You were wanting to get back to the children, but for the time being –
>
> *Jane:* I knew that I couldn't then – I just made the most of what there was available. I really enjoyed that time. I was very very thin and I got tired ever so quickly. I sat down a lot and drank coffee sitting in café windows looking out watching the world go by! And I wandered, just sort of ambled

. . . I think it probably aided my recovery because I was happy and contented and I was seeing things that I never thought I'd have the opportunity to see at that stage.

P.M. In a strange way it was the beginning of a new life, wasn't it?

Jane: Well, it was, yes. Things were very different after that. I think I grew up then. I actually began to develop and grow up. (Pause.) When you've nearly lost everything, or think you might have lost everything, then everything becomes so much more valuable.

P.M. And every day is precious.

Jane: Each day is an entity in itself.

In this strange interlude which was a kind of rebirth, she developed a new and separate sense of herself which also, sadly, had implications for her marriage. The new life which she discovered began to draw her away from her husband. 'When I came back I think basically I just wasn't the same person I had been when he married me . . . there was no way I could travel backward – I tried, I did try.'

When they eventually separated 11 years later, she was determined to start again with the children in a new place. It was a lonely hard struggle to re-establish herself as by a series of circumstances she was very poor to begin with. However, gradually she saved enough for her own home to become a possibility. Not surprisingly, handling the children on her own, particularly in adolescence, had not been easy, but now they were virtually all fledged, and she had time to be herself again.

Jane thought that Ralph had come through the earlier time of separation very well because he had been given the rather special experience of living with Celia, and had been the one most in touch with his father and with her, knew where she was, could understand more what was happening, and knew the doctors who had been very good with him. Bridget too, seemed fairly unscathed and she and Jane have a very close relationship now, can talk very freely and enjoy each other. Justin was harmed less than might be expected, having by ten months become attached to Mrs Knight but had settled back home easily. It was John who seemed to suffer most, having been at that very vulnerable age of 18 months, too young to understand or to hold an image of his mother for long in her absence.[9] He was cared for by his grandmother (nearly a day's journey away) so fared better than his namesake in the Robertsons' film,[10] but even so there was a total disappearance of his former life and he could well have felt his sense of trust had been betrayed. When he came home six months later he would sit under the table and bang his head against the wall. 'He's very much a loner. You could never put your arms around him or cuddle him if he was upset or if he'd hurt himself; he'd just stand up absolutely rigid and he wouldn't let anybody get close to him.'

So there were worries still, and scars, but Jane was still on friendly terms with her ex-husband. She had the same lovely serenity, dignity and sense of fun, but seemed more fulfilled as a person.

> *Jane:* I feel very much at peace now . . . Things keep coming at you, but really and truly I think I feel very much at peace. I feel lonely at times but – I think I'm having a love affair with my house actually!

She had created a beautiful oasis and it did look much loved. At breakfast next morning, trying to sum up our earlier relationship, she chose the words quoted at the chapter heading. She set me on my way to Ringshire and sent messages to Celia and Felix Stone.

I had always loved driving along their high ridge and recalled the rather perilous exhilaration of visiting once at the start of a blizzard, when Celia, edging the door open to me against the driving snow, exclaimed, 'You must be mad!' However, now we lunched in the garden in late summer warmth, the valley stretching away benign before us, and I saw again with pleasure Celia's sculpture of three swans, their curving heads arched together. Her own chiselled good looks seemed to defy age.

Felix had been supportive in the fostering experience but less involved. He joined in the discussion for a while after lunch and then left for a Saturday afternoon's flying. A picture of Ralph emerged as they talked both of the enjoyment and the uncertainties of fostering. They had also twice fostered two sisters whose unsupported mother twice had to let a baby be adopted to preserve her existing family. Felix remembered Ralph more clearly – 'He was a very, very ingenious little chap' with a will of his own which had led to some tussles, mostly dealt with by diverting him. They had learnt a lot as they went along about putting the foster-children at ease. Ralph had enjoyed school.

> *Celia:* On the first day Rupert was just cross, but Ralph was all smiles, 'Hullo, hullo – we did this, we did that.' (Jane had recalled being told that he had said, 'Well, that was school today, what's tomorrow?'!) He just wanted things to happen all the time.
>
> *P.M.* And did he seem to understand, do you think, about his mother being in hospital and why he was living with you?
>
> *Celia:* Yes . . . He must have thought about it, but it was almost as if he could

categorise things and could put it in a pocket or something till tomorrow or another day. That could be his personality, or that he didn't know how to cope with it, I don't know, but I was never aware that he was brooding.

P.M. He wasn't in tears at night?

Celia: No – he seemed to need a lot less sleep than Rupert. When Rupert was fast asleep Ralph would be sitting up making ingenious things out of a box or tying string to the end of the bed and making pulleys. So he was so absorbed – but whether he really was absorbed or whether he needed to be absorbed because he didn't want to think about his mother, you can't tell. He'd know, I expect.

(Jane had given another picture of Ralph's absorption when she had arranged to meet him and her husband in a café near the hospital on her first time out. 'They were sitting there and Ralph had a book and was showing it to the woman sitting at the next table, and he was so full of this book and telling her all about it and I walked in and said, "Hullo Ralph" and he said, "Hullo Mum" and went on talking to this person. And he suddenly looked up at me and said, "You're not in hospital!" He knew it was me but it hadn't registered.')

Celia: This capacity to get absorbed . . . should take him a long way in life, shouldn't it. But I wonder, on reflection – I didn't think of it at the time – that he closed off his worry about his mother in doing the things he was doing.

P.M. Shut himself off.

Celia: Well, some people do have that capacity, don't they, in emergencies. Others collapse more openly, but he was just naturally that way inclined anyway – to be busy.

P.M. Well, people have different ways of coping with their anxieties.

It seemed likely that Ralph, with a previously secure family life, used his natural intense interest in things as a means of diverting his mind from unhappiness about his mother. Many other children in care (such as Mark and the Waldos) who are less sure of their parents, find it hard to concentrate because of their worries, and their education suffers.

Ralph had the assurance of regular visits from his father. These he enjoyed and he usually let his father leave without tears.

Celia: He did get upset on one occasion. He stamped and shouted – I think it was because he had thought he was going home and he wasn't. I don't know how that came about because you always took such care to keep him informed in advance . . . I didn't know if there was something underlying or whether he just wanted his own way that day, because he always came back quite happily.

73

P.M. He really seemed to settle with you, didn't he?

Celia: Yes he did. We settled with him. He was interesting and we gained really, because he was interesting – I'm not surprised Felix can remember Ralph, he was quite a lovely little boy . . . We seemed to get to the nub of Ralph even though he would defy us quite a lot, but we could get close to him because he liked doing the things we liked doing.

Her ways of helping him communicate with his mother had often just arisen naturally.

Celia: It seemed to come spontaneously out of what we were doing. 'Oh, that would be a good idea, we could send that to your mother.' It seemed to be a reasonable, normal sort of atmosphere.

She had felt less confident in helping him with his feelings.

Celia: The easy part is to occupy the child and give him food and a bed and warmth and play (records) at night, but the part you don't know – 'Is he feeling hurt or –?' – the real part.

P.M. Knowing what's going on inside – dealing with that. And in a way he was a proud little boy, wasn't he? He perhaps kept his feelings to himself.

Celia: Yes, I think he would only cry in anger really. He was very upset with his mother, perhaps, but he had this strong will-power.

It would have worried her if he had cried because of his tendency to do things rather than cry. 'He had all those things sorted out at five – on the surface anyway.' She had been more frightened than she had conveyed to me at the time at the thought of Ralph's potential unhappiness, and had always talked about his mother in a positive way. We had needed to keep his faith going (and our own) that she would recover, but perhaps did not tune in enough to his worries. Celia had talked more with the girls as they questioned her more. 'I found myself just sitting at the table with them, tears falling on the letter they were writing to their mother.'

She had had other uncertainties, including the vexed question of managing the naughtiness of someone else's child.

P.M. Well, you wonder, is it ordinary naughtiness, or is he upset, and if I give in –

Celia: Is he going to always expect me to give in?

P.M. Whereas in a way if you can avoid unnecessary battles you probably get on better.

She had mostly used diverting tactics, but had been nonplussed when she had called for Rupert at school to take him to the dentist and Ralph had screamed that he wanted to come too, and she had complied with the teacher's dictum that he was not going. We agreed a lot of hassles are unnecessary.

Celia: It would have been a lot easier to have taken his hand as well and brought them both back.

It is not easy to prepare foster-parents for all eventualities, and one can only hope to be at hand to support them and discuss worries. The National Foster Care Association now provides material for preparation courses, and group preparation and support make foster-parents less isolated.[11] There had obviously been one misunderstanding between us in that Celia had uppermost in her mind a maxim, 'Don't have a close attachment', and thought this originated from me. I would not have wanted her to feel restricted, knowing Ralph would need her affection, but perhaps had warned her initially that it can be hurtful when foster-children return home. Would this kind of misunderstanding be avoided, I wonder, by the use of a written agreement between the parties to the placement such as is recommended in the BASW report, *Guidelines for Practice in Family Placement?*[12] Otherwise I think we naturally established 'a working partnership' without becoming legalistic. The Ryders were also willingly involved so that the placement met Holman's preferred 'inclusive' fostering model.[13] This inclusion of all the fostering participants, foster-parents, children, natural parents and social worker, enables emphasis on a child's need to obtain a true sense of his present identity and past history within a framework of affection, and also facilitates rehabilitation if possible. Both Aldgate's[14] and Fanshel's[15] research has shown that frequent contact with natural parents (together with purposeful social work activity) is one of the main factors influencing a child's return.

Celia looked back on her motivation to foster which sounded a healthy mixture of self-interest and altruism.

Celia: I was completely housebound. It wasn't enough to look after one child and it didn't seem we could have any more, so I thought, 'What a shame, this huge place; one boy – there should be five boys really.' It sprang from a feeling of dissatisfaction with the little nucleus of spending all that time with one, and then we justified it by saying, 'Well, it's much better too for Rupert,' and looking back I think we all learned a lot from it.

P.M. But it was your feeling you'd got more time and energy and affection to spare.

Celia: Also I felt (pause), 'Fancy being given all this and then have just this one child.' That seemed basically wrong, not to be using it more and sharing it.

P.M. Well, it's natural to want to share something good.

Josselyn[16] presents the complexity of motivations to foster, and Towle[17] suggests that it is not really possible to judge outcome by motivation – the capacity for foster-parenthood can sometimes only be known through the experience of doing it. It is recognised now that foster-parents have needs of their own which can legitimately be met by fostering; as Towle puts it, 'the decisive point is that foster-parents seek children out of some unmet need, but that does not necessarily have sinister implications.' It seems important, however, that the placement of a particular child feeds into the mainspring of the foster-parents' wish to foster, otherwise they will not derive the satisfaction which encourages them to continue. Kay[18] warns how foster-parents can be wasted as valuable resources if their needs are not recognised and they are used inappropriately.

Celia and I had also derived mutual pleasure from our partnership (talking at times about art as well as child care).

> *P.M.* I was the only social worker you had, so you didn't have a chance to compare me with anyone else.
>
> *Celia:* No, I never thought of you objectively really, you were just my anchor. I knew if anything happened I couldn't cope with that you'd know what to do, but I didn't think of you critically in any way . . . I thought this week when you telephoned and I said, 'Yes, come, or stay to lunch', I seemed to be quite closely attached to you. So it's part of it, I think. I wondered afterwards when I tried to analyse it to myself, you supplied a sort of intellectual need that I had at the time as well. I wasn't out in the world and I felt rather drained of that kind of conversation. So perhaps that contributed to it. You brought me some nice children.

Ralph particularly had been well matched, and the special experience which Jane Ryder felt he had been given had in turn added to Celia's sense of herself as a mother. Celia said, 'Ralph was very like his mother,' and Jane said of Celia, 'She was his sort of person.' So it seemed that they had been able to share him and enjoy his individuality without the jealousy that can be inherent between mother and foster-mother. I was disconcerted to think that they had both found the task of responding to the feelings of their charges more difficult than they had conveyed at the time. It is perhaps such a relief when foster-parents appear to manage very serenely that one does not give them enough opportunity to admit their difficulties.

The rest of Ralph's and Justin's childhood had not been without further trauma, but they had reached young adulthood and late adolescence apparently intact. This was a tribute obviously to Jane (and themselves) but was also evidence perhaps of the quality of care they had received in their foster-homes in that critical period of early separation.

Caring is the greatest thing, caring matters most.
(last words of Friedrich Von Hügel)

5
Lorraine and Helen and their Grandmother

It's surprising how valuable a cuddle can be.

Traditionally, grandparents can be an important source of supplementary or substitute care, in good times as well as in trouble. Even when nowadays they may no longer live in close proximity in two–generation units of the kind described by Young and Willmott,[1] the ties of affection still often provide an alternative base which can be turned to with confidence. Literature and autobiography are rich in childhood memories of the relaxed and enjoyable security of comforting grandparental figures – as well, of course as some who were remote, awesome or disapproving. Gorky's particularly vivid account of his childhood[2] paints a terrifying picture of his grandfather who beat him till he was insensible and then brought peace offerings to lay on his pillow; but also of the compensatory haven provided by his grandmother, that 'endlessly kind indefatigable old woman', 'whose eyes caressed me with musing tenderness, conveying much more than words'; 'all day I would trot at her heels . . . it was as if I had grown to be part of her.'

In social work practice also grandparents figure importantly. Their fares can be paid from Section 1 money[3] to prevent a child's reception into care, and it was seen how Bridget and John Ryder stayed with their grandmother for six months. On the negative side, Stevenson[4] warns against the assumption that family placement is necessarily the best solution as a child can be caught up in bitter family antagonisms; also the hostile antecedents of an abusing parent are often a contraindication against placing the abused child with grandparents. However, Rowe et al.[5] give encouraging evidence of the success of long-term placements with relatives.

Lorraine and Helen's maternal grandmother, Mrs Alice Moon, was a much loved cornerstone of her large family network. When their parents separated, their mother, Mrs Yvonne Revel, left Lorraine with her mother in Paxton, and some months later was planning to do the same with Helen. Mr and Mrs Moon could not afford to care for two extra children and were approved as foster-parents for them so that a boarding-out allowance could be paid. Mrs Revel had earlier left Helen as a baby of 18 months with the owners of the corner junk-shop (along with some of her furniture and other possessions) hoping they would adopt her, but Mrs Moon had intervened.

I arranged to meet Mrs Revel and Helen (by then aged three) off the train from London. It was snowing as I waited at Paxton station, and Mrs Revel, blonde and heavily pregnant, sailed towards me. 'Welfare?' she asked with an upward inflection, as she might have queried 'Porter?' or 'Taxi?', and pausing only imperceptibly, swept on with Helen to my car outside.

The children knew their grandparents and my main function was to support Mrs Moon as she integrated them into the family. Lorraine was eight, shy and pretty with long fair hair, while Helen, dark-haired with a fringe, was more extrovert and demanding of affection, and would often sit on my knee. Their mother visited about twice a year on their birthdays, and by the time I left three years later there seemed little likelihood of their returning to either parent, and they grew up in care in this family foster-home.

Helen wrote to me twice and sent me her school photograph. There was then a long gap until a recent Christmas card from Mrs Moon telling me that Lorraine was happily married with two children, and that Helen was engaged. 'So they are on their way through life, and they are very proud of me and you and everyone who has helped to care for them.' I guessed that Mrs Moon was perhaps wanting me to share in her own pride and satisfaction in bringing them up.

Lorraine's husband, Jason, is a serviceman, and I visited her in their married quarters near Paxton, a collection of rather anonymous houses that have seen many families come and go. Lorraine, now a good-looking young woman of 23, was welcoming but reserved at first, and I had competition from Pamela, a talkative two-year-old, the baby Adam's crying and a friendly dog. However, Lorraine breast-fed Adam very naturally, which quietened him, and Pamela and the dog went out to play intermittently. She was inventive in her frequent reappearances – 'She has all her marbles' – and I nursed the baby once or twice while her mother attended to her. Lorraine insisted on good behaviour, perhaps for my benefit, but was patient and affectionate with her and they seemed companionable together. She was obviously enjoying being a mother.

Lorraine: I think I'm a natural . . . I fed her till she was eighteen months.

P.M. That would give her a good start. It's a very easy way of comforting them, isn't it?

Lorraine: Especially when they wake up at night.

In company with a number of other young people in the study she was determined not to inflict on her children her own parents' pattern of divorce or separation.

Lorraine: I always said I'd never get divorced. If I got married it would be forever.

P.M. You wanted to make sure before you got married.

Lorraine: I thought he was right for me after the first week. But I wanted to be sure of him before I had a family.

She felt the experience of being in care had been less hard on her than for children who went to strangers, though she still missed her parents. She had seen her mother infrequently, but she and Helen spent all their holidays with their father in London as he had been given custody of them after the divorce.

Lorraine: I felt it was my fault they'd split up, because I was the cause of their getting married in the first place.

P.M. Well, you blamed yourself that they split up, but perhaps it might have happened anyway.

Lorraine: Oh, it would. They always had arguments. I'd stick up for my Dad. I used to be in the middle, kicking my Dad's legs. There are lots of things I can remember. Looking back now I think they're funny.

P.M. But they weren't very funny at the time.

Lorraine: No.

It was not till she was 15 that she began to sort things out for herself about her mother.

Lorraine: It didn't trouble me too much when I was younger because my Gran was always there when I was upset.

P.M. She would comfort you.

Lorraine: You don't want it when you're 15. At nights I used to cry in bed.

P.M. It's sad to think of your crying in bed with no one to talk to about it.

Lorraine: I went very into myself and wouldn't talk to nobody. I was never a person for showing affection for anybody anyway.

P.M. Weren't you? Not even your Gran?

Lorraine: No, not even how close I am to her now, I wouldn't show her if I was upset . . . I'm very independent.

P.M. Early on you had to cope and look after yourself.

Lorraine: I was looking after Helen and Leo (one of her brothers) at the age of five. (Her mother had been cautioned for leaving the children on their own.)

Lorraine had mainly talked to her grandmother about her uncertainties, although later she was able to question her mother who was very open with her. Recently her mother had been writing her life-story and had given it to Lorraine to read, perhaps to justify herself. Lorraine had been upset for her mother by what she read of her way of life, and better understood why she had subsequently become a compulsive drinker.

She had always wondered what it would be like to grow up with both parents. Their grandparents had treated them as daughters and had become *de facto* parents – they called them 'Mother' and 'Father' and their own parents, 'Mum' and 'Dad'. In considering adoption by grandparents and other relatives, the Houghton/Stockdale Committee regretted that existing relationships could be distorted by adoption,[6] and this was the basis for their recommendation of guardianship (which became custodianship in the Children Act, 1975) rather than adoption by relatives in circumstances where greater legal security was desired.[7] However, for Lorraine and Helen there was no secrecy about their natural parents or desire by the grandparents to exclude them; they just naturally parented the little girls and brought them up and the children chose the names that felt appropriate. In the preliminaries to our discussion now, Lorraine had shown me her wedding book. I noticed that her natural parents rather than her grandparents featured in the family group, and her distress at the latter's accidental absence from the photograph was indicative of whom she regarded as her 'real' parents.

Lorraine felt she still had her grandmother to turn to, and visited her as often as she could. She dreaded the thought of losing her.

P.M. It is frightening to think of someone you have depended on so much – that they can't stay with you forever.

Lorraine: . . . now I can't stop thinking about it. I don't know what I shall do if anything happened to her. I suppose I'll have them two to help me out.

P.M. You'll have your own family to love and to look after you, but she's special, isn't she?

Lorraine: Yes, she always has been. Ever since I can remember.

Living as she had within her own family, the involvement of social workers had seemed a mixed blessing and she had not liked all of them. The routine annual medical had become an issue at 15 when her grandmother had said, perhaps partly teasing, partly a bit hostile towards the Department, 'It's a check-up to make sure you've got no bruises or anything. To make sure I'm not beating you.'

Lorraine: I said, 'Right, I'm not going anymore.' I thought, 'My Gran won't beat me' . . . I was adamant that I wouldn't go and I was too big for my Gran to drag me there.

P.M. It made you feel different, I suppose. Or did it seem an insult to your Gran that the Welfare should be interfering like that?

Lorraine: I always felt different with the Welfare. Not so much when I was a child, but more when I was in my teens . . . Because when you're young then the Welfare people seem more like friends.

P.M. Yes. And do they stop being friendly when you're in your teens?

Lorraine: No. I think you stop being friendly towards them.

However, she thought that her last social worker had not been friendly or interested in her, but had talked to her grandmother about her in front of her without speaking directly to her at all. She had met her husband on her seventeenth birthday and had asked if she could come out of care before she was 18 as she was embarrassed to have a social worker visiting when her young man was in the house. Unlike the Waldos, coming out of care had just brought her a sense of relief, because she already had a continuing family base as well as courtship and marriage to look forward to.

Lorraine's determination to make her marriage work and her feeling that she was 'cut out to be a mother' were uppermost in her present sense of herself. She said she 'couldn't be happier if she tried', though against this saw herself as shy still and as a loner who could not show her feelings, and she compared herself with Helen who was more sociable and could keep a conversation going. It was not difficult to reflect back her picture of herself as a 'good-enough' mother, and I added that she seemed able to show affection to her children, and had kept a conversation going with me.

That afternoon I talked with Mrs Moon before Helen came home from work. They still lived on the edge of Paxton and I remembered how their crowded little house with its open view up a wooded hill was often a hub of family traffic. However, Mrs Moon was waiting on her own, dressed up to greet me, red-haired and small of stature, a loquacious, indomitable character, full of courage and humour, and she welcomed me as warmly as ever. With Mr Moon's quiet support she had reared these two grandchildren in the wake of her own four children, and I had supported the start of this venture. It seemed important to her that I had come back to see how she and the girls were now, and she was eager for conversation.

She had survived several major illnesses and was gamely fighting old age. Her sense of fun had come from her father.

Mrs Moon: I love to make people laugh. My dad was a comedian, he loved making people laugh. You would have liked my father, if you had met my father. He met Lloyd George – shook hands with Lloyd George, and he met Sir Conan Doyle – and schoolmasters come down to his house to discuss – he was marvellous discussing, anything, my father was.

She showed me family photographs, including ones of her 12 grandchildren, and Lorraine's Pamela. 'That's my little baby, look, my little granddaughter – my great-granddaughter' (the generations merged into one). 'She's fantastic. There's Lorraine on her wedding day. There's me and father in Jersey. There's Helen on her 18th birthday. Oh, and father studying the horses! There's me coming out of Pompeii – you go in them gates there. That's two Italian soldiers. There's me and my friend dancing.'

Her enjoyment of life made her a magnet for the family and there were many instances of her various grandchildren's attachments to her. Behind her pleasure and pride in her large family, however, there was a shadow which perhaps made her emphasise her success the more. This was her sense of failure in her only daughter, Yvonne, whose way of life was a constant heartache.

Mrs Moon: I don't know, there's something gone for me, somehow. She's hurt them so much.
P.M. Well, you took a lot, didn't you – and you did a lot for her.
Mrs Moon: Well, you don't know half of it. One year she hit me, on the floor. The two children were hysterical . . . She'd had a drink, see. She sat down there, and her father the other side, and she was sucking this bottle of whiskey – just like a baby with a bottle of milk. My heart was breaking then, it was.

Mrs Revel had later imputed sexual ideas to Helen just because she had come downstairs in her nightie and dressing-gown in male company, and with her native wisdom Mrs Moon was quite aware that Mrs Revel had been projecting her own feelings on to Helen. The girls had always come down to the fire with towels wrapped round them after a bath.

Mrs Moon: It's natural enough. I think the filth is in the mind, not in the eyesight, what you can see, but what you are thinking. And I told the girls, 'Don't you worry about that, there's nothing filthy in the human body,' I said, 'We were born without nothing on'.

P.M. And you thought she thought Helen was having the sort of thoughts she might have had herself.

Mrs Moon: Of course it was – definitely – don't get 'em thoughts unless you've got 'em yourself, do you. No.

P.M. It must be hard for you, Mrs Moon – I expect she's a disappointment to you, is she –?

Mrs Moon: Well, the only one, wasn't it, and I don't see where she went wrong . . . because we always brought her up like we have my boys, always the same. (She returned several times to this theme.) I don't know what's the matter with her, I'm sure, but there you are. These girls do it from the best of homes, don't they?

Parents often expect social workers to blame them for their children's behaviour. If they do have a part in it, they are more likely to be able to see this (and feel helped themselves) if they feel the social worker is sympathetic and recognises their difficulties. It was extra hard for Mrs Moon as a foster-mother to feel that her grandchildren's unhappiness was caused by her own daughter.

P.M. It's a sadness for you, isn't it, because you've got a big family, and a loving family, but you've got this thing that goes on worrying you.

Mrs Moon: You've got to, haven't you? It's yours – your flesh and blood, never mind what's she's done. I still worry about her now. I'd love to see her all right, you know, with the children. Not so much Lorraine, I think Lorraine has accepted her as she is, but Helen can't you see. She's a bit – well, how can I put it – Helen likes everything just so. She wants to live, or try to live, a class above her own. Not that she's stuck up, she just wants to get on . . .

P.M. And she hasn't accepted about her mother.

Mrs Moon: No, I don't think so, love, honestly. I said to her, 'Well, we all do silly things.' 'Not many mothers leave their children,' she said. 'Even animals cling to their children.'

P.M. So it's still hurting her.

Mrs Moon: Yes. 'Even an animal will look after its child, and fight for its child.'

There were echoes here of Lady Macduff's lament, 'For the wren, the most diminutive of birds, will fight – its young ones in the nest – against the owl.'[8] As a small child, Helen had noticeably missed her mother. She would hide herself in the gap between two armchairs, draped over with a blanket, and at school she seemed in a world of her own, 'miles and miles away'. R.G. who had followed me in this family, too, had suggested a Child Guidance appointment. Mrs Moon was not convinced this was necessary – 'I don't think there is anything wrong with her – more than what she's missing her mother' – but agreed. The psychiatrist told her what happened.

Mrs Moon: She drew a mother pushing a pram when he asked her to draw the first time. Next time she drew a mother with a baby feeding on the breast – she was only a little kid . . . So he sent her out . . . and said, 'There you are, Mrs Moon, there it is.' I said, 'I don't need anyone to tell me what it was – I had a mother too.' Commonsense isn't it.

P.M. You knew –

Mrs Moon: He smiled. 'You're a marvellous substitute,' he said, 'but you'll never be the real mother.' I said, 'I don't want to be, it's my daughter's children' – didn't want to be the real mother, I was their grandmother.

P.M. Well, so you are, but you've also mothered them, haven't you?

Mrs Moon: Oh well, they are like my own now, you know. I love them as I love my own. Lorraine knows that.

P.M. In a way the real mother is the one that looks after you.

Mrs Moon: Yes – that's what Helen says. I said, 'Your mother's coming down,' and she said 'That's not my mother, that's my mum – you're my mother, you brought me up.' That's her own words. (Helen had been a bit distant as a child.) I couldn't reach her for a long time. I think she resented me for a while . . . I didn't push it – I just tried to make her happy . . . She come to me of her own accord and put her arms around me.

P.M. Well, she was perhaps pulled in her mind, was she?

Mrs Moon: I think she was . . . she had gone through a lot, mind, because she was in a Home before she came down here. Her mother give her to these people to look after for a week, and while she was on holiday they had a row – the wife left the husband with all the kids and he stuck them in a Home. That was in London . . . And then she was given to that man down the road in that second-hand shop. 18 months old, and I didn't know . . . till he come up and said he wanted her (Mrs Revel) to sign the adoption form. 'I've got your granddaughter.' 'You've what? Well, you can bring her back up here right now.' So she been through a lot.

This kind of uncertainty is one of the possible hazards of direct placement by the mother for adoption. Mrs Moon had been torn herself, holding back at first from too much involvement, in case the girls' parents wanted them back. Sixteen years later she still felt some unease.

Mrs Moon: I feel guilty inside, if I tell you. I don't think I feel right inside. But they're like my own. I'd give my life for them willingly.

P.M. What do you feel guilty about?

Mrs Moon: I suppose I do think I robbed they mother of they love – I shouldn't be having it really. I've got my own children looking after me, I shouldn't have them as well – because they are not mine, really, they are only my grandchildren. I don't feel it's right somehow.

P.M. You can't stop people loving you, can you?

Mrs Moon: No. And I love them so much too. But I love all my grandchildren – and that little *great*-grandchild, well! I do whisper in her ear, 'I love you,' and she whispers back, 'I love you, too.'

P.M. You did so much for them it seems hard that you should feel guilty for doing what needed to be done, and which you did freely – you didn't try and steal their love, did you?

She had wanted me to share in her pleasure at how well the girls were doing, and this was the other side of the coin – the complex feelings that are part of grandparent fostering. These are well examined in the DHSS publication, *Foster Care: A guide to practice*,[9] which also notes the potential awkwardness of social workers' statutory involvement in a family's care of its own. However, Rowe *et al.*[10] found a more positive attitude to social workers amongst relative foster parents, and Mrs Moon averred that she had not resented our part in the shared care and would have been hard pressed financially without the Department's help. She thought social workers should spend more time talking to the children, should be *young* and natural with them, and should be able to know when a child was unhappy without asking too many questions. She had seen me as available to her, 'And you didn't push yourself too far, to put anybody off.'

I looked with her now at the rewards for her of her labour of love. 'Lorraine's a good mother – everybody do say that about her, the doctors and nurses and all. She takes them to the Clinic and she feeds them on the breast.' She thought breast-feeding helped to produce 'affectionate, feeling children'. Helen was very thoughtful of her, and 'she's got a nice young man. I think she'll be happy with him. He won't go on the wrong road . . . All my children are good to me, and they father.' The phrase in the Christmas card, 'They are on their way through life', had been Mr Moon's.

P.M. You must feel that, that you set them on their path and they're doing well.

Mrs Moon: Yes. Father wrote that. He's rather quiet, but he's got the right way of talking.

Mr Moon arrived home and greeted me warmly but did not take much part in the conversation. Helen also arrived, a sophisticated version of the six-year-old Helen I remembered. She was a little guarded at first and reluctant to talk with me on her own, so we had a three-way discussion as she seemed to want her grandmother's support. She was well able to express herself and gave me a run-down of the five social workers she had known, soon warming to the business of assessing them. 'The only decent one after you was Miss G.' She had liked R.G. but not her successor, who became nervous if spoken to and apparently sat with a pad writing down what was said!

P.M. That must have felt funny. Perhaps a bit like my having the tape-recorder on.

The next one had been failed on her appearance (greasy hair and hippy clothes) and her manner. When Helen, prompted by her grandmother, had asked if she could go on a school trip, her response had been, '"Don't you think you have had enough, Helen?" That tone of voice as well. I remember that. It turned me off straight away.'

Then there had been a man, already known to the family, which made him *persona gratis* to Helen. She thought appearances were important. 'People grade you by your appearance . . . you don't have to look perfectly smart all the time, but – just nice – just nice.' She had looked forward to R.G.'s and my visits, but dreaded the next two's coming. She recommended 'just mixing in . . . rather than put people in situations and awkward spots when they're asking questions and they've got to answer them, even when they can't, probably because people are listening, or because they feel too embarrassed to say it.' She mainly remembered sitting on my knee and playing with a brooch and a ring I wore, and that I had fair hair which made her think of her mother. She spoke bitterly of the infrequency of her mother's visits, and gave her version of the visits to the psychiatrist.

Helen: He asked me to draw pictures and I just drew what come into my head, and both of them were pictures of my Mum, or drawings of a mother with a child, and he assumed from that that I was missing my Mum.

She refused to go again because he had also asked whether her grandmother beat her. R.G. had realised how indignant and upset she was.

Helen: She was like that, she could see without asking 'Are you upset?' or that sort of off-putting question.
P.M. And you said he *assumed* that you were missing your mother, so that was a guess – that perhaps was right?

87

Helen: It was a guess that was right – even though I didn't know what sort of Mum she was like, I wasn't in a position to judge whether she was a really lovely Mum or a horrible Mum. I just knew I was missing her.

P.M. Mm. And do you think you were missing her as a person, as you say you could hardly remember her, or was it just the feeling that she was –?

Helen: It's the love you get from a Mum, I suppose.

P.M. Mm – that she ought to be looking after you.

She did not receive visible affection either from Lorraine who, although fond of her, pushed her away when she put her arms round her.

Helen: And I didn't get much love off Mother, because she's not that type of person. She doesn't like putting her arms around children and cuddling them up or anything.

P.M. (Pause.) So it was – demonstrative affection you were wanting – cuddling.

Helen: Yes. That's why I used to sit on your lap, because you used to love me.

For a few seconds I had thought she was refuting everything Mrs Moon had said, till I remembered that 'love' often meant 'cuddling'. Even so it was a tense moment for all of us.

P.M. Because she didn't put her arms round you, that made you feel she didn't actually love you.

Helen: No, I knew she loved me.

P.M. So when you say, 'She didn't love me,' you meant she didn't cuddle you?

Helen: Yes, that's all.

Mrs Moon: Well, you see, I didn't want them to get too attached, or me to get too attached to them. I didn't know whether they mother and father was going to go back with they children. I didn't know I was going to have them all the rest of they life.

P.M. So you were holding back.

Mrs Moon: It must have been something holding me back inside, because I am a lovable person really . . . I know I've got the love inside. I may not show it with kissing and all that.

Helen: She do show it in the things she does . . . she'll do anything for you. She'll show her love like that, but she just don't like to be wrapped up.

Mrs Moon: No, well you must think. I didn't want to get too wrapped up in you girls. I was thinking in a few months, or a few weeks, you'd be took away and I know if I get attached to something I don't like losing it.

P.M. You were frightened of being hurt in case they were taken away.

Mrs Moon: Yes. I didn't expect to have 'em. I thought they'd get back together or when she married again she'd want them. I didn't want to get too involved in that way because I'm very possessive and once I did, I wouldn't want to give them back to her. I didn't want that to happen to my own daughter, not to give her own children back to her. I thought there couldn't be nothing worse than that.

P.M. So you were torn . . . And perhaps you're worried what I will think, now that Helen has said you weren't affectionate with her.

Mrs Moon: No. Oh no . . . I couldn't love them more. I think she's too big to be kissed – unless she's going away somewhere, I get hold of her and kiss her.

P.M. Perhaps you never get too big to be kissed.

Mrs Moon: Well, I am an affectionate person really. I'm not cold.

P.M. Maybe it's gone on with you, because you were scared in the first place of taking their love from their mother.

Helen: I wouldn't like it now if she changed – it would be weird.

P.M. Yet you've wanted it.

Helen: I get it from another source now.

Mrs Moon: I can't bear anyone being torn away from me once I get to love them. I put my mind against getting too fond.

P.M. And yet you were deep down.

Mrs Moon: Of course I was. They were like my own children to me. Still are.

P.M. So it seems sad that you weren't free to show it more.

Mrs Moon: Well, I wasn't. I never knew – my daughter said she'd come and fetch them. Well, I kept waiting for her to fetch them.

P.M. Year after year?

Mrs Moon: Yes. Till it got – well, nobody's going to fetch them now, they're here for good.

P.M. I'm thinking that the social workers who came later on should have helped you with that, to make you feel it was all right to be loving and affectionate with them – because you'd become like their mother.

Mrs Moon described how she had tried to keep them in touch with their parents.

P.M. You were trying to do right by everyone, weren't you? You were pulled in all directions.

Mrs Moon: I didn't know which way to go, see.

She speculated that there must be a lot of other foster-mothers in a similar predicament, and I told her that there was more recognition now in many areas of social work practice, of the need to protect attachments, so that foster-parents who have cared for children for several years can be helped to feel secure (legally and emotionally) in loving them. Mrs Moon should certainly have had more social work help with her conflicting feelings, but it is perhaps more difficult to free relatives to love foster-children 'as their own'. It was not easy to help

her now, as she made her heartfelt defence in response to Helen's
longing to be shown physical affection, and I was in the position of
trying to empathise with both at once.

A pan had boiled dry while we talked, which lightened the
atmosphere. They were both saying affectionate things about seeing me
again, when Mrs Moon recalled an incident which was not to my credit.
I had provided twin beds for the girls, which had to replace a double
bed, and Mrs Revel complained about this on one of her visits.

> *Mrs Moon:* (Laughed.) And you said, 'I'm not getting them for your
> convenience. It's for the children.'
>
> *P.M.* I've always been ashamed of that . . . I should have been more
> sympathetic to her.
>
> *Mrs Moon:* No. I think I knew what you felt – she was thinking of herself and
> not the children, and you was a bit angry about it.
>
> *P.M.* I suppose I was minding what she was doing to the children. But I
> might have helped her more by trying to see her point of view instead of
> ticking her off!
>
> *Mrs Moon:* (Chuckled.) I laughed at that, I did, on the quiet.
>
> *P.M.* Well, I wasn't very proud of having said it! Life wasn't easy for her and
> she was wondering about her place here.

Indeed, with hindsight, had I tried more to understand the unhappiness behind Mrs Revel's hard veneer, she might have done more for the
children.

Eventually, Helen and I talked together as Mrs Moon prepared tea in
the kitchen. She said how much Larry (Mrs Moon's youngest son) had
helped her. He had been ruthless about her feeding bottle which she
still had at seven or eight.

> *Helen:* And most children have finished years ago. He got hold of my bottle
> and chucked it in the dustbin. I hated him for it, but he done me good.
>
> *P.M.* Well, you're telling yourself he did you good, but you perhaps missed it
> at the time.
>
> *Helen:* I went and bought another one with my pocket money! Then he
> chucked that one away. It became a sort of game. But I adored Larry for
> helping me out . . . We're just like brother and sister . . . But myself, the
> only sort of thing what I ever missed was love.
>
> *P.M.* That's a big thing to miss, isn't it?

She had the love she wanted now from her fiancé, Luke, but was cross
with him at times if he didn't cuddle her.

> *Helen:* It's surprising how valuable a cuddle can be.

90

P.M. Well, it says a lot – if you're wanting comfort.

The Department had paid fares to London for Lorraine and her to see their father and she felt she had become a better person through seeing him.

Helen: If I hadn't seen my Mum and my Dad, I think I would have been even more disturbed than what I was . . . I had love inside me for my Dad anyway, and love inside me for my Mum, but to be able to see 'em –
P.M. And does that love inside you go on?
Helen: Oh yes, I still love my Dad. I love him twice as much now – because my Mum told me something – (long pause)
P.M. You love him twice as much –

Haltingly, she told me how her mother, jealous of her love for her father, had quite recently told her, in brutal words, that he was not her real father. She was bereft, but moved that he had none the less always treated her as his daughter, and she and Luke were shortly going to London to ask his permission to be married.

P.M. It was cruel to hear like that. You must have felt she was taking him away from you.
Helen: She wanted to hurt me. Mother thinks, because she can see herself in me – she calls me a carbon copy – growing up in a better way than she did, she's jealous of me, because I'm doing better than she did.

Luke had comforted her distress, and I put my hand on her knee when she said she did not know how he put up with her as she was so moody – usually because she wanted a cuddle. She saw herself as possessive of him because he is the first person whose love she has 'really clasped'. I wondered if this might make for difficulties, but they are able to talk out their differences freely. 'Luke's very true to me and we're determined to make a good life together. Me, more so, because my Mum went wrong.' She wanted a few years of togetherness with Luke before sharing their love with a child.

P.M. It seems important that you know you've got all this love inside you and you can talk about it. You know what you're looking for and you've found someone you care about. I can see you've got deep feelings that get hurt – it makes you vulnerable to be a loving person, I think, but it also means you get great happiness from it.

Before I left Helen fetched her wedding dress, which she was making herself, and sat on the floor beside me to explain the pattern. She walked with me back to my car and promised to send me a wedding photograph. When I kissed her goodbye, she said, 'Even that means something – or a hand on the knee,' and I was conscious again of her unsatisfied need for tenderness. I hoped she would find it in good measure in her marriage. It seemed promising that she had not succumbed to what Suttie[11] called the 'taboo on tenderness' (in which the longing for tactile affection becomes repressed because of the distress of early 'psychic weaning' in our society from the fondling relationship with the mother). Instead, her painful awareness of her need meant that she remained open to giving and receiving affection. Evidently, at 19, she was still missing the mother's love she had never had; her grandmother as a surrogate mother had substantially met her needs, though holding back on physical contact. However, in lieu of touch, the language of feelings was used in this household, and so Helen had words and concepts available to express herself in her relationship with Luke, and to tell me now what she was feeling.

Lorraine had perhaps earlier learned to deny her need for overt affection, but now her own children were drawing this out of her, as was her husband.

As a postscript, I received the promised photograph of Helen's wedding, and also heard that Lorraine's husband had returned safely from the Falklands conflict. She wrote, 'I always hid my feelings from the family. Then when I met Jason I gave him all the love I had never given to anyone. So you can understand how lost I would have been without him.' They did indeed seem to be well 'on their way through life'.

> It may seem incredible that so harmless and amiable an emotion as tenderness, the very *stuff* of sociability, should itself come under a taboo.

> Touch is a more fundamental reassurance than sight or sound.
>
> Ian D. Suttie[12]

6

Michelle

I often think, I'm 30 and I've had a 15 year old son. . . . One day he might come and knock on the door.

The decision whether or not to relinquish a child, of whatever age, for adoption must be one of the hardest a mother can face, knowing that all the potential of mutual love and the pleasure and satisfaction of watching him grow up would accrue to other parents. Even recently Rowe[1] still maintains that it is often 'the most thoughtful and responsible single mothers who decide on adoption as offering their child the best chance in life'. This view is controversial and needs to be seen in the context of continuing lack of government support for measures such as those recommended in the Finer Report[2] to increase financial, housing and day-care provision for single-parents. Poverty thus continues to compound the inherent emotional complexities.

For Michelle, whose words also began the Introduction, the odds were heavily weighted against her keeping her baby. Like Lily in chapter 4, she was only 14 when she became pregnant. Her mother was sympathetic but was not a free agent. She was divorced from Michelle's father, remarried with another daughter and a new baby, but separated from her second husband and living in her brother-in-law's farmhouse in a small village. This uncle of Michelle dominated her predicament. In discussion with me he was punitive in attitude and refused to let her remain under his roof, so that regretfully her mother had to ask for care.

With changed attitudes to illegitimacy it is rare now for a pregnant teenager to need to come into care, but in the 1960s this was still a feature of our work and we usually maintained several specialist foster homes for the purpose. Apart from Jane Ryder, there was a gentle widow, who cosseted and cocooned each girl through her pregnancy in a comfortable little house with honeysuckle round the door and a lavender hedge. However, she was not free, and after an introduction, I placed Michelle with Mrs Blythe, who lived further away than I would have wished. She was a resource envied by other areas which sometimes borrowed her. However, although gifted, she had a tendency to blow up any alleged misdemeanour (by girls already feeling in deep trouble) into a drama, in which the social worker was also made to feel on the mat, until the crisis was resolved in repentant tears and hugs. Her kind and genial husband was a long-distance lorry-driver who often added a welcome lighter touch.

When Michelle's son, Adrian, was born, I took her mother to see them both in hospital. Attitudes and plans for adoption sometimes change dramatically once a baby is born, but Michelle's mother, though sad to think of her first grandson's being adopted, was not in a position to say that Michelle could take him home. So he, too, came into care, temporarily, prior to adoption.

Michelle's uncle continued to reject her, ostensibly on the grounds that she would be safer in care. It was particularly hurtful for her when she had just parted from her baby, and was needing mothering herself, to be denied the comfort of returning home. She found herself a job with horses, living with her employers, Mr and Mrs Dunn. She was torn still over the decision about Adrian, but settled well as part of this cheerful, easy-going family. It was a blow, therefore, when Mr and Mrs Dunn applied to foster younger children and statutory references revealed that Mr Dunn had a police record for a Schedule 1 offence against children.[3]

Because of her newly-found happiness there, I hoped that Michelle would be allowed to stay. The offence was some years ago and not directly related to the safety of an adolescent girl. It was hard, therefore, when the County Children's Officer decided that I should remove her. That year the influential Dorset inquiry into a sexual assault on a foster child had shown how one child's injury can affect the image of a whole service in relation to current and potential clients.[4] Consequently the Children's Officer thought we should not risk leaving Michelle in a household with someone who had been sexually irresponsible. Previously he had often supported us in making controversial decisions, but this occasion illustrated usefully for me that 'the boss' has wider responsibilities than has the social worker fighting for a single child in care. However, he softened his dictum by offering to come with me to talk with the Dunns. He was a much loved and admired figure in the county, and it was typical of him to face the consequences himself of an unwelcome decision. I valued his support on our joint evening visit, though I was still left with the difficulty of not being able to give Michelle a full explanation, on grounds of confidentiality. She found herself another residential job on a farm high up on a windswept, stony ridge, and the farmer's wife seemed equally unfriendly, particularly when Michelle drowned her sorrows on Adrian's first birthday. Her next two jobs, working with horses in a neighbouring county, were much more enjoyable, and she met John, a farm assistant, whom she later married. She was a girl of great spirit and usually found these jobs on her own initiative, while I varied my working day talking with Michelle in the stables and drinking sherry with the MFH.[5]

Michelle eventually returned to her mother (by then in different accommodation) after an appendix operation, and was discharged from care. She wrote to me quite often when I left Ringshire, and I was glad to hear of her engagement and marriage to John and of Sharon's birth. There followed several miscarriages.

On my project visit I drove on a perfect early spring afternoon across the Ringshire border. There was a faint wash of green over the bare trees and the ploughed earth felt warm. Michelle and her family lived in a solitary farm cottage on the side of a sheltered valley, and she and Sharon were looking out for me on the farm drive. Sharon was six and because of their rather isolated setting was used to plenty of Michelle's undivided attention. She was excited at the prospect of a visitor but also naturally wanted to share our conversation. Michelle told me later that everybody they had seen knew that I was coming. '"Mummy's friend's coming – a lady called Miss Mann." She's so chuffed if anybody comes!' I gathered that Sharon did not know yet about Adrian and so Michelle and I could not talk freely at first about him. When his name slipped out Sharon asked at once who Adrian was, and Michelle answered, 'Somebody Mummy used to know.' She had told John before they were married, and his mother. 'I don't know if she ever would have found out . . . I just thought it was nicer to tell her.'

Michelle's recollections of care were somewhat mixed. She had not been very happy in her foster home, partly because of her pregnancy and its likely outcome, and partly because she was perhaps too independent-minded to be a favourite with Mrs Blythe. She had more understanding now of her mother's difficulties in bringing up four children on her own. 'I think she had a hard time really. Now I'm married I can see that.' She was glad that her mother had again remarried and was very happy and contented at last. She bore surprisingly little grudge against her uncle for the major part he had played in separating her from her mother just when she specially needed her. Michelle thought it would have helped if she had seen her mother more often. 'That was the only thing really. I think I was quite happy. I just made the most of it, I suppose. I knew it wasn't going to be forever.'

She was generous also about the decision to move her from the Dunns.

Michelle: It was just unfortunate I couldn't stay with them.
P.M. It must have seemed very hard at the time.
Michelle: Well, because it was a family, and I was pleased it was a family.
P.M. And they were fond of you – they made you part of the family.
Michelle: And it was the stage when I had to sign Adrian over. I can remember that.

Adrian had been placed for adoption and when Michelle was asked to give her consent (now called agreement) I accompanied her when she signed the form in front of a magistrate.[6] Raynor's study[7] of mothers who had parted with their babies for adoption found that most saw this moment of signing the consent form as the decisive point of legal relinquishment rather than the later interview with the guardian *ad litem*, or the making of the adoption order itself. It had therefore seemed the more unkind to have to move her from a supportive family at this stage.

Michelle: I didn't really want to leave Guy (Mr Dunn).
P.M. You must have been fed up with me for moving you, weren't you?
Michelle: Well, I could see your point of view. You obviously had to look for records, and that came up, and I thought, 'That was a long time ago that that happened.'
P.M. They told you, did they?
Michelle: Oh yes.
P.M. I wasn't sure. I felt I couldn't tell you – it was confidential to them. I imagined it must seem pretty arbitrary.
Michelle: Oh no. They would explain things to me, and that's how we got on so well most likely – because we talked to one another straight.
P.M. I'm glad they told you. It must have been quite hard for them to tell you. At least you understood a bit.

Michelle had lived with her decision to have Adrian adopted for 15 years now. She asked if I was still in touch with anyone from Ringshire who had kept an illegitimate baby, naturally wondering what the outcome might have been for Adrian and herself if the decision had gone the other way.

Michelle's question might be answered more convincingly by other research studies. For example, as Packman[8] summarises: 'The cohort studies of the National Children's Bureau suggest that illegitimate children who are adopted fare better socially and educationally than their counterparts who remain with their families and better even than legitimate children in their own homes.'[9] The children studied were then seven. Lambert and Streather,[10] comparing them at 11 years, found that adoption had undoubtedly still provided a form of parental care which had given one group an environment vastly different from that of a considerable proportion of the other group. In terms of social adjustment alone (and this should not be underestimated) the unadopted illegitimate children did not appear to be worse off.

Apart from these studies involving directly contrasted groups, there is accumulating research evidence here and in the United States of the high success rate generally in adoption placements.[11] On the other hand the difficulties inherent in bringing up a child unsupported are implicit in the large number of illegitimate children who come into care. Fifty per cent of all children in the *Children Who Wait* study were illegitimate, and they were thought to be one of the two groups most likely to be at risk of remaining in care till they were 18.[12] Earlier Packman[13] also found that illegitimacy was a predominant characteristic of children in long-stay care. A charge needs to be acknowledged here that some adoption agencies seemed more concerned then (or even now) with supplying childless middle class couples with illegitimate babies usually from working class backgrounds. This does not nullify the success of adoption *per se*, but puts it in a wider political context and relates to the debate over the permanence movement (chapter 3).

Michelle was still sad about losing Adrian but felt basically that it had been the right decision.

P.M. It was such a hard decision, wasn't it?

Michelle: Yes. I think I did the best thing, myself, at that age anyway. But these days there are not many girls in that situation, because abortion's so easy, and people are either more careful or – there's so much more contraception.

P.M. So it seems hard to you now, does it, that it had to happen that way to you.

Michelle: Mmm.

P.M. I certainly think it would have been very difficult for you if you had kept him.

Michelle: Did you want me to keep him? You always did secretly, didn't you?

P.M. Well, I think one always minds so much for someone like you having to

97

part with a baby.

Michelle: Actually I said that to John the other night – I said, 'Well, obviously Miss Mann wouldn't have said in so many words then, but . . .'

P.M. I think you made the right decision, but I suppose I was very sad for you.

Because the decision needs to be the mother's own, the social worker can only help her explore all the possible alternatives, though for a 15-year-old the choices often seem limited. It is also a fallacy to think one can be totally non-directive, and Rowe[14] asserts that it is impossible for the caseworker to avoid the responsibility of playing a part in the decision about the child's future. I can remember Michelle asking me directly what I thought she should do. She must have picked up an inner wish on my part that she could keep her baby, although we both knew that in the circumstances it would be in his best interests to be adopted. She managed to hold to this resolution even when the Dunns, out of sympathy, offered to let her have Adrian there. This would have been a short-term solution – shorter as it turned out than we imagined – and she would have been faced with further *ad hoc* solutions on her own, at an age when parenthood is premature, with no family back-up, and when less accepting attitudes to illegitimacy still prevailed. It appeared later in the interview that her feelings for her mother were central to her decision.

Michelle: Mum said to me I could come home to live as long as I didn't bring Adrian home. I gave up Adrian and I still wasn't allowed home.

P.M. That was very hard.

Michelle: Otherwise I think I would have kept him.

P.M. Would you? So you gave him up in order to get back with your Mum?

Michelle: Mm. But Mum wasn't in her own place. Then I started with horses and that was that. I just thought, 'I'm not allowed to go home –'

P.M. That was very hurtful – that part of the bargain wasn't kept. Was it your uncle again who said –?

Michelle: Oh yes. Well, I suppose I did blacken the family.

I tried later to lighten any shadow of the black sheep. She was very preoccupied now in trying to extend her family.

Michelle: I think that's my only thing – I wish I did have a few more children! Because I've had three misses – all boys.

P.M. Ah. And that makes it extra hard, does it?

Michelle: Yes it does – quietly to myself . . . And some people say, 'Perhaps you can't carry boys.'

They had also applied to adopt (a child younger than Sharon) having decided they could not face the insecurities of fostering, but had heard nothing more after a preliminary interview over a year ago. At 30 she felt impatient at the delay. An adoptive mother in Timms's *The Receiving End* writes of her feelings that social workers often seem unaware of the meaning of time to people applying to adopt. 'Time assumes disproportionate importance which has to be experienced to be understood.'[15]

Sharon was also impatient – for our promised walk – so I suggested that we might talk later. We walked up the fields in the warm still air to see the horses, Sharon running and dancing ahead of us. She was a country child, as fond of horses as her mother before her. Susan Hill[16] wanted to give her daughter 'a rich treasure-store of country memories, sights and smells, sounds and colour on which she could draw for the rest of her life'; she recalled a city friend who 'feeds off a memory of running through fields up to her waist in buttercups, on a day's outing to the country when she was six years old'. Sharon at six was already versed in country ways, and confident in her small world of valley and woods and the activities of the farming year. She greeted her father with excitement when he arrived home on his tractor.

John was quiet and gentle in manner and they seemed an affectionate trio. As we ate a meal together I heard how he ran the 350 acre farm single-handed, and enjoyed the autonomy allowed him by the previous landowner's widow. Afterwards, he returned to his ploughing while the light lasted, with Sharon riding high on the tractor beside him.

Michelle and I were then freer to talk about her recollections of care and of Adrian. At the time she had just thought, 'I'm pregnant and I've got to get on with it,' but had often thought since that she would have preferred an abortion. I suggested that she was feeling I should have raised the question, but she had in fact left it rather late in going to her doctor. She thought a social worker now should discuss this as one of the options.

We recalled her time in hospital. She had found it hard having to care for Adrian herself, knowing she would have to part from him. I remembered her pride that he had been the biggest baby in the ward, and she became tearful at the memory of her mother's visit. The hurt was still there. I turned off the tape for a while and moved beside her on the sofa to comfort her.

Michelle: I was just thinking of Mum really. When she came to see him she

99

kept saying, 'I wish you could keep him.' I've often said to John that one day Adrian might come and knock on the door. Because when they're 18 they're allowed to, aren't they? If ever that happened I don't think I'd close the door on him.

P.M. Does it worry you to think that he might come?

Michelle: No . . . If he did come, obviously he'd come to find out why I couldn't keep him. That must be the first thing in their mind – 'I wonder why my mother couldn't keep me?'

P.M. To see what you're like, I think. To find out a bit more about himself too.

Michelle: Mm. John and I do talk about it, that he might come. John's very easy to get on with and to talk to.

Michelle and I had talked a lot about Adrian after she parted from him; I had taken a photograph of him for her to keep, and she used to sleep with one of his 'bootees' under her pillow. Adoption (and abortion even more) is often seen by the mother's family as a tidy solution, so that she is not given sufficient opportunity to talk about the child (or potential child) she has lost, in case she gets 'upset'. The social worker may be the only person who allows her to mourn. Seeing Michelle's tears now, 15 years later, I wondered if I had helped her enough to grieve at the time for him, though for many mothers this particular sorrow leaves an abiding ache. She had one friend now who knew about Adrian and it helped to be able to talk about him.

P.M. It's a relief when someone does know – if you're preoccupied with something.

Michelle: Yes. I often think, 'I'm 30 and I've got a 15 year old son - or rather I've had a 15 year old son.'

P.M. You wonder what he looks like.

This was even harder for her to imagine because of the uncertainty about his paternity. She had kept the photograph I had given her of him until she married. 'I kept it for a long time . . . it got a bit creased.' The possibility that he might turn up on her doorstep once he was 18 arises from Section 26 of the Children Act, 1975.[17] This allows adopted people over that age access to their birth records, which give some clues towards a possible hunt for the birth parents' whereabouts – a development unforeseen when Adrian was adopted. Michelle had not kept his existence a secret from John (though she was still looking for an appropriate moment to tell Sharon) so was not vulnerable on that score, but feared an implicit reproach in his likely questions.

Statistically, the chances were slender that Adrian might be one of

100

the few people each year who start a search for their first mother. In a two-year period after Section 26 came into force, between one and two per cent only of all adopted adults who were eligible had come forward.[18] As there are more than half a million adopted people in Britain today, this minute percentage still represents, of course, a considerable number of people. Two studies, by Leeding and by Day,[19] both showed that the main reason for making the application was the need, often long felt, to establish or complete a sense of true self-identity. It was mainly information they wanted. A minority of applicants, after an interview with a counsellor (mandatory for those adopted before November 1975) intended to try to trace their natural parents. However, as in the earlier Scottish study by Triseliotis,[20] only a handful of those who decided to make this search had managed to do so.

Two findings from the larger study by Day could well be a comfort to mothers in Michelle's position. First, that those interviewed showed 'compassionate understanding of the situation of the natural mother, both at the time of parting with her child, and as affected by retrospective legislation'. And second, that 'hostility towards a natural parent was rarely expressed by applicants'.[21]

If it was probable that Adrian could understand and 'forgive' Michelle, it was also necessary for her to be compassionate towards herself.

P.M. I'd be sorry if because of having Adrian you feel there's something bad about you now – that it takes away from what you feel about yourself . . . You were saying that you'd blackened the family? This was still a shadow . . .

Michelle: Oh yes – then, but not now. At the time. Fifteen years ago it wasn't like it is today, nobody takes that much notice now, and so many more girls are keeping their babies now. And parents have got a different outlook to life as well.

P.M. I don't know whether you feel I should have done something more to help you keep him.

Michelle: If I'd kept Adrian the person that I wanted to marry would have had to take me on and Adrian. I still think it was a good thing that I did give up Adrian, although that may sound funny now.

P.M. I'm sure it was the sensible thing – for you, and probably best for him, although there's the sadness for you, and there'll be a bit of him that's always sad. But in a sense you were giving something *to* him.

Michelle: I know you would have helped out, but I would have had to find somewhere to live with the baby – and money . . . (She was frightened,

101

too, of being in the house on her own.) And even when you're married and bring the baby home, it's hard work!

She had been depressed briefly after Sharon was born, but had breast-fed her successfully –

> *Michelle:* – till she was six months. I was glad that I breast-fed her . . . she wasn't cuddly. She is now, she often comes to have a cuddle . . . She loves helping, she loves to be involved in what you are doing – she's always with me or close by. She stayed with John's sister for four days and – oh, it was horrible! Sometimes you can't wait to get rid of them for half an hour, you think of all the things you can do when they're not around – and you can't do it, you can't get on with it – you're thinking, 'I wonder what Sharon's doing!'

Apart from her underlying sadness over Adrian, and the disappointment of her miscarriages, she seemed very happy in her present life. She was still much in love with John and proud of him. He had helped her in many ways, and was with her when Sharon was born: 'I can see him now, the mask on and tears streaming down his face he was so happy.' She too was determined to make her marriage work, having experienced the breakings and remakings of her mother's marriages. 'When I say, "make a go of it", it sounds as though it's hard work being married – I don't mean it like that. I think it's important that you have a Mum and Dad.' She was on good terms with her mother now and rang her up when needing support. She also seemed fortunate in her parents-in-law. There had been another important event. Around the time of her marriage she wrote to tell me of a reunion and holiday with her father after a long gap, and this had meant much to her. She had been disappointed that I could not get to her wedding.

> *Michelle:* But I think it's nice – do you think it's nice to keep in touch?
> *P.M.* Yes I do.
> *Michelle:* I was in your care, and you've come today and you've seen John and I happy, and Sharon – do you feel nice?
> *P.M.* I do feel nice – it's lovely to see that you're all right. Because you've come through a lot, haven't you? I always used to think you were someone with a lot of spunk and go – that you coped very well with your situation. You can take a lot of credit yourself for the way you are now.

I wondered if my project letter might have made her anxious that my coming and recollections of Adrian would upset her. 'Oh no, I was as chuffed as anything, and John was over the moon – he couldn't wait to meet you. He knew it was from you by the handwriting . . . He did say,

"Will it worry you?" But it didn't worry me.'

In the event my coming had brought tears and I had a qualm about bringing up old hurts on a single visit. However, it seems that she can talk to John quite freely about Adrian. Also, as the hurt was close to the surface (activated by her miscarriages and, ironically, by her own application to adopt) I hoped it might help to talk with me about it, as apart from her mother I must be the only person she knows now who actually saw and held Adrian. I felt there was a degree of unfinished business here, of which in a sense I was still part.

As a postscript, Michelle wrote 18 months later, rejoicing that she had become pregnant shortly after she and John heard that they had been approved as adoptive parents. So one way or the other there were hopes of another child.

> Mother, I love you so.
> Said the child, I love you more than I know.
> She laid her head on her mother's arm,
> And the love between them kept them warm.
>
> Stevie Smith[22]

7

Steven and his adoptive parents

I used to dread it when you came . . . I used to say, 'Oh, she's coming, she's going to take him away.' My heart used to beat so quickly . . . I kept wondering if the mother had changed her mind.

Each adoptive family is an entity in its own right, not just one of a category. Particular and widely differing circumstances have brought together these unique individuals. Even so, Michelle's story, her feelings about losing Adrian and his possible reappearance in the new life she has made for herself provide a background to the three chapters which follow. In contrast these take the viewpoint of children, now grown up or nearly so, who were adopted, and of their adoptive parents.

The Houghton Report which was the basis of the Children Act, 1975 held that the child is the focal point in adoption.[1] The natural parents and the adopters have needs and wishes which must be respected and which can be well met by adoption, but the Report recommended that the child's welfare should always be the first consideration.[2] Since this concept became law,[3] courts and agencies have wrestled with more precise definitions of 'the welfare of the child', notably where there is a conflict of interests.

The changes in the law relating to adoption and to children in care recommended by the Houghton Committee reflected the changing face of adoption in the 1970s,[4] but also set in motion future radical changes in policy and practice. The framework of the law needed to encompass a new adoption service which would become part of the mainstream of social work practice. From being a specialist activity, principally occupied in placing healthy white babies with childless couples, adoption has become one of the options to be considered for any child or group of siblings in need of a permanent substitute family. A familiar if complex cluster of factors contributed to these changes, of which three might be mentioned. These were, *first*, the dramatic reduction in the supply of babies offered for adoption, due to the increased availability of contraception and abortion, and to the more relaxed attitudes to illegitimacy which have made it possible for many single mothers to keep their babies; *second*, the discovery in the *Children Who Wait* study of the large numbers of children still growing up in care, who were thought to need new families; and *third*, the encouraging and timely evidence on both sides of the Atlantic of the high success rate in adoptions, including those of older children.[5]

Now that adoption can be seen to meet the needs of many children who are older or handicapped or of mixed race, it is also characterised by more openness. This has developed pragmatically, because older children have longer memories or they may have an obviously different ethnic heritage; but also from the conviction behind the access to birth records provision that adopted people have a right to and a psychological need of information about their origins.

A traditional secrecy, however, still governed adoption legislation, policy and practice when Michelle and the other three young people in this group were in need of an adoption solution. Steven was the youngest to be adopted. His first mother was unmarried, older than Michelle, but still living with her own mother who strongly opposed any idea that her daughter might keep the coming baby. So before he was born, his mother made a private arrangement with Mr and Mrs Scott through an intermediary (a director of the firm where she and Mrs Scott worked), and they were able to collect Steven from hospital when he was ten days old. Unlike other young people in the study he did not have to come into care, but went straight to his new family, though he became, of course, a 'protected child' until the Adoption Order was made.[6]

John and Anne Scott already had a four-year-old daughter, Rachel, born to them. I first came into their lives when Miss T., the Diocesan social worker who was helping Steven's mother, alerted us that a 'third party' placement was being planned. In common with a number of other Departments,[7] Ringshire pursued a policy of trying to reduce the incidence of private adoptions, and I was asked to visit the Scotts to discuss with them the possible disadvantages attached to this way of adopting a child. A few years later the Houghton Committee examined the disadvantages from all points of view and concluded that because 'the decision to place a child with a particular couple is the most important stage in the adoption process', independent placements should not be allowed once the new registration system for adoption agencies, with its greater safeguards of good practice, was in force – which it now is.[8]

At the time I could only point out to the Scotts the drawbacks from their point of view, such as the natural mother's proximity, and the lack of a medical examination of the baby and of any social or medical history of his parents. They were not deterred by my warning and were determined, rightly as it proved, to go ahead.

When they notified the local authority of their intention to adopt Steven, I visited for the three-month period of welfare supervision before the court hearing.[9] This traditionally has had a dual purpose: to ensure that the placement is in the child's best interests, and to help the applicants 'to deal with the social and emotional implications of their new role'.[10] It is always difficult to reconcile these inspectorial and counselling functions. Because this was an independent placement my visits were the more likely to be seen as inspectorial (although it was quickly apparent that Mr and Mrs Scott would probably have been accepted if they had applied to an agency). But equally, because there had been no agency involved beforehand to help them prepare for adoptive parenthood, there was much to discuss in a short time. Such difficulties will be removed to some extent in future when welfare supervision will be carried out by the placing agency; the worker will then already have gained the trust of the adopters and be in a better position to support them.[11]

In spite of Mrs Scott's great fear that Steven's mother would change her mind, an Adoption Order was made when he was six months old. Anne Scott, outwardly cheerful, generous hearted, extrovert and the talkative partner, bore with my visits which she could have felt a threatening obstacle to what she so dearly wanted. I must have managed to convey that I was with them as, after the Order was made, I was invited to Steven's christening, which also included 'A Service of Blessing upon the Adoption of a Child'.[12] This little inter-denominational service has a prayer for the natural parents, and there is a moving moment when all members of the new family together place a hand on the child's head in welcome. The court hearing in its brevity can seem an anti-climax after the prolonged anxious wait, and some adopters find this service a fitting expression of their thankfulness. In most people, whether believers or not, there is a need for ritual, for some kind of symbolic act, so that things felt and experienced inwardly may be seen to be done.

Every Christmas since then I have received a nice fat letter containing news and photographs of Steven and their cheerful family life. He was a remarkably beautiful child and I have been able to watch – at a distance – his growth into attractive boyhood, through all the stages of cuddly toys, first school satchel, cub uniform, school plays, and holidays abroad in Holland, Belgium and Austria.

On my project visit I was invited to an evening meal and Mr and Mrs Scott and Steven were gathered in the front porch to greet me. They were living in the same comfortable house in a small private estate in Paxton, the back garden now occupied by a swimming pool Mr Scott had made. Steven, nearly 15, not surprisingly was rather shy to begin with in the limelight of pleasure and pride which surrounded him. However, he seemed fairly relaxed and natural and to be on easy terms with his adoptive parents. There was general conversation during dinner and Rachel, married three weeks earlier, came briefly to see me, bringing her wedding photographs.

Mr and Mrs Scott were naturally eager to convey to me the success of the adoption, and theirs did seem a very happy and united family, unusually trouble-free, with Steven a true and much loved member of it. He had presented fewer problems than Rachel before him, and Mrs Scott was glad to realise that any adolescent difficulties were not necessarily related to adoption. He was not as enthusiastic about school as they might have wished, but was taking his 'O'levels that year and had hopes of qualifying for a furniture-making course.

Mrs Scott's memories of the welfare supervision period were dominated by her recollected terror that Steven's mother would want him back. On each visit she dreaded that I had brought bad news and she would ask, 'Is everything all right?' before I reached the front door.

Mrs Scott: You know he's not yours till you've been to court. You know that, you understand that. But even so, when the car used to come up the drive there was just that feeling.

The visit of the guardian *ad litem*[13] towards the end of the waiting period had aroused more fears. She could laugh at herself now.

Mrs Scott: I can always remember him coming. It was just after Christmas and we'd blown this packet of balloons up, and as I came in all these balloons wafted about all over the place and I was trying to catch them . . . I thought, 'Oh goodness, he's not going to say he's in the right home is he, all these balloons floating about.'
P.M. I suppose because there weren't any social workers involved before Steven was placed, you weren't used to the idea of our coming. It must have seemed a bit of an intrusion.
Mr Scott: We had to accept you were coming because we knew you had to come.

Mrs Scott: No, that didn't worry me one bit. Once you'd come over the doorstep and everything was all right, I was pleased to see you. But when you used to come through the driveway I used to think, 'Oh, what is it now? Open the front door quick.' That was the biggest fear.

P.M. I knew there was always a fear whenever I made an adoption visit, and that this was uppermost in people's thoughts – 'Is the mother going to change her mind?' But I don't think I knew you were feeling exactly as you're describing now each time. What could I have done to make it easier for you?

Mrs Scott did not suggest one obvious answer. With large caseloads it was not easy to work to an appointment system, but a telephone call in advance to reassure her would have saved unnecessary anxiety. I certainly believe now that regular appointments wherever possible are more productive than unscheduled visits. I wondered if talking more about her fears might have helped.

Mrs Scott: I don't think anybody could have consoled me till I'd gone to court, and I just couldn't wait to get there. Then I thought, 'It's all over, he's mine, nobody can do anything about it.' If you'd come and said, 'Everything's all right,' I still couldn't have accepted that until the actual court hearing. Nobody could tell, only the mother, and if she changed her mind it was her prerogative to have that child back. You know that, you've been told it, and you say you understand it, but when you've actually got that baby and you know you can't do anything about it – I didn't realise how tense I'd got till afterwards in my own mind.

P.M. It must be awful waiting.

Not surprisingly, she thought adopters' main need during this period was to feel confident they could keep the child placed with them. She had wept at nights sometimes when she tucked Steven up, to think he belonged to no one properly – 'He seemed to be in no-man's land. We loved him dearly from the start.'

Now that Freeing for Adoption Orders are available some adopters will be spared this kind of uncertainty.[14] The natural mother will be able to choose between the present procedure in which she gives her agreement to adoption by a specific couple after the child is placed with them, or the new freeing procedure in which she can make an early decision. In that case the legal position is clarified before the child is placed and the parental rights are vested temporarily in the agency. This alternative might still seem to leave the child briefly in 'no-man's land', but in the knowledge that he is 'free for adoption' the adopters will be freed to commit themselves emotionally in the period leading up to the Adoption Order, and a child of any age will sense this.

John and Anne Scott had not wanted Rachel to be an only child. Mr Scott had been firm that fostering would not be right for his wife who would quickly attach to any child however impermanent. They had chosen a private arrangement fearing they would not be accepted by an agency having already had Rachel born to them.[15] Also the gap was growing and they thought agency procedures might be slower. We recalled my attempts to dissuade them.

> *P.M.* I used to wonder sometimes when you wrote to me, if you were telling me that I had been wrong, and how well it had worked out!
>
> *Mrs Scott:* No, I just felt I needed to keep in touch with you so that Steven had a link if ever he wanted to talk to somebody at any time – there would be somebody, apart from us, that he could turn to that I was sure would know him . . . It was nice to keep in touch and it was a relief to think, well, you were there. You knew how he was getting on every time I wrote, and we used to show him the letters you wrote.

I wondered if Steven had found it strange that his mother sent me bulletins, but he said he just treated me as one of her friends. There was a great emphasis on normality in this family.

> *Mrs Scott:* It doesn't seem that he wasn't mine, you don't think about him being any different.
>
> *Mr Scott:* We treat him as our own child.
>
> *Mrs Scott:* Well, he is. (Adoption) was something that was never kept a secret. It was just spoken about quite normally. There's nothing to be ashamed of and we're not ashamed, nor is he. It's just we're lucky to feel we got him. It hasn't made any difference to you has it?
>
> *Steven:* No.
>
> *Mr Scott:* We always do things together and we always go places together. We go abroad, which is more of an education for the children.

The Scotts were obviously wanting to minimise the 'difference' in adoption. Kirk[16] (himself an adoptive parent) was writing about childless couples who become adopters when he constructed his theory that they deal in one of two ways with the series of 'role handicaps' which they meet (reinforced by unintentionally hurtful comments from other people about 'own' children or 'real' parents). Some reject while others acknowledge the difference in growing a family by adoption. For about a decade social workers were much influenced by Kirk's belief that adoptive families built on the latter approach were more likely to achieve the kind of easy communication which enables the child to build a true sense of identity, and consequently be better prepared to describe himself to others.

However, although it is well established that knowledge about origins is an essential component in a child's sense of identity, there is growing evidence that an equal, if not more influential, factor in building a comfortable sense of self stems from the friendly interaction and daily feedback he receives from his parents.[17] This suggests that it is more useful for the social worker to try to help adoptive parents feel confident in the authenticity of their parental role, and to respond to whatever anxieties and fears they raise, rather than to urge acknowledgement of difference. Attitudes to difference also become less of an issue in current practice where adoption is sometimes likened more to a marriage – a marriage between families who are often already established and children who bring emotional luggage packed with images of other parent figures.

John and Anne Scott, too, had begun to prove themselves as parents before Steven joined them, so it was not the wounds of childlessness which led them to reject the difference. Perhaps it was more their desire that Steven should not feel disadvantaged in any way compared with Rachel, and they were pleased that all the grandparents had supported them in this. It soon become apparent, however, that although the fact of Steven's adoption had been accepted naturally, there had been very little discussion about his birth parents.

We had talked during the welfare supervision period about what they would tell Steven; we had limited information but Anne Scott did at least know his birth mother by sight. There are more books now for young children which help adoptive parents to explain[18] as it is a notoriously difficult task to tell a child who was adopted as a baby that he was actually born to other parents, and the Goodacre sample showed how difficult adoptive parents found 'telling', even those who were convinced of its necessity.[19] More recently Triseliotis found that about three-quarters of the adopted young people in his study had experienced little or no discussion about their families of origin or the circumstances surrounding their adoption.[20] Raynor, too, found a serious lack of communication after the first telling.[21] Perhaps it is more helpful if social workers acknowledge the difficulties inherent in this kind of discussion, rather than exhort parents to undertake it. It may also be appropriate to respond to likely ambivalence in the current interaction with the worker, so that uncomfortable feelings become more accessible and a prickly subject more graspable. Jenny Lee,[22] an adoptive mother and social worker, writes of the need to be alert to the child's (and adopters') sense of loss that may lie behind the comments and the silences.

Mrs Scott had told Steven he was adopted when he was very small and the word was quite often mentioned naturally so that he would be used to the idea before he went to school. Steven recalled an exchange with another boy at school who was adopted which had prompted him to ask his mother for confirmation. However, in spite of this initial openness about the straight fact, it seems that the subject was not developed as Steven's potential understanding of the implications grew. I had imagined there would be an advantage in the Scotts having some slight first-hand knowledge of Steven's birth mother.

P.M. And have you been able to tell Steven what she looks like?
Mrs Scott: No, it's never cropped up really. When he wants to know we could say.
P.M. Have you ever wondered, Steven?
Steven: Yes. I'd like to know what she looked like. Just out of interest really.
P.M. But you haven't liked to ask perhaps?
Steven: Well, I'd like to.

Mrs Scott had felt sure he would ask if he wanted to know as theirs was a family without any real secrets, and any problems were talked about quite openly. The lack of communication between them about Steven's first parents was not unusual. McWhinnie, Triseliotis, Seglow *et al* and Raynor have all shown that it is a common fallacy for adoptive parents to assume a lack of interest if there are no questions. In spite of a pressing need to know more about their origins, adopted adults and children in these studies had frequently sensed this was a difficult subject for their parents and so had felt unable to ask. Triseliotis[23] found that this need to know had become particularly urgent in adolescence when the respondents were trying to establish their identity as individuals. For the adolescent who is adopted this customary task demands an extra effort as he has to integrate two sets of parents in his understanding of himself. Even the most loving adoptive parents cannot protect him from the pain of knowing that he is someone who was relinquished by his birth parents; but if they are confident enough in their own parenthood they can help him to internalise a picture of his first parents which he can live with. A child's outer certainty about his adoptive parents' friendliness towards him can be matched by his inner feelings and images of them and of himself as loving and lovable. But he will have no outer reality to correlate with internal images of his birth parents, particularly if he was adopted as an infant, and so will need help in building up a picture by talking about them in some detail – the kind of people they were, what they did and how they looked. Without discussion there can only be fantasies, which may be hurtful – as Steven's proved to be.

> *P.M.* In a way my coming brings it all up, doesn't it, and I don't want to force a conversation from you about it, or her circumstances, if you haven't talked about it to Steven.
>
> *Mrs Scott:* No, that part of it has just never cropped up as yet. I suppose it will.
>
> *P.M.* Well, I don't know what it's like for Steven, but young people who are adopted often do want to know and don't find it easy to ask for fear of what their adoptive parents will feel – whether they'd mind. I think it's natural to wonder –
>
> *Mrs Scott:* Of course it is. I mean you all wonder.
>
> *P.M.* – what the person who gave birth to you looks like and why it wasn't possible for her to keep you. I guess life was pretty difficult for her, and I guess you know more about it than I do.
>
> *Mrs Scott:* She wasn't married. I think she felt she couldn't give him much of a home and adoption was the best thing in the circumstances at that time. But she'd every chance of getting married after that.
>
> *P.M.* She felt she was giving him a better start by asking you to look after him. She seemed to know best, didn't she? She made a good choice.
>
> *Mrs Scott:* We hope so anyway.
>
> *P.M.* Is it difficult for you, Steven, talking about it with your parents?
>
> *Steven:* No, not really. Sometimes I ask, sometimes wonder. If she didn't want me, I don't want her.

With one voice Anne Scott and I hastened to correct this misunderstanding. I let her continue the explanation.

> *Mrs Scott:* I don't think it was that she didn't want you. She couldn't look after you as she wanted you to be looked after. I suppose she had her ideals as to how she would like her baby to be brought up, and obviously she couldn't do for you what somebody – if you'd have had a father, which she felt you needed, so that you had a normal home life.
>
> *P.M.* I suppose it's easy to assume she didn't want you when she didn't go on looking after you. It would be sad if you did feel that, because no mother finds it easy to give up her baby for adoption.
>
> *Steven:* I don't hate her . . . I can face it really. I just accept it.
>
> *P.M.* She was in a difficult position and she had a difficult decision to make. I was talking to a girl yesterday whose baby was adopted 15 years ago, and the memory of it was still hurting her, that she'd had to let this boy go, and

she knew that somewhere there was a 15-year-old son who wasn't hers. I'm sure your mother did want you; she was just trying to think what was the best thing to do.

Mrs Scott: I suppose nowadays it's different from when we had Steven. Girls couldn't keep their children like they do now . . . it was frowned on to some extent then . . . I think parents look at it in a different light now.

She thought the difficulties of not having a husband to help were in part financial ones, but having someone to back one up was important too. John Scott had been to Steven's school once or twice to sort out problems, and he helped him with his homework. His first father remained a shadowy figure in this conversation, referred to only by his absence.

There was an opportunity to mention him when Steven said, 'I wouldn't mind having a look at my birth certificate.' Mrs Scott was surprised to realise he had not seen it as the family's birth certificates were kept in a box to which they all had access, particularly when passports were needed. The box was fetched and we looked at Steven's 'long' birth certificate, issued by the Adopted Children's Register, but which otherwise had the usual details in the adoptive family's name. There was also a 'short' birth certificate which omits any reference to adoption and can be used more suitably for purposes such as job applications.

I explained to Steven his right under the new legislation to apply for a copy of his original birth certificate when he was 18, and the kind of information it was likely to give. The column for his first father's name would probably be blank. I had virtually no knowledge of him myself, and as neither Steven nor his parents sought to make him more substantial I did not persist at that point. It had been agreed beforehand that I could talk with Steven on his own and had I done so he might well have expressed his curiosity more freely. However, I decided they would be relieved if we remained together, and that the initiative to talk might come better from Steven. Mrs Scott said that he had my address and could always write to me. Rachel was also said to be someone he used as a confidante.

As the first mother's name and address had been known to his parents there would be no need for Steven to apply for his original certificate unless he wanted more information from the records than his parents could remember, or if he would find it easier to discuss the implications with an adoption counsellor. We talked of the possibility that his first mother might have married and might or might not have

113

told her husband about him, and Steven was quick to say he did not want to cause trouble for her.

Common parlance assumes that 'real parents' are those who gave birth to a child, and Anne Scott used the word 'true' mother. However, I was able to say that research[24] has shown that the adopted adults studied almost invariably regarded their adoptive parents as their 'real' parents.

> *P.M.* In a way this is your real Mum and Dad, they brought you up.
> *Steven:* I think of them as my real Mum and Dad.
> *Mrs Scott:* Of course you do . . . We are as far as you're concerned and we're concerned. We love you and we wouldn't see anything happen to you or hurt you. We'd be the first ones to step in to protect you, and put you on the right road as far as we could see it.

More than anyone, Triseliotis has wrestled with the whole question of the adopted person's self-image, and he selected for his most recent research three areas which are said to make a big contribution to identity building. These are '(i) a childhood experience of feeling wanted and loved within a secure environment: (ii) knowledge about one's background and personal history, and (iii) the experience of being perceived by others as a worthwhile person.'[25] There was no doubt that Steven had been blessed with an abundance of the first of these ingredients, and his family also gave him a basis for the third. His parents had not seen the second requirement as important, but as has been seen they were not alone in this.

I wondered if there had been mixed feelings about my return. Steven apparently had a last minute qualm before I arrived and asked, 'They can't take me away can they?' The social worker's power to remove can it seems leave an uncomfortable shadow long after the statutory power has ended. There seemed some advantage in our joint conversation as it perhaps showed Mr and Mrs Scott that Steven did have a natural curiosity to know more about his first mother, but had assumed privately that she must have rejected him. Anne Scott agreed: 'It's a good thing really to air it . . . if it's under the surface then I think it should come out and you should talk about it.'

I told them how I had often wondered what the future held in store for children I was working with or for, so that it was rewarding now to see Steven, grown and thriving.

> *Mrs Scott:* Well, it's nice for you to see the finished article.
> *P.M.* Not finished, but happily on his way.

114

Because it seemed likely that this family would keep in touch and use me as a resource if necessary, and because I was conscious of my own lack of knowledge about Steven's first father, as an insurance I called the next day on Miss T., now retired, when driving through her village. Her enormous caseload was receding, but she remembered Steven's first mother and was able to give me a pleasant if sketchy picture of her. She could, however, summon no image of the putative father. Still, any information she had at the time would be recorded in her reports, stored now with Social Services, and presumably in the guardian *ad litem's* report, so would be available to Steven later if he became more curious – perhaps in courtship, marriage, or as a potential parent himself.

Then every member of the family, together laying a hand upon the child, shall say
We receive this child into our family with joy;
Through God's love *he* comes to us,
With God's love we will care for *him*,
By God's love we will lead *him*,
And in God's love may we all abide for ever.
from *A Service of Blessing upon the Adoption of a Child*

8

Louise

I wonder if she ever thinks about me or whether she's forgotten all about me
. . . I think I would like to find her, and my Dad and sister, to find out what
they're like . . . She might really like to see me – or she might not.

When Louise was born her mother, about whom she speculated here,
was 42 and caught up in divorce proceedings. There was already an
adolescent daughter and her mother could not envisage starting again
with another baby on her own in middle age; adoption therefore seemed
to offer the best alternative for her. However, she had been born
prematurely – into a family in disarray – and as if unsure of her
welcome had a somewhat tenuous hold on life. Ironically, instead of
being placed straight away with an adoptive family prepared to take the
risk of committing themselves to her, she was fostered until it became
clear whether she would be healthy enough to satisfy the adoption
medical requirements which then prevailed.

Louise was placed with Mrs Knight (who keeps appearing in the
background). She had previous nursing experience and was one of our
safest answers then for babies awaiting adoption, particularly those
needing special care. However, this time we probably asked too much
as she was already immersed in Cherie (p.7) who was also delicate and
needed extra patient feeding. Whether or not Louise sensed that she
had not yet come home, her crying at night disturbed Cherie and Mrs
Knight untypically asked us to move her just as I took over the
supervision of both babies from M.R.V.

Normally this was a most placid foster-home. A visit to Mrs Knight
in their attractive thatched house facing the village green often provided
a restful punctuation mark between more demanding assignments.
Sunk in an armchair beside the fire, plied with coffee and lulled by Mrs
Knight's soft lilting voice, the only pressure was usually that of
wondering what the future held for the current baby on one's lap.

Plans for adoption were mostly made centrally but, still cautious, the
Adoptions Officer was not yet prepared to place Louise, so unexpected-
ly I had to find her other foster-parents. Mr and Mrs Boylan, whom I
had come to know during their recent application to foster, were willing

to take Louise on a temporary basis, although they and I both knew it was an ambiguous request. Louise at once began to thrive with them, but when an adoptive couple was found for her she became seriously ill with bronchitis. This happened more than once and the Boylans nursed her at home when she was too ill to be moved to hospital. Once when Mrs Boylan had a hospital appointment away from Paxton, Mrs Knight looked after Louise for the day, and when I collected her that evening her temperature had rocketed again. On Mrs Knight's advice I took her straight to hospital where she was at once admitted. I heard a suggestion that she might need to be taken to the county hospital 30 miles away, but when I begged that she might stay within easy access for the Boylans to visit, the paediatrician, already an ally, agreed.

I was by now convinced that Louise should be allowed to stay with this family. Philip and Vera Boylan had inevitably become attached to her, as had their two children, Kate and David, and they asked if they could adopt her. It seemed to me that other adoption plans were now irrelevant; that Louise's fragile progress was bound up emotionally as well as physically with the Boylans' care of her, and that this attachment should be protected. In his comment on the welfare of the child and the local authority's duty now to consult the child's wishes and feelings, 'taking into consideration his age and understanding',[1] Freeman writes, 'A child may express feelings even when he is too young to express wishes,'[2] and so it seemed with Louise.

I was supported by J.B. who had succeeded M.R.V. as Area Officer, but had to fight the rest of the 'hierarchy' every step of the way. 'What a depersonalising word to call people,' Parsloe suggests,[3] and indeed they were valued and helpful colleagues who usually backed one's hunches and gave one considerable freedom. The concept of psychological parenthood was respected in the Department then, ahead of its more specific formulation,[4] but adoption policy and practice still gave some weight to other factors. It was certainly awkward that the foster-parents and Louise's mother both lived in Paxton; and the planned adopters were also said to have a very slight advantage socially. However, Mr Boylan, as a local government officer, had plenty of scope for moving geographically (and in a senior position in his own department did not take kindly to delayed decisions).

Goldstein, Freud and Solnit later argued their principle of the 'least detrimental alternative' for children,[5] and Solnit has made the point that we should not destroy a decent quality of life for a child now on the supposition that we could promise something better in the future.[6] The benefits of a fresh placement need to be considerable to outweigh the harm of separating an attached child from bonded parents.[7] So, without benefit of these formulations, it was eventually agreed that the Department would support an application from the Boylans to adopt Louise. I continued to visit during the welfare supervision period, accompanied them to court for the adoption hearing, and was asked to be Louise's godmother. The family moved almost at once from Paxton and I became a godmother mainly by correspondence, though her parents brought Louise to see me when she was about eight – a shy but attractive tomboy.

Philip and Vera Boylan and Louise all agreed to see me for my project, but unfortunately the parents were in Paris for a week's holiday when I was in their part of the country. In a telephone conversation Vera Boylan said she was quite willing that I should talk with Louise (her husband was more worried that she might be hurt); she said she was no doubt biased, but to her Louise seemed very well adjusted, and I came to a similar conclusion when I visited her in their comfortable modern house on a private estate.

Louise was now 15½ and very pretty. She opened the door to greet me and my immediate impression of her very pleasing personality – warm, friendly and spontaneous – was reinforced during the afternoon. She bubbled away with an easy natural charm and laughed infectiously. This sparkle, however, was also balanced by a quieter, more thoughtful side. Her adoptive sister, Kate, was with us throughout, perhaps representing their parents, and she was helpful in talking with Louise about her early days as a foster-baby. I recapped her story as I remembered it.

> *P.M.* . . . and so you came to your Mum and Dad, and you were to be placed for adoption – but each time there was any mention of your going anywhere else you got ill.
>
> *Kate:* You must have wanted to stay with us.
>
> *P.M.* That's how it always seemed to me. And your Mum and Dad were getting fonder and fonder of you and were saying, 'Can't we keep her?' and Kate and David were saying, 'We don't want her to go.' This was where you were beginning to belong.
>
> *Kate:* And I suppose with her being so ill as well it made the bond stronger – she had bronchitis and pneumonia – you get more attached . . . and one night we thought you'd died on us. Do you remember that?
>
> *P.M.* Yes . . . That gave us all a fright.

Louise took the opportunity to talk about adoption. A social worker had been to her school recently.

Louise: She talked about units for unmarried mothers with babies and when it came to it they often didn't want the baby adopted.

P.M. And did that make you wonder why your first mother hadn't somehow managed to keep you?

Louise: Yes.

P.M. It's natural to wonder, isn't it, when it's the woman who gave birth to you. (I enlarged on her mother's difficulties at the time.) I think she thought it would be very hard to give you a good life – on her own.

Kate: Didn't she have a grown up daughter? . . . You might have some nieces and nephews somewhere.

Louise: I think sometimes, 'What would I be doing now, if I hadn't been adopted?' . . .

At other times she had felt a sense of difference from her adoptive family. 'When I've gone to bed sometimes – and you've been downstairs – I'd think, "That's what they'd be like if I wasn't here."' Her thoughts kept returning to her first mother.

P.M. I suppose it still hurts a bit – the thought of her.

Louise: Mm.

P.M. I don't think you can ever quite escape from that – however much one explains or talks about how difficult it was – there's still a hurt there you have to live with.

Louise: There's that letter that explains – gives information.

As was common practice in adoption, a letter had always been sent to adoptive parents after the Order was made, confirming information about a child's natural parents which had been given verbally but which can fade with the years or not be heard in their preoccupation with the child. Vera Boylan had shown this to Louise who fetched it now to look at with me. She mulled over her first parents' physical characteristics – 'I think sometimes, where do I get this or that from?' From the letter Louise enjoyed identifying interests which she had in common with both of them. '"She was a teacher." (Louise had thought of being a teacher at one time.) "She liked sports, swimming, amateur dramatics; she wrote articles for a magazine, enjoyed reading, listening to the wireless." I like all those.' The father had worked for an engineering firm – another possible career interest of Louise's.

The thoughts of adolescence turn naturally to queries about oneself, one's origins, identity and ideals for the future. For the adopted adolescent, in establishing her sense of self, such reflection needs to be based on reliable information. One of the respondents in Triseliotis's earlier study said unhappily, 'You look at yourself in the mirror and you can't compare it with anybody . . . I am a stranger to myself.'[8] He found that even those who were happily settled in their adoptive families still wanted information about their birth parents to complete their picture of themselves.

Louise regretted that adoption had cut her off completely from her first mother as though the latter were of no value. Kate thought that if any vestigial claim were allowed to a natural mother Louise would have felt torn between her two sets of parents. I tried to make a distinction for her between the process of law which had legally terminated the relationship with her first mother, so that she could really feel part of her new family, and her own continuing feelings which no law could dissolve. Such feelings of course are even stronger when older children are adopted, and the Barnardo's New Families Project amongst others has shown how some links can be kept with members of the original family.[9] Adoption offers a security of commitment which helps many new parents to be generous about a child's other loyalties.

> *Louise:* I think I would have liked to see her or if she could write to me, and yet at the same time I don't think it would be fair to Mum and Dad. I wonder if she ever thinks about me or whether she's forgotten all about me.
> *Kate:* I don't think she can have forgotten altogether – I don't think anybody can.

Our discussion naturally led on to whether Louise might try to see this mother once she was 18. She had read accounts of one girl who had been disappointed in a mother who had no room in her life for her, and of others similarly disillusioned who had set their hopes too high. Their experience served to caution rather than deter her.

> *Louise:* I think I'd like to meet her . . . I'd like to meet both of them, even though it might be a mistake and I might regret it.
> *P.M.* I think everyone who is adopted has this curiosity, but it seems that often it's wanting to find out more about you, more than wanting to have a lot to do with them.
> *Louise:* Yes, to find out about my sister –
> *Kate:* To see if she's better than me!
> *Louise:* - and my Gran, my aunties, or if I'd had cousins. I had thought when I was 18 I'd find her – but I don't really need to. It would be nice, but at the same time I think it would upset Mum and Dad. Mum said she wanted me to know that I was adopted, but that Dad didn't want me to know until I was older.

P.M. I think he was worried that you'd be hurt.

Kate: He is always trying to protect you. He thinks it hurts you more than it will. I think you should be told like you were – when you were very little – so that you knew the word.

Louise: I think if I did try and find her, I'd like someone else to ask her if she would like to see me – or if my father would like to see me.

Kate: Well, Dad and Mum have always said if you wanted to find her they'd help you – as much as they could – to trace them.

Louise knew her original name, and Mr Boylan apparently remembered the house where her first mother lived. The new law about birth records (which had set her thinking more in this direction) would also provide a chance, when the time came, to talk to a counsellor about the implications of her search, and advice on how to approach it. Fuller information about her first parents and the circumstances of her adoption should also be available.

P.M. If you were wanting to see her what would you be hoping to get out of it?

Louise: What she was doing and how she was. I think in a way I'd just like to see them in the distance – though it would be nice to talk to them to see if they think about me. That's from my point of view, but for them it would be a shock – and yet they might want to find out who I am, and so might my sister. Would I be able to find my sister as well, and my relations?

P.M. Well, there's nothing to stop you trying if you wanted to, except the reservations you're having now, wondering what it would mean to them.

Louise: I thought that if I found my mother then I would want to ask questions about my father. And because they're divorced she might not say nice things, or she might not want to talk about it, or she might resent me for asking questions.

P.M. I think it's something you need to think a lot about and talk a lot more about, and you can always talk to me if you wanted to. I'd always be there to help you go about it.

Louise: I think I would like to find her, and my Dad and sister, to find out what they're like.

P.M. And to give you more of an idea of who you are.

Louise: Yes.

P.M. It takes some working out, doesn't it – helping you think about what sort of a person you are and who you are – though the person you are comes as much, or more, from the family you've grown up in . . . It sounds as though your Mum understands that you've got this sort of curiosity but that your Dad is worried you might get hurt, whereas you're worrying that you might hurt them.

Louise: I thought they might think that I wasn't happy because I wanted to.

Kate was helpful in trying to explain the ambivalence of their parents' position: they did understand her curiosity, they *might* feel a bit upset or slighted, but had always said they would help her search, in spite of her father's wish to protect her. I had my own memories of her first mother; a sad woman, very preoccupied with herself and her troubled affairs, and there was not a lot of warmth there to offer much basis of hope for a glad reunion. But Louise's recurring question was whether her mother ever thought of her, as if she needed to be thought about to affirm her own value, and this she might need to pursue. Self-discovery is not without its pain.

Louise: She might really like to see me – or she might not.
P.M. Yes, and you'd have to cope with the possibility of her feeling she had another life now – we don't know if she's married again or what she's doing.

Louise thought it might hurt more if her first mother told an intermediary that she did not want to see her, than if she just turned up and received a cool welcome. The idea of seeing her at a distance, in natural surroundings, had attractions. She would see her more as the person she really was, not a possible façade; whereas if they met they would both be nervous, each wondering what the other would think.

Louise had been quite pleased when my project letter came.

Louise: I didn't mind at all. In a way I thought it was a way to find out and talk it over. I think it would be nice to talk to a group of people who had been adopted.
P.M. You feel you might have a lot in common if you talked with them?
Louise: Yes, to find out what sort of things they thought about. I don't think you can talk to people about it unless they've been through it as well.

She was perhaps not sure that I really understood. I suggested that her family had been through it too – they had grown together as a family.

Kate: But there again we don't know what it's like to be in your shoes – we can only surmise, but when you're in that position yourself it can be entirely different.
Louise: I remember sometimes I used to think they were getting on at me because I was adopted . . . I used to think they didn't love me sometimes when I'd been naughty and I used to keep getting into trouble.

Kate had shown considerable empathy; she was sensible now in seeing that many upsets can be identified with adoption rather than seen as part of the ordinary ups and downs of family life – 'really we've all been treated the same'. Louise thought she was lucky to have been adopted as a baby, but had wondered if her parents ever regretted adopting her, feeling she might not be as lovable now as when she was a tiny baby. She had certainly been beautiful then, and Kate and I tried to assure her of her present undoubted good looks – and her attractive personality. Louise acknowledged that everyone saw her as an outgoing person. She made friends easily and enjoyed making people laugh. 'I think it helps if people are friendly, but I think you've got to be friendly or you just don't get anywhere . . .' She was full of jokes –

> *Louise:* . . . but I think there's a side to me that's very quiet and serious . . . every so often I like to be on my own, so I go out and talk to the rabbits, or just into the garden.
> *P.M.* That sounds a good sort of mixture – to be able to cope with being on your own, and it's a great gift to be able to get on easily with people.

Kate also described how the neighbourhood boys would line up at the gate to talk to Louise – as much because she showed an interest in their football and other activities as for flirtation.

> *Louise:* I just see them as friends. I don't think there's any substitute for having a serious talk with a friend – and I see boys sometimes as a lot better friends than girls.

In her last letter to me Louise had been counting the weeks till she left school, and she had a place now in a College of Technology, subject to her 'O' levels. She seemed to have a happy capacity for relationships with her peers and a close bond with Kate. (David was now a sailor and I did not meet him.) She was imaginative about both sets of parents' feelings, though apparently a little less confident of her adoptive parents' unqualified affection than they were likely to assume. Despite this slight uncertainty, she appeared to have blossomed in this family and to be a very likeable, thoughtful adolescent, with a capacity both for fun and for deep feelings. She thanked me for answering her questions and I think was able to use my visit for her own purposes.

Philip Boylan called to see me some time later when he was in my direction. He expressed contentment in the outcome of the adoption, and affection and pride in Louise. He told me that when she was younger she had thought I was her first mother – this mysterious godmother person who wrote and sent presents. In the course of their relationships social workers are often the subject of transference fantasies and can be seen as comforting or depriving parents, but this was more part of the search for her own identity – and was I not a teacher too? Philip Boylan was sympathetic to her need to establish an accurate shape to her imaginings.

An adopted person's need to know about his origins is neither a criticism of his present family nor a threat to his loving relationship with them. It is just a basic human need to see one's place in the whole scheme of things.[10]

9

Georgie and his adoptive mother

A sorrow and a joy . . . Tell them I had a hard time, but I got through it. You don't get through it without hard work – and a deal of patience, really, which I haven't got – or didn't know I had.

Georgie, the last member of this little group, was adopted by his foster-parents, Mr and Mrs Cox, when he was eleven. He came to them at five years old from another county, an unhappy, angry small boy, disturbed by the discontinuities of his care till then. His father had been a Sergeant in the army; his mother had tried on her own to care for him in temporary lodgings, but reluctantly soon had to request care. Georgie spent two years in a residential nursery, returning there when two foster-homes could not manage his anger. (Some readers may remember the little barbarians in the background of the Robertsons' film, *John*; they were longer-term children in a nursery which, with multiple care-givers, was, typically, not geared to meet the emotional needs of toddlers.)[1] He then went to Mrs Silver, a special foster-mother who under some incomprehensible policy could only keep children till they were five.

Meanwhile, Mr and Mrs Cox had applied to us as foster-parents. Mrs Cox, in her fifties, had married too late to bear children (having nursed her elderly father till he died) and was then considered too old to adopt a baby. They answered an advertisement from our neighbouring authority and were offered Georgie. They agreed and weathered a protracted introduction which was too long for anyone's peace of mind. Kerrane[2] has described a revised shorter plan of introductory meetings which the Barnardo's New Families Project in Glasgow found raised less anxiety than their previous lengthy programme. Their aims include '(1) the chance for both child and family to have a gut reaction to each other, (2) the opportunity to be familiar enough with each other and the surroundings to allow some continuity of experience for the child, and (3) an opportunity for the child to withdraw and separate from his previous caretakers and friends'.

Georgie, however, was eventually placed, and I took over the supervision on behalf of the care authority. The Coxes lived in a small village near Paxton in a cottage which hugged the hill behind. Georgie immediately attached himself to Mr Cox (who had grown-up sons from a previous marriage). There had been no visible male figure of any significance in his life before and he followed his foster-father like a devoted shadow. Mr Cox was self-employed and Georgie spent hours with him in his yard across the road, often sitting contentedly in the frame of an old taxi.

While the bond grew with her husband, Mrs Cox had to wait patiently (sometimes desperately) for Georgie to begin to trust her. She had so much love in her to offer a child and Georgie appeared to hate all women. A marriage needs to be strong to withstand the potential divisiveness where the partners are split into good and bad parents.[3] Bowlby[4] suggests that a child's ambivalence is intensified in separation, and if he cannot hold together both his fury that a mother has left, and his longing for her, he may deny one feeling and over-state the other. Georgie's anger, which was perhaps cumulative, certainly seemed predominant, and was displaced on to his new mother. (It is hard to be punished for other people's failures.) He tested her grievously, outspokenly rebuffing her. He sought physical contact but used it to hurt her, wrenching and biting her hands, or nearly throttling her. She was bruised both inwardly and outwardly by him. He often shamed her in front of visitors (who perhaps need to be kept to a minimum when a child is settling). When at last he began to trust her he regressed, trying to catch up on some of the mothering he had missed. He wanted her to dress him and would try to suck a bottle on her lap. In her study of children adopted from residential nurseries, Tizard[5] found that 'babyish' behaviour was not altogether unwelcome for adoptive mothers who had hoped originally to adopt a younger child. Both Rowe and Jewett[6] write about the older child's need to be cuddled, rocked and babied when he is trying to experience earlier 'lost' stages in his new family. The worker may also have to legitimize his new parents' tender responses, so that they are not pressured by other people's (or their own) opinions of how children should behave at certain ages. Some warning, prior to placement, of possible 'babyish' behaviour can also reduce discomfort for the parents.

My main task was to support Mrs Cox. I tried to comfort her, to help her understand some of Georgie's perplexing behaviour and to maintain hope in her. As their relationship grew she was very able to talk with him herself about his circumstances. She and I would always look at any current pressing problem (his aggression, his biting and chewing, his rejection of her cooking) and sometimes then review the hurdles she had already surmounted. Initially he had lacked physical co-ordination and would walk warily, 'with the gait of one who finds no path where a path should be'.[7] So it was good one day to see him run freely down the field opposite their cottage and fling his arms round Daisy, 'the goat I love the best', and later reach up his arms more gently round Mrs Cox's neck. Mostly, however, he would not let her kiss or hug him and this was a continuing sadness for her.

There was a setback when tests showed that Georgie had epileptic tendencies, but this was medically controlled. There was also some Child Guidance help. Adoption plans were delayed, partly because Georgie was such a handful, and the Coxes welcomed support, both emotionally and financially. We encouraged our neighbouring county to assume parental rights[8] so that Georgie's placement would be more assured, and as a result they managed to trace his natural mother who had earlier disappeared. I went to see her. She had married, and despite some depression was managing a new family. She was moved to see a photograph of Georgie and left the room to hide her tears. She told me of her struggles to care for him. She had visited him at first in the Nursery, and painted a picture Thomas Hardy might have penned of herself sheltering in the church porch opposite while she waited for the strict visiting hour to begin. She had long imagined him as having been adopted, but was pleased to think he was at least settled permanently in a foster-home. Georgie was adopted at his own insistence a couple of years after I left Ringshire. Five years later Mr Cox died, just after Georgie had joined the army at 16. Mrs Cox had been away for the night, and she wrote to tell me how in the morning neighbours had found her husband's body on the hillside, with his dog sitting guard beside him.

We had a number of telephone calls and I heard how helpful Georgie was when his mother developed cancer (from which mercifully she recovered). 'He's a lovely boy. Thank God I've got him.' Later she was proud of his campaign medal for service in Northern Ireland. She feared for him there – 'Oh my heart, the first time he went away.' She loved him dearly, but there was inevitably some ambivalence; partings were the more painful because he still would not kiss her. 'Hallo, you old cow' or 'you old bag' was his only endearment. He wrote to me two or three times about his army life and how he spent his 21st birthday on duty in Belfast.

Georgie was in Germany when I visited Mrs Cox for my project. I had called to see her in her new cottage the previous year and found her quite contented. She had always been a keen gardener and showed me her garden above the cottage with wide views of the surrounding country. The cottage itself was crammed with plants and ornaments and everything she needed close to hand. She was very much a countrywoman, enjoyed the friendliness of village life and the proximity of her neighbour who was a friend of many years' standing. She is a good raconteur and described a recent surprise party for her 72nd birthday. She had been invited to her old cottage and found it packed with her friends and relations all singing a birthday welcome to her. 'And I thought "Has anybody been so lucky?" and the phone was ringing all day.' Her immense pleasure in this had been marred, however, because there had been no card or telephone call from Georgie – 'My own son was the only one that I didn't hear from.'

P.M. I don't think you've ever doubted that he loves you – he just finds it so hard to show it, doesn't he?

Mrs Cox: He can't show it – he's always been like it hasn't he, ever since he was a child.

P.M. And that's always been a disappointment to you.

Her sadness about his present neglect of her this time outweighed her pleasure and pride in him which for some years had seemed to predominate in her ambivalence. On the one hand was her pride in what she had achieved after a long struggle, her good-looking soldier son, with friends in the army, a passable fluency in German and a German girl friend, and on the other her hurt at his harshness and his handicap in showing his feelings.

Mrs Cox: He's got so hard . . . I put it down to war training, getting ready for war.

P.M. So he cuts off his feelings.

Mrs Cox: Mm. He must do. I don't know how he goes on with his girl – I feel sorry for her really . . . Perhaps she'll reform him. Perhaps she'll be the making of him. I hope she will.

P.M. Well, you feel you've made something of him, don't you – when you think what a difficult child he was.

Mrs Cox: Oh I have – definitely – not much perhaps, but I haven't done badly I don't think, do you?

P.M. No, I think you can feel proud of him.

Mrs Cox: Oh I do. But I don't feel so proud of him now, when everyone else says, 'Have you heard from him lately?' and they are all so down on him.

P.M. So you feel you have to stand up for him and yet you're hurt.

Mrs Cox: I try to make excuses – I've always made excuses for him, haven't I – always, at school and everything. Oh I do wish some other woman would take him on – I'd like to see him happy before I go.
P.M. You went on hoping that you would see him grow up – that you'd be able to see him through.

Her husband had helped her, and so had her faith.

Mrs Cox: You'll think me funny to say this, because I go on so, but I'm a Christian, or hope I am.
P.M. Why should I think it funny?
Mrs Cox: And I know I have had help – I don't just believe it, I know I have. I prayed that I wouldn't go before he was grown up and able to look after himself. Well, that's come –
P.M. He's a grown man now, and independent.
Mrs Cox: He's a man. I could leave him, he could do without me now . . . But I would go happier if he was married and had a woman to look after him – there's always something. I shall want to see my grandchildren – that's what I'd love. I'd be able to go then, when I'd been able to see his children.
P.M. That would crown it for you, wouldn't it?
Mrs Cox: Oh I'd feel I had really accomplished something then.

Georgie only came home now about once a year.

Mrs Cox: And you feel, when you're my age, 'I wonder how many more times am I going to see him.'
P.M. You feel you haven't got time to spare.
Mrs Cox: If I live another five years I'll only see him five more times.
P.M. Yes, that's hard to think of. And you think he's wasting the chances.
Mrs Cox: I mustn't think about it, because I think it's his life and this is mine – I've had mine, haven't I?
P.M. Well, he's given you a lot of happiness, but he's also given you a lot of hurt.
Mrs Cox: He has, but then that happens to every mother – whether they are adopted or not.

She thought she understood him more than other people, but added sadly, 'I still don't understand him, not properly,' and she was very conscious of *his* ambivalence.

Mrs Cox: He sometimes gives me the impression he doesn't care twopence about me – that if I were to die tomorrow he wouldn't turn a hair. And yet, you see, when I think that, something happens that I realise that he does –
P.M. Well, you've done wonders for him, and brought him on, but maybe he's still a bit handicapped in his feelings – because he got hurt when he was little –

129

Mrs Cox: Oh yes, terrible things –

P.M. – that he's somehow protected himself – from feeling too deeply . . .

Mrs Cox: You don't know whether he feels anything or whether he doesn't. You feel does he and is afraid to show it, or doesn't he care?

P.M. I think he's often shown you he does care.

Mrs Cox: Yes he has. But then like now he makes me feel that he doesn't.

It seemed to me that it was hard for both of them – for Mrs Cox who had unselfishly delayed the chances of marriage and motherhood till so late in life, to be rewarded by such a struggle for any affectionate appreciation from her son; while for Georgie it was perhaps uncomfortable to be the object of so much intense longing. He seemed to want to avoid any strong display of emotion.

Mrs Cox: The most I ever get when he goes is, 'Well, I don't want to go back but I got to – well,' (Got up and hit me on the arm.) 'Cheerio, old thing, look after yourself.' . . . And even when he first went in the army, George (her husband) and I took him to catch a train at Paxton, and he wouldn't let us on the platform. That broke my heart. I wanted to see the train go . . . and I tried to lean over the rails to see if I could see –

P.M. Ah. Perhaps he thought he might be upset.

Mrs Cox: I never slept all that night. I was thinking, 'What is he doing now?'

Neither of her menfolk would ever hear of her getting old, perhaps responding to her own regret that she was. Georgie was very tall now:

Mrs Cox: He can hardly get in here now. And he picks me up under one arm. He gets his funny moods like that . . . He'll pick me up and put me on the settee there, or carry me upstairs. He's very strong.

P.M. Well, it's a funny sort of way of showing his feelings, but –

Mrs Cox: I just laugh. I try to be skittish and pretend I'm young again, and have a laugh and go with him. And sometimes I think, 'Oh Georgie, you are hurting me,' because I'm an old woman now. But I try to forget it because I don't want him to think I'm an old woman. (Laughed.) He knows I am . . . but he treats me like he would, well, any other girl really. My husband was the same too – they won't hear of you being old.

P.M. They don't want to think of losing you.

Mrs Cox: I always remember my husband's words to this day – if ever I said anything about getting old, he'd always say to me, 'My darling, you'll never grow old, you'll always be just the same.'

Mr Cox had made her feel special. Georgie was rougher in his attempts to keep her young.

Mrs Cox: I've often got bruises on my arm, up here, after Georgie's been home. He forgets that it hurts, and he seizes you. He wouldn't deliberately hurt me now – it's just that he forgets how old I am and I bruise easily – I don't say anything.

P.M. Well, you could say something – couldn't you?

Mrs Cox: Oh I could hit him sometimes. (Laughed.)

P.M. Yes – I'm sure you could.

Mrs Cox: But all the same I wouldn't be without him. If I had my time over again I'd do the same thing – that's saying something.

P.M. That's a big thing to say – after all you've been through with him.

Mrs Cox: Well, I would – because he's given me some joy – though sometimes I think he hasn't given me any.

P.M. When you're feeling down you feel he hasn't given you anything.

We talked about her struggle at the beginning. I reminded her that she had nearly given up early on but had not told me (till years later) in case I thought she was unsuitable to look after him. I was sorry not to have made it safe enough for her to tell me then.

P.M. You didn't know what I'd think if you told me.

Mrs Cox: I ought to have known better, knowing you, but I was always so terrified someone *would* take him away. I must have been blooming bad, mustn't I, because I could never have meant it.

P.M. It was before he took to you, wasn't it?

Mrs Cox: Yes. He did get me down. Well, you see, every morning, there was I full of joys to have a little child, and the first time I put him to bed I said, 'We're just in there, and the door's open. If you want me in the night you know where I am, you've only got to call.' And he comes in next morning and glowers at me and says, 'I hate you.' And of course, into bed beside my husband – that happened every morning – and the looks he gave me –

She had eventually told her husband one morning she could not stand it any longer.

Mrs Cox: And of course that was where he was a help to me. He said, 'Well just stand him a little longer, it'll turn' – and it did.

The patience which her husband had urged (and supported) had been rewarded.

Mrs Cox: I'll never forget that time – he was such a baby and he looked out the window and saw a woman in the road going by, and said, 'Huh! a woman. I hate women,' and then he turned round and said, 'I don't hate you, Mum.' Oh the first time he said that, oh that was good.

P.M. You felt you'd turned a corner with him.

Other foster or adoptive parents reading this may recall similar moments of triumph when they have survived a child's testing of them. Mrs Cox would have been helped by the kind of group support that is now more available to foster-parents or adopters of older children, where hope is engendered by people who have come through similar experiences, and uncomfortable feelings of exasperation and anger are recognised and accepted. Bowlby,[9] writing about ambivalence, also admires the ability of parents who can accept a child's 'I hate you's' with equanimity. And reminding us of the most basic fact, that hostility elicits hostility, Woodmansey[10] suggests:

> not to lose one's own temper with one's children (provided that this is a genuine freedom from anger, and not a defensive emotional withdrawal) is perhaps the greatest test of emotional maturity. Yet how common is the inverted view that the child should control his feelings, but that the parent need not.

The social worker has a classic role in helping substitute parents hold on during a child's initial testing to find whether he will be rejected yet again. But this involves empathising with the desperate pitch the care-givers can sometimes reach. It is not easy, when one is afraid a placement may be disrupted, to help a mother say that she has nearly reached breaking-point; but just saying it may ease her enough to persist. Mrs Cox reached this point before she knew me well enough to trust me, so it was important that Mr Cox was able to help her through. Foster-fathers may be seen less often and can sometimes be thought to play a subsidiary role, but in fact their support or lack of it can be crucial.

Mrs Cox's earlier ambivalence was demonstrated again when she recalled her terror that Georgie would be taken away from her. A woman doctor had magnified this fear after a school medical. 'She was very bossy, and she said, "Oh that's not the sort of child *you* want at all. You want a nice cuddly little child, you don't want him. I'll see into that." And do you know, it went through me.' She had made her way straight to our Area Office. 'I couldn't ride, I pushed my bike up there, choking with tears I was. I was in an awful state. I wasn't crying really because I'm not a crying person, but I was very upset!' J.B. had assured her that Georgie would not be taken away from her if she was happy with him. 'I'm *not* happy with him,' she had said, 'but I'd hate to lose him.'

An understanding of ambivalence is a basic tool for social workers and one which needs sharpening as we learn how to recognise and respond to underlying mixed feelings. That doctor was possibly prompted by some hostility towards social workers as well as by concern for Mrs Cox on whom they had apparently landed such a difficult child. Their own GP had been an ally. 'I'll never forget the day I took him to the doctor and he said, "You've done wonders with this boy" – he says that to this day, my doctor – "he doesn't need them (tablets for controlling his epilepsy) any more. He's all right now."' This had been another moment of triumph for her. 'I was on top of the world.'

Georgie was a firm member of the family by the time he was adopted at 11. He had earlier listened intently when I told him of my visit to his birth mother, but he refused the offer of meeting her himself. Mrs Cox had generously thought it might benefit him to see her before he was adopted – 'And I could have met her, and perhaps she would have liked me – or perhaps not, but she would have seen who was having her son. But he wouldn't, he was quite firm.' She had talked sympathetically to Georgie about his birth mother, 'I've always told Georgie it wasn't her fault, not to blame her. Poor devil – lovely little boy like that, and then to pass him on to someone else – you wonder why these things are allowed to happen. He blames his father more – he swears if ever he meets him he's going to shoot him.'

As with any feeling so vehemently expressed, this may have contained within it the wish for (or fear of) the opposite. An understanding of defence mechanisms – the various ways in which we protect ourselves from uncomfortable thoughts and feelings – is less fashionable now, but still indispensable to social workers if they are not to be constantly misled or superficial in their reactions.[11] Georgie apparently expressed an outward indifference to his natural mother (Mrs Cox did not know what he had done with the photograph she sent him) but did not seem to harbour resentment against Mrs Silver, whom they continued to visit occasionally. His warmest and least complicated feelings had probably always been for Mr Cox.

Mrs Cox: Oh he loved him – it was the greatest blow to Georgie, losing my husband.

P.M. It was a blow for both of you.

Mrs Cox: He was in a state when he came home. (He had been brought half-way by the army, the other half by the police, arriving late at night.) He must have been crying most of the way home, but he didn't want anyone to know (he sat hiding his face) so we had to pretend not to see. My heart bled for him but I couldn't do anything. I didn't make a fuss – I said,

'Hallo, my son, it's rather a sad home-coming, isn't it?'

She had learned painfully not to try to hug him, and I wished I had been able to help them more over this.

Mrs Cox: He didn't desert me when George died, he offered to come home. He had only just joined, and he said, 'Shall I give it up and come home?' And I said, 'You please yourself, but I don't think so, because you like it there.' But he said, 'You'll be alone,' and I said, 'I'll get used to it, and you can write to me' – in those days I thought he would.

She had known poverty at first after her husband died, living on £7 a week till his affairs were sorted out. Georgie had written needing money for new trousers and she had somehow managed to send him £10 which was all she had. 'I hadn't got a penny to my name. I thought, "I'll have to do without anything this week." I made do – ate cream crackers rather than buy a loaf of bread.'

She was still living on a narrow margin, and Georgie was unpredictable about helping financially when he came home on leave. She would draw money to stock the freezer with his favourite food for the month, but his enormous appetite and midnight feasts would empty it in a few days. 'He's a big fellow – he works like a man and eats like a man.' Although his pay was about five times her pension, he sometimes paid nothing. Like the exhausted reed warbler feeding her giant cuckoo foster chick, Mrs Cox did not falter or refuse, and was philosophical about the apparently unfair distribution of money between them. 'Never mind. I think to myself, "Money's no good to you." I work on the idea that money's only lent to you while you're here – everything's lent to you, so what's the good to hang on to anything – I mean it's not life or death, your money or your goods!'

Georgie's welfare and wishes were still paramount to her (though he was perhaps not being groomed for marriage to anyone with ideas about women's liberation). However, she was confident that I had come to see her for herself as well. She was typically generous about my work. I suggested I could have made it easier for her to tell me difficulties.

Mrs Cox: No, you helped me enormously – you don't know what a help you were to me – that was why I was so pleased when you said you'd come to see me. I tell my friend nobody knows what she did for me (this friend came in briefly to meet me). I don't know how I could have got on without you.
P.M. Well, we shared a worry about him didn't we?
Mrs Cox: We certainly did.

She had kept in touch, seeing me as a friend. 'I could tell you things – perhaps I didn't tell you everything, but you heard most of it!' She hoped my students would benefit from hearing the story of her struggle. 'Tell them I had a hard time, but I got through it.' She regretted that some foster-parents were unable to use social work help, perhaps seeing it as interference, but was herself convinced of its necessity. It is some years since Kay[12] presented arguments for casework help for foster-parents, and the growth of the National Foster Care Association has rightly emphasised their status as colleagues. But the two are not mutually exclusive. If a sign of professionalism is the willingness of social workers to receive supervision and appropriate help for themselves, there is no reason why they should withhold their casework skills when their foster-parent colleagues are disheartened or discomforted by the stress of caring for other people's children. As Kay suggests, if anger can be shown and expressed to the caseworker, the need to direct it on to the child is reduced. Berry[13] too has suggested that if the worker can accept the care-giver's pressure of negative feelings, the positive side which is usually there has room to breathe.

Mrs Cox had come through her experience still periodically hurt and disappointed in her hopes, but with some gratitude and satisfaction.[14] He had been 'a sorrow and a joy' to her. 'If it wasn't for Georgie I'd have nobody now – that's what's such a blessing, I've got him.' As Abelard wrote – 'and hearts that sorrowed will be satisfied'.[15]

I had been shown photographs of Georgie in army uniform – 'He's a handsome fellow, there's no doubt about it' – and Mrs Cox was eager that I should see him when he came home on leave. In the event my return visit to see Georgie came in the aftermath of a late-night quarrel in which he had violently threatened his mother, leaving her shaken and distraught. She was very distressed on the telephone and hoped I would still come and see her even if Georgie was unwilling. She had recovered when I visited, having been much comforted and strengthened by hearing her husband's voice saying, 'What are you doing, my darling? Don't give up now when it's so near the end.'

Georgie and I talked fairly briefly on our own. He was not pleased to see me, perhaps wondering if I might reproach or reprimand him. His gun was prominent and his big frame and hostile brooding presence filled the cottage. He eyed me warily as we talked. He was now a Lance Bombardier, with a small group of eight men to look after, and greater responsibility when in Northern Ireland. 'There you're in real charge and make decisions as to what to do . . . If someone pulls a knife on you

– and you don't know what to do – do you shoot or whatever?' I had heard he was engaged to his German girl friend but he was unforthcoming about her. 'My mother exaggerates a lot of things.'

He said he did not think much about his childhood, but had resented the feeling of being 'controlled' by my male successor, whose questions and visits made him feel different from his friends who had more freedom. Surprisingly he had joined the army to be his own boss.

> *Georgie:* I don't trust nobody personally. I never have done – not a hundred per cent.
>
> *P.M.* Isn't that a bit lonely?
>
> *Georgie:* Not really. I like being on my own. I've two or three good friends and the rest of them – well, they're all friends really, they're just one big community. And there's not many you can really trust, especially from the army point of view.
>
> *P.M.* Well, I suppose looking back, people have let you down when you were very small.
>
> *Georgie:* They certainly have . . . When I left school 'Oh, he's a potential hard case' and that's it. That was the hardest bit for me . . .

I pursued the question of trust and he did concede, 'I trust my mother of course, but work-wise I don't trust nobody.'

He disclaimed any interest in his birth mother and had no wish to see her. 'If she turned up on the doorstep I'd just say, "Off you go, I don't want to see you."'[16] I reminded him of my visit to her. She had apparently hesitated later over signing her consent to his adoption, but Georgie had no doubts about where he had wanted to be.

> *Georgie:* I was in a frame of mind that I just wouldn't have stayed with her.
>
> *P.M.* Well, she'd be a stranger to you.
>
> *Georgie·* That's what I mean. That's how I'd treat her, as a stranger as well.
>
> *P.M.* Yes, and you probably don't want me dragging her up into the conversation.
>
> *Georgie:* That's right.
>
> *P.M.* I suppose all I'm wanting to say is that I did meet her and she was very much wanting to know how you were and I showed her a photograph of you. She was sad to think that she hadn't been able to bring you up. It wasn't that she didn't want you.

Georgie could not recall how he had perceived me between the ages of five and nine. 'At the time I thought, "Somebody's coming to see me today," but I didn't know why.' I said I was trying to discover from consumer views like his how to help my social work students do better than I and it seemed important to make one's reason for visiting clear.

He played down his reaction to his father's death.

Georgie: I was surprised and upset, that's all. I soon forgot about it. I'll never forget him – it sort of hit me later on, not at the time. It took a few months really.

P.M. To realise you wouldn't see him again?

Georgie: When I saw all his stuff going out of the house . . . all the stuff he'd collected all smashed up and sold – it wasn't on.

P.M. Are you saying you didn't miss him for himself?

Georgie: When I came for a few days on compassionate leave it didn't sort of hit me at all. I don't know how to explain it myself, but people coming in and out and all the old things going, it was all changed . . . I still think of him. I'll never forget him though.

P.M. You were fond of that house.

Georgie: It wasn't the house, it was 16 years of collection, 16 years of memories. It was seeing them getting pulled about and ruined.

P.M. Well, it was a part of your life that you really remember. But it seems to me that you can't easily say that you're fond of people.

Georgie: I've always been independent, you know I've always been that. I can look after myself.

P.M. And do you think you're happy that way?

Georgie: Yes.

P.M. Does it feel safer that way, that you wouldn't perhaps get hurt?

Georgie: That's right.

He had been slow to answer my project letter.

Georgie: I don't mind answering questions, it's just that I'm not very good at that sort of thing.

P.M. Well, it feels like an interrogation, rather than you and me talking as people who used to know each other.

I just touched on the recent row and heard his viewpoint.

Georgie: She does get carried away sometimes. I don't think it's all my fault either, it's just that she's getting old and she won't accept the fact. She jumps to conclusions all the time. I can see it building up sometimes when she's going to start on me.

P.M. I suppose it's a responsibility for you that she's so fond of you and it's a lot to live up to.

Georgie: Sometimes I just can't tell her things and we'll argue –

We were interrupted, I think to Georgie's relief, by a visit from some cousins. He was becoming less taciturn, but was wary of anyone in authority and I did not see him for long enough to bring out the side of him which has given Mrs Cox some happiness and helped her to persevere.

Georgie's story bears out the belief of some writers, for example Bowlby, Winnicott and the Robertsons, that certain impairments resulting from early deprivation do have a long-term effect on the capacity to form relationships. It seems as if the damage of his first five years had only been partially modified by 16 years of consistent affectionate caring since. The study by Tizard[17] of children adopted from residential nurseries shows more encouraging findings in terms of parental satisfaction and reported mutually satisfying relationships (when the children were eight); the findings, however, do not deny that some early experiences may result in kinds of behaviour which it is difficult to alter. She mainly shows that a group of ex-nursery children who were deemed likely to respond to adoption did better with adoptive parents prepared to devote considerable time and attention to them than did those who returned to natural mothers who were often harassed by disadvantaged circumstances. There is no shortage of evidence now that adoption offers the best alternative for many older children in need of substitute families, and can lead to considerable parental satisfaction. Mrs Cox's share of the story shows how much patient endurance and loving commitment there can be in someone who is highly motivated to be a parent. (A minimum criterion of success taken by Tizard was the stability of the placement.) Possibly this laid too much of a burden of expectation on Georgie who put down roots but felt unable to respond outwardly to such an intense need to give. He did, however, find a secure base and a sense of belonging, and took pride in the cottage which one day would be his.

One point of policy is very apparent. Had Georgie's birth mother been given more help to keep him, or had his placement in a permanent family not been delayed till he was five, a lot of suffering would have been spared.

From a socialisation viewpoint, it is necessary in a placement to set the developmental needs of a child alongside the needs of members of his new family. I have the advantage of a long view now. When Georgie was five, Mrs Cox was 55 and they both had a lot of catching up to do. He had no grounds for believing the world was a reliable or satisfying place, and she had unselfishly delayed the pleasures of marriage and parenthood until it was urgent for her to make the most of mothering Georgie. At ten he was something of a terror at school and a tearaway with his friends, while she at 60 was beginning to tire physically. When

Mr Cox died, Georgie was 16, making his bid for indepenc
search for identity within the structured environment of the
loss of his father in adolesence will have revived memories
losses, but he probably found it unsafe to show or share his gri
of appearing weak.[18] He seemed anxious about his mot   ιu
telephoned her frequently. Mrs Cox was then 66, and this major loss of
her husband just after Georgie had left home, will have compounded
the other potential losses of ageing, particularly the reduced sense of
being needed. Now, while he at 22 was pursuing his separate life and
career, at 72 she too was partly disengaging. His aggressiveness was
now to some extent diverted into official channels, and he had never
been in trouble with the police. Mrs Cox had won his trust, but he was
perhaps one of those men who find it hard to integrate the feminine side
of their make-up and thus see gentleness as weak and unmanly, so that
she was left still hungry for a more tender response from him.
However, she had some comfort in feeling she had accomplished a
demanding task and done it with love. She was to some extent
philosophical that he had to live his own life, and as her neighbour had
said when she was with us, 'I think you hold on to your children by
letting them go.'

So it seems. As a postscript I heard two years later that Georgie had
left the army to be nearer his mother when her health deteriorated. He
was applying to join the Prison Service but would be in this country.
'It's lovely to know you are not alone,' she said.

Perhaps it is roughly
Saying what God alone could perfectly show –
How selfhood begins with a walking away,
And love is proved in the letting go.
C. Day Lewis[19]

10

Deborah and her foster-parents

Well, I suppose she wasn't growing up. I suppose this is it. You get great satisfaction from seeing your children grow up and making strides of independence and when you haven't got it – or when three members of the family have got it and the fourth one hasn't – the poor fourth one really suffers.

Deborah was a child of incest, her parents a young brother and sister of moderately low intelligence. There seemed no chance that they could bring her up and in those days she was considered unadoptable because of the question mark over her development. Mr and Mrs Murray who had one small son, Jonathon, agreed to take her as a long-term foster-child. They were both qualified in different helping professions, and lived in an attractive Ringshire village in a roomy Victorian stone house with a secluded rambling garden. Deborah was four when I took over the supervision and by then her physical and mental retardation was becoming apparent in her small stature, her lack of speech and a slight spasticity. Earlier it had perhaps been harder to anticipate handicap just because her appearance was so 'normal'. There was a second son in the family, and I have a seaside photograph of the two Murray boys busily excavating, while Deborah, aged five, sits quite happily apart, building her own small sandcastle. She looks alert, bonny and trusting. Another shows her running laughing across their big lawn to be caught by her foster-mother; a more poignant one pictures them on Paxton station, Deborah dwarfed by an enormous suitcase, on her way to a special boarding-school for children with speech difficulties.

The offer of a place there had presented a dilemma: would she benefit more from gaining some verbal ability than she would be set back by separation from her foster-parents? Our decision to accept was debatable but was influenced by the degree to which her lack of speech inhibited her ability to think and to communicate. A few years later Younghusband et al.[1] recommended that more special classes were needed for children with speech and language disorders in order to avoid residential placement.

As she grew older her retardation became more visible. After I left, Mrs Murray seemed to welcome the birthday and Christmas cards I sent Deborah, and for a while wrote giving me news of her, and of the birth of a third son. After a gap of some years I was startled by a letter signed 'Deborah', from an undecipherable address, misspelt and oddly worded but conveying a rather desperate message that her mother was ill, that she herself had three more weeks there before going to another town in Ringshire, and that she wanted to die.

I discovered that the Murrays had moved out of our area; that Deborah at 16 was about to leave boarding-school and move to a hostel as the Murrays felt unable to continue being a base for her. In this crisis she must have dimly recalled me as someone who had known her in her foster home. I spoke to her on the telephone and wrote to Paul and Diana Murray, guessing what it must have cost them to make their decision. They had cared for Deborah for nearly 16 years while she slowly grew more handicapped than they had originally expected.

I answered several little letters from Deborah and sent her photos of herself in the foster-home, then heard nothing till I telephoned to ask if I could see her for my project. I was sad to hear that she had been moved to a hospital for the mentally handicapped, having started a fire in her hostel.

The Murrays agreed to see me and asked if I would visit them before I saw Deborah. I wondered if our meeting might be difficult for them though I hoped my letter at the time might have helped to ease any sense of failure (Mrs Murray had replied then that it expressed exactly what they were feeling). However, they were very friendly and talked with generous frankness. Their modern house, on the edge of a town, contrasted with the rural, timeless quality of their last home. They talked of the increasing difficulties of caring for Deborah and explored with me their different perceptions of why the fostering had ended.

Mrs Murray: I think the relationship broke down more and more really. The older she got the more withdrawn she got and the less we communicated really. I think, with hindsight, I was the wrong person to have Deborah.
P.M. What makes you say that?
Mrs Murray: Well, I think having two, and then three, lively, reasonably bright boys, I found it very hard to relate to her mental level.
P.M. There was such a big gap.
Mrs Murray: There was such a big gap, and also with her being a girl as well . . . but I say that with hindsight.
P.M. Yes. You weren't to know in the first place – I don't suppose anyone

realised how handicapped she was going to be. What were you told when she was placed with you?

Mrs Murray: Well, originally, that there was every chance that she would be normal.

The social worker had told them that research into children born of incest was suggesting that they would not necessarily be handicapped.

Mrs Murray: They didn't say, 'Don't have any worries.' And I suppose really almost from the word go it was pretty obvious she was going to be –

Mr Murray: He did sort of say that there was a question mark over it . . . this was one reason why she was not available for adoption; it was a question of seeing how she turns out. He more or less said would we consider her as a foster-child knowing that there was this question mark.

P.M. What were you hoping for yourselves at that point?

Their motivation had been mainly altruistic, a social service rather than a response to a pressing need of their own.

Mr Murray: We had just one of our own at that time and we had a home and there were kids who needed homes and we felt perhaps, you know, we ought to offer a home to somebody – and of course we had unmarried mothers later on . . . We felt it was something we could do to help certain categories of people really.

Diana Murray was more conscious of having wanted to extend the family, and her hope that fostering might have a bonus effect was fulfilled when Luke was born a year later. She had nearly miscarried and for several weeks Deborah was cared for within the extended family.

It seemed as though the difficulty in communicating with Deborah had possibly been the main stumbling block.

Mrs Murray: There was always the feeling that either there was nothing in her at all, or else there was so much in her and none of it was coming out.

P.M. It was very frustrating not knowing whether there was something there, and whether it was all bottled up.

Mrs Murray: Yes. Which I suspect is what eventually happened through all the years – a complete breakdown in the end.

P.M. It got disheartening.

Mrs Murray: Yes, we didn't ever seem to get any response and it is very hard having a one-way communication.

Deborah had also become very difficult to handle.

Mr Murray: Eventually . . . you could correct her in a normal voice saying,

'Stop doing that' or 'You mustn't' or whatever, but she would go off the deep end, stamp out, throw stones – temper-tantrums really.

Mrs Murray: She got very violent.

This surprised me as I remembered Deborah as a docile child.

Mrs Murray: Well, she was either very docile or she went completely the opposite if she got roused . . . it got worse the older she got . . . and you got to the point where you did everything not to rouse her.

The distant special school had not been able to improve her speech very much – most children there had a higher IQ – and she returned to a local one. Gradually she began to speak a little.

P.M. I was surprised to get that letter from her – when I left she had virtually no speech at all and certainly couldn't write. I was thinking some of her skills must have developed.

Mrs Murray: Yes, she could write reasonably well and she could read a limited amount. (She recalled an early assessment by an educational psychologist when Deborah was three.) She thought she would develop to about a 12-year-old. She said, 'She'll be able to read the *Daily Mirror* – look at the pictures and the big stuff . . .' I think she was absolutely right.

Mrs Murray thought that Deborah suffered from the realisation that Benjamin, their youngest son whom she had seen as a baby, had grown up and overtaken her and there had been tension between them.

Mrs Murray: Of course in a way the boys used her – included her in their games but got her to do the running and fetching for them. In a way she enjoyed that, and of course in other ways she didn't.

Because she became so troublesome, the Department had suggested she went to another boarding school, from where she came home for weekends and holidays. Once Paul and Diana Murray began to think they could not face the responsibility of her at home indefinitely, the age of 16 became a critical milestone.

Mrs Murray: She was going to leave school at 16 and whatever was going to happen then was going to have to be a big decision for the rest of her life, because if we kept her at home after that it was going to be very difficult for her to see any reason why she should be moved on. Jonathon had left home at that stage, so we said to her, 'Well, Jonathon's left home now, which is what happens when you leave school, and you're going to leave home.' We tried to wrap it up, not that 'We're pushing you out entirely' – which I suppose was the truth really –

There had been a painful time before Deborah left school when the

143

social workers were unable to find an alternative placement and so nothing could be said to her.

> *Mrs Murray:* The school was very much gearing everybody to leaving. And of course she didn't know what was going to happen, which was when she wrote (to P.M.) and said she wanted to die . . . This is when I felt everybody was falling down.

As so often happens with a fostering breakdown, other circumstances accelerated a deteriorating relationship. The family had reluctantly moved less than a year before when Paul Murray was offered a new job, and his wife had become very depressed (more so than I had gathered from the social worker at that time). She suffered a grief reaction at the loss of their much loved home and village, and her depression must have compounded and been compounded by her sense of failure over Deborah.

> *Mrs Murray:* I was very miserable, and really very depressed.
> *P.M.* At the change – and losing all your friends –
> *Mrs Murray:* It was just the general uprooting, I think . . . We were all at sixes and sevens and very unsettled, which again didn't help Deborah.
> *Mr Murray:* I really wondered whether I had made a terrible mistake . . . It was probably the longest you'd lived in one place.
> *Mrs Murray:* Yes, and the children had grown up there and it was a super old house . . . and a sort of family community . . . this is a town mentality not a village mentality.
> *P.M.* It can give you a real sense of loss, can't it –
> *Mrs Murray:* Oh absolutely.
> *P.M.* – to leave a house and a community.
> *Mr Murray:* I suppose it's this bereavement thing really. (He was taking part that afternoon in a forum on dying and bereavement.) I'm sure bereavement symptoms manifest themselves for any form of loss. Not just somebody actually –
> *P.M.* – actually dying –
> *Mr Murray:* – actually physically dying, but any loss or deprivation must produce similiar symptoms . . . and I think this is maybe what happened, looking back on it; the sort of depression and the sort of grief and the feeling that the world was never going to be the same again.

An understanding of the wide incidence of bereavement reactions is becoming more generally accepted, and this was a welcome explanation from someone in a related profession. Parkes[2] uses Fried's[3] study of rehoused people to show similarities in the process of mourning a loved person and the loss of a home. Marris[4] suggests that our ability to cope

144

with life depends on our capacity to make sense of what happens to us, and that the process of normal grief seems to be a working out of two conflicting impulses – either to return to the time before the loss, trying to recapture and reconstruct it and the image of the dead person (or lost thing), or alternatively to reach forward to a state of mind when the past is forgotten, where life is bearable and understandable. This conflict is painful as each impulse checks the other. He too writes helpfully about the impact on people in slum clearance schemes:

> If we can understand a change of home, like bereavement, as potential disruption of the meaning of life, we may be able to see more clearly who will suffer grief, and what might help them to retrieve a sense of purpose.[5]

Diana Murray had been helped to find her way back to meaning by a part-time job in their local surgery, but it had taken three to four years for her fully to recover her previous equilibrium. We spent some time talking about their move and the effect on both of them. It was sad that Diana had not had more social work help at the time. Because they had moved areas their new social worker must have met her in a low state, not knowing her previous strengths of energy, resourcefulness and cheerful capability. She could not remember the social worker's name.

P.M. I suppose with the move and everything, whoever you had didn't realise what you had been through with Deborah – and the long haul you'd had with her.
Mrs Murray: Yes, I suppose that was it.
P.M. They came in at the point where you felt you couldn't go on.
Mrs Murray: They didn't know me from the past, so if I was being very odd, they wouldn't think, 'Well, she's being a bit odd.'

If she had time to look at it, the social worker could have gleaned something of Deborah's troubles and the Murrays' long endeavours from the now bulky file. More usefully, perhaps, if she had had time to listen, she might have responded to Diana Murray's current low spirits, disorientation, and her likely sense of poor self-worth.

They had planned to keep in touch with Deborah but had found this hard to sustain, and I wondered if the social worker had tried to help them value their importance to Deborah in spite of her ambivalent behaviour towards them. They were reluctant now to resume contact.

Mrs Murray: The last time I saw her we took her out for the day and really she didn't want anything to do with us at all. So we didn't feel there was any point in going on, which I am sure was probably shattering for her in a way,

145

but there doesn't seem to be any point of contact at all.

P.M. That would be hard when you had steeled yourself to go and see her – to feel you couldn't communicate with her.

Mrs Murray: She did ring once from the hostel and said, 'Can I come home?' and I said, 'Well, what's the point, you weren't really happy here were you, or not recently?' That was in fact the last time we heard from her, which was a year ago.

It is possible, judging from the sequence of events, that this final break with her foster-parents might be not unconnected with the fire Deborah started in the hostel. That might be thought too dramatic an interpretation, but when someone has limited speech, her behaviour is more than usually a communication in itself. Her apparent outward rejection of them when they visited – she had gone in when they left without a backward glance – was perhaps her way of coping with her hurt that she was no longer living with them. When I telephoned for information and permission to visit her in the hospital to which she had been moved, her current social worker told me how Deborah, usually uncommunicative, had one day thrown herself on her bed in tears and said, 'I wants me Mum.' This had prompted a visit to the Murrays.

Mrs Murray: She tried very hard to persuade me to see her again, but I went back through the case history with her . . . you can't tell from what's on paper. I said I didn't think it would be any help to Deborah to start up the relationship again. In a way it was better for Deborah hopefully to get some relationship in the place where she was and not look back to us . . .

P.M. I think it is terribly difficult to go and see someone who has lived with you who is not living with you now, because you feel badly in yourself.

Mrs Murray: Yes, in a way I have enormous guilt feelings about Deborah and I suppose I always shall – according to the psychiatrists we have done everything you shouldn't do – blighted her life –

P.M. You're blaming yourself rather than saying you had a difficult child, and a more difficult child than you thought you were going to have.

Mrs Murray: Well, a more difficult child I suppose than anyone could foresee – but whether the difficulties were provoked by us in our situation, who knows? (Deborah had increasingly withdrawn from the lively activities of their three sons and became very aimless.) I suppose if it had been your own natural daughter it would have been different, I don't know. Perhaps it wouldn't for me. I don't think I'm a very motherly sort, and I suspect Deborah needed a very motherly, ample-bosomed sort that would give her great long cuddles and be very patient.

Because physical touch is one of the most effective means of non-verbal communication it is certainly easier for any care-giver who is at home with or finds pleasure in plenty of bodily contact. And although Mrs Murray had her at ten months, Deborah had never really felt like a child of her own. She was anxious now about my visit to Deborah.

Mrs Murray: In a way I don't want ideas about home again stirred up – which is really why I asked you to come and see us before you see her.
P.M. Yes, and I imagine you felt that if I saw you before seeing her I wouldn't be putting pressure on you.
Mrs Murray: Yes, well true, yes. Because really we'd thought a long time. I didn't say yea or nay while (the social worker) was here, and said we would write. It took us a long time to write the letter, and I don't really want us to go through it all over again. Or from Deborah's point of view. I'm still very concerned about Deborah's happiness, and what the situation is – news of her really, but this is slightly my undoing. Perhaps it's no good us seeing her and being involved, but I'm interested to know what has happened and what her condition is. I'd be very interested to know what you find.
P.M. And you feel that seeing her is no good because it upsets her? Or because originally you didn't get any response?
Mrs Murray: Yes. I don't think it would achieve anything – we've got no point of contact.

An earlier social worker had apparently helped them to withdraw gradually.

P.M. I suppose it would be bound to be upsetting both for you and for her; the only advantage would be she would feel you really hadn't forgotten her.
Mrs Murray: Yes.
P.M. And I suppose because you're scared of what she might want, it's harder to do anything smaller – to write to her, or –
Mrs Murray: I have always answered every letter Deborah has written to *us*. She's owing us one if anything.

She was ticking me off here. Paul Murray supported her. Conscious that the fostering had not come to a satisfactory conclusion, and willing to question their own part in it, he still felt the outcome was inevitable, 'unless presumably we were prepared to become a hospital or home for mentally handicapped people, and that would then become a full-time job'.

They may have felt I was slow to appreciate how wearying Deborah had been to live with, and the struggle they had to help her maintain some basic standards of caring for herself.

Mr Murray: She was sick one night and she just lay in it all night. Most normal kids would have got up and banged on the door and shouted 'I've

147

been sick' and we'd have . . . She would accept that standard of living without batting an eyelid, whereas most people would find it distasteful really.

They had been amazed to hear of a plan to send Deborah to a hostel to equip her to live in a minimal support unit – to teach her the 'social graces' such as looking after her clothes and washing herself, which she could already do at home.

Mrs Murray: It made me wonder what in the world had happened to her.

P.M. Well, I imagine no one else has found her any easier than you did.

Mrs Murray: Well, they have left her where she is which is quite significant – whether they feel the hospital is the place for her. When she was growing up I felt really a mental hospital was the only place which was going to be able to cope. The last social worker but one said she would lead an independent life one day, and knowing her as we did I just couldn't see that – she wasn't responsible enough, too unpredictable. I always had the feeling that one day she would be raped.

At the hostel Deborah had talked about boy friends who almost certainly had not existed.

P.M. Perhaps she needed a fantasy boy friend.

Mrs Murray: Perhaps she did . . . I often wondered whether to Deborah our life was a sort of blur and she never knew quite what was going on – maybe it was all a bit much.

P.M. I suppose whenever something doesn't work out you go over and over in your mind thinking, 'What was it?' And it's no one's fault really, is it? It's just been very hard for you to have to make that decision.

When we discussed whether they might have had more social work help with Deborah, initially Diana Murray could not visualise what more a social worker might do to help in what Bayley[6] calls 'the daily grind' of caring for a mentally handicapped person, and her actual management.

Mrs Murray: Being a foster-child one felt one couldn't take the risks that perhaps one would with one's own child. I felt she had to be continually supervised and I wouldn't let her go out on her own, but maybe it was the wrong thing.

P.M. That must have been quite a strain.

Mrs Murray: Yes, and another thing I always found difficult . . . how much do you treat them as their mental age or as their physical age? I suppose no social worker is going to say, 'Well, take what risks you like and no one will come back at you if the child gets run over,' because I didn't feel she was capable of crossing a busy road.

She thought it would have helped her to understand Deborah better if she had talked more to people who had specialist knowledge of mental handicap, such as teachers or staff in special schools or hospitals. She had found one headmaster more helpful than any of the social workers, and there are obvious implications here. CCETSW has pressed for better training for this work,[7] and Stevenson and Parsloe[8] suggest that students need far more help in transferring knowledge across client groups; also that once in post, when informal specialisms can occur, they need 'a chance to stick at something for long enough to gain confidence in deepened knowledge and skills'. Subsequently Stevenson[9] recommends the setting up of a 'unit' of specialist workers within each area office. More recently Anderson[10] discusses the principles of how a social worker may hope to relate to the mentally handicapped themselves, their parents and other family members, and begins to look at the fine balance between practical and emotional support.

Help with access to resources is one clear means of support, and Paul Murray thought that because Deborah was a foster-child the Department had pulled out all the stops to get appointments with specialists or places in schools or hostels, whereas natural parents might often be left to struggle on their own. Families with mentally retarded children need multi-disciplinary help, as is recommended in the Court Report,[11] while the duty 'to ensure that the services they require are made available to them' falls on social services departments. The emphasis increasingly is on providing such services in the community,[12] but their distribution is still very uneven. We were beginning to foster Downs syndrome babies in the 1960s, but bolder policies are now pursued and variously aged children with a whole range of mental handicaps are placed for adoption. There are also preventive measures to help natural parents, either initiated by social workers[13] or by the parents themselves. Nicola Schaefer,[14] the mother of a brain-damaged child, writes vividly of her initial solitary fight for resources and the self-help group she started, but also of the exultation at each minute step of progress in her child. Mental handicap is, of course, another form of loss – most bitterly experienced by parents who feel cheated of a 'normal' child, as described by Olshanski,[15] Ballard,[16] and others. Deborah made more advances than many, but her achievements were perhaps inevitably diminished in contrast to those of the Murray boys. Paul and Diana Murray had the Department behind them, but the kind of group support from other foster-parents now available in some areas

149

might have made their struggle less lonely and discouraging.

Deborah would not be considered 'unadoptable' now. A permanent placement, however, might be delayed until a child born of incest is at least a year old if the possibilities of any major defects are to be established. Turvill[17] discusses the increased genetic risks, the main one being recessive diseases, and the BAAF pamphlet on *Genetics in Adoption and Fostering*[18] examines these. Wolkind[19] has shown from follow-up studies that less than half of the children appear to be 'normal' at the ages studied (ages six and eight). In placement 'the emphasis would be on providing as much information as possible so that prospective adoptive parents have a very clear idea about the likelihood of physical and mental as well as emotional problems which might arise.'[20] Diana Murray saw that adopters of an older mentally handicapped child would at least know what the range of problems were – an advantage they had lacked. She thought social workers should present a very realistic picture, outlining all the difficulties rather than looking on the bright side.

> *P.M.* There must have been times when you felt pretty fed up with the Department, to have been landed –
> *Mrs Murray:* No, I don't think I did because they had said it was incest and nobody could foresee, and it's no good blaming anybody.

Deborah had not talked enough to ask questions about her natural parents. 'You couldn't *talk* to Deborah and get any answers back – sometimes she gave you the answers that you wanted to hear.' They had told her from the beginning that she was fostered and had kept her real name in the foreground, but were not sure whether she really understood the difference. She had always called them 'Mummy' and 'Daddy'. Her natural mother who had three more children, all of whom were adopted, had been in touch with the Department to ask about Deborah and to know whether or not she had developed normally.

Before I left, Diana Murray talked more freely of her continuing interest in Deborah and hoped for news of her through me. She hesitated to ring the hospital direct in case they expected more of her than she felt able to give. I had had a small hope that I might help them feel able to resume some contact, however minimal, but realised now it would not be fair to put any more pressure on people who had already suffered considerably. They both had a strong sense of duty and I did not want to lay any extra moral obligations on them. Their agreement to see me was part of a general disposition that had led them both into helping professions and to contemplate fostering.

Mrs Murray: I suppose it's my attitude that one tries to be helpful and hope anything you can do may help other people – but I suppose with Deborah it came unstuck . . . I suppose it was bigger than I could cope with.
Mr Murray: But that was probably the nature of the case.
P.M. Well, the compensations weren't enough to overcome all the difficulties.
Mrs Murray: Yes. I think that probably was it.
P.M. And it must have got increasingly harder . . . And it *is* very hard because it would have been so nice if you could have felt that you had wanted to help and you'd achieved it. But you can think, though, that you gave her a good start and did all you could for many years.

Sixteen years' perseverance in fostering against formidable odds surely does not constitute a failure – some studies of outcome in foster-care give five years' continuance of the placement as a criterion of 'success'. I felt Paul Murray had resolved the outcome to some extent in his own mind, but that at one level Diana still felt wounded by it. However, in general she seemed much happier again in herself and I was glad for her.

I drove on to see Deborah. There was a friendly relaxed atmosphere in her relatively small-scale hospital for the mentally handicapped, which had a charitable foundation and was pleasing architecturally. She was waiting for me in a day room, still small in stature and quite recognisable as the Deborah I had known. She was heavier, though, in features and body, and to me had a rather subdued, sombre air. She smiled readily enough and on the suggestion of the Sister took me to another room, walking with a stilted gait that was a mixture perhaps of institutional living and her own slight spasticity.

I did not attempt to tape my conversation with Deborah as it hardly merited that term. She smiled shyly and nodded, shook her head or said 'I don't remember,' and once or twice repeated my words. Her non-verbal communication was one of wary friendliness. She looked at me quickly when I said I had been to see Mr and Mrs Murray, but asked no questions. I gained the impression that she could understand much more than she could verbalise. She responded quite eagerly when I asked if she would like to go into the town, led me out of the building, directed me in the car, and took me to an upstairs tea-room. Once there she was polite and biddable and seemed to want to please, but I did not feel I really got through to her.

In answer to questions she said she had not been able to think what I

151

looked like but had recognised me. I talked about her letter to me when she was unhappy at leaving home and she just hung her head and nodded. I said it must be hard for her to understand that she didn't live at home now. I told her that her foster-mother still thought about her and wanted to know how she was, and had asked me to ring to let her know. When I asked Deborah if there was anything she would like me to say to her, she just shook her head. I felt that she did not have a lot of hope in relation to her foster-parents nor indeed from me. She became preoccupied with her watch and we returned to the hospital so that she would not be late for tea.

Deborah said goodbye and I had a word with the Sister, at her request. She asked how I found Deborah; her own assessment was that she was quite happy there. She had a sense of fun and the best means of communicating or getting her co-operation – for example to have a bath or wash her hair – was by making a game of it. She had been moved from another ward where she was said to have threatened to attack a nurse with a pair of scissors. She had revisited that ward and made her presence felt by running the taps in the bath and leaving them on. (Her forms of protest seemed to have a certain elemental quality – fire first and now flood.) This Sister seemed friendly towards her and found her no trouble, but did not feel she was making much progress.

The short-term plan for Deborah was a day training centre. Longer-term they hoped another hostel might take her, but as a 'fire risk' she would need to show some settled behaviour first. Her lack of motivation made progress towards even sheltered employment an uphill task, and as Heron[21] points out, the current economic situation and consequent high unemployment make 'even the best-equipped of the mentally handicapped occupationally marginal'.

The Sister said they would welcome any contact from Mrs Murray and she need not fear that much would be expected of her. Apparently Deborah still visited an aunt of Diana Murray's, and was said to come back from there quite happily. I had to accept the perception of someone who lived with her every day that she was reasonably happy, though my own impression was more a sense of hopelessness.

When faced with silence we search for non-verbal messages – in behaviour, in facial and bodily expression, and mood outwardly and inwardly observed. Our attempts to empathise then need to be tentative and can be open to misinterpretation, but they can at least be informed by knowledge and experience, laced with common sense, and the subjective clues we detect in our own reflected feelings. Our imagination can be fed, too, by those novelists who attempt to portray a person from within. In *The Albatross* Susan Hill takes us on a journey through the confused and frightened mind of a mentally retarded adolescent boy, Duncan, and illustrates a typical imbalance between strength of feeling and paucity of verbal expression.

He was beyond thinking now, only walked steadily on through the darkness. But feelings gathered inside him, like matter in a wound, and began to press outwards, until he wondered what he might do . . . He felt the words surging up inside him, and tried to choose the right ones, and not to stutter and stammer, because he needed to explain everything to her . . . He could only say, 'I might do anything.'[22]

The lives of Deborah and the Murray family had overlapped for 16 years and were now separate physically, though each would carry internal images of the other. Social work education is sometimes not best served by a university setting where understanding of feelings can be overshadowed or even dismissed by emphasis on academic achievement. Most social workers know, however, that the possession of a keen intellect does not of itself protect a person from being hurt – nor, at the other end of the spectrum, does the lack of it.

Suppose we define a person as an irreplaceable centre of minding. By this means we do not dispose of the mystery of personality, but point to where the mystery is.

Helen Oppenheimer[23]

11

Liz

Politics to me is about fighting for socialism, and to a socialist feminist – 'the personal is the political'.

Liz wants me to say that as a socialist feminist she disagreed with my first draft of her chapter. She disliked its apparent psycho-dynamic bias and was angry that I had failed to understand how her life experiences have produced the strong person she is now. Omission of the chapter was one solution but we both felt the book would be incomplete without her. What follows is a revised version which Liz accepts, *faute de mieux*, with the proviso that my perspective does not do justice to her view of reality.

Liz was four when her mother was admitted to hospital, labelled schizophrenic, and she came into care as her elderly grandmother was also ill and unable to look after her. The loss of these two main people whom she never saw again was followed by the death of her first foster-mother (with whom it had been hoped she would grow up). Her second foster-parents (whom she did not like) moved near London – without her – after 18 months, and then her third foster-mother also died. By then Liz was ten. She stayed briefly with M.R.V., who as Area Officer had long been closely involved, while J.B. looked for another foster home amongst people who knew her, such as school friends.

Mrs Violet Forrest, sister of 'Auntie Rose' who had just died, offered to take Liz. She and her husband were the epitome of 'respectable working class' (conservative in outlook, with segregated sex roles) and Liz spent eight years of her life in care in this rather unfertile foster home. Mr Forrest was in fact a keen gardener and in summer a colourful militia of bedding plants, dragooned into rows, marked out his immaculate garden on their housing estate, while a healthy nursery of seedlings and cuttings flourished in the greenhouse behind. However, feelings and behaviour were regulated like the antirrhinums and French marigolds, and there was little scope for the real Liz to emerge.

She was 15, undoubtedly bright and well settled at the grammar school when I took over the supervision. It took me a while to establish myself with Liz and the Forrests. I was Liz's fourth social worker and saw her through to within a few months of 18. It is traditionally important to recognise feelings about the previous worker(s), though the sense of loss will obviously vary according to the quality of relationships. In this instance my predecessors remained interested and available in the background.

I visited Liz's mother in hospital, unsure of what I would find. (She had been admitted before the Mental Health Act, 1959 with its stated policy of open doors and community care. Now she would surely have moved out, at least to a hostel.) She was in a long-stay ward, small and child-like. Her image of Liz was of the four-year-old she had known and her main concern was whether she had shoes to fit her. I tried to give Liz a less frightening picture of her mother and hoped to ease her inevitable fantasies about this unknown 'mentally ill' woman. She was naturally reluctant, however, to see her, although an opportunity ironically presented itself when she visited 'Auntie Vi' who became a voluntary patient briefly in the same hospital. (Liz has no recollection that a meeting was suggested.)

Liz was also ambivalent about her father, another shadowy figure in the background. He was said to have secretly married his pregnant cousin in order to give Liz his name, but had then returned to look after his blind father, and her parents had never lived together. He was non-committal about his actual paternity but accepted financial responsibility when Liz came into care and faithfully visited the area office to pay his parental contribution. A solitary man, he expressed no wish to see her until she was 13, when he came to live in Paxton after his father died. Liz was reluctant to meet him but agreed a couple of years later. She was then excited at the prospect but angry with me in the event. The chemistry did not work and she was also probably disappointed in his lack of education. The foster-parents welcomed him hospitably, though Mr Forrest offered horticultural analogies to me about the difficulty of grafting grown trees.

When I left Ringshire I made Liz a retrospective life-story book. This involved a number of expeditions: to the hospital where she was born, and the deserted, strangely silent scatter of farm houses where her parents had separately lived. I photographed her earlier foster homes and the streets down which she would have walked to school. Her father was interested and produced family photographs. Liz was then living in the present and was reproachful that I had omitted some of her current friends. (She says that friends have always been more important to her than family.)

When Liz left care she kept in touch by letter about her life at university and later with requests for references. I saw her a couple of times – when she came to stay *en route* for an interview for a social work course, and when she got in touch very depressed during her professional training year. I was spending Easter in her neighbourhood and went to see her. She had ended a long-standing relationship with a man from her degree course and simultaneously lost their house in the country and her cat. When I saw her for my project she had experience of working in a social services department, in a community arts project in a multi-racial area and, after a hard year of unemployment, was about to start a new job in community relations in London.

Liz, now 30, was living in a university city. She had many friends and was active in a variety of community work groups. I climbed the stairs to her flat at the top of a tall eighteenth-century house. She made coffee for us in mugs, saying with a rueful grin, 'Shades of Auntie Vi!' (Mrs Forrest had always produced her best china when I visited.)

I was seeing Liz at a watershed in her life, on the day before she actually moved to London to take up her exciting new appointment and after a year's unemployment. She described the hardships, frustration and anxiety of living on the edge of poverty. At night she had frequently lain awake worrying about how she could pay her bills. 'I've been stale as well – when my stomach's churning in a meeting because I bought ten cigarettes rather than have lunch – and you can't concentrate because you've got to find the electricity bill by next Friday – and yet I'm in some sort of political meeting which I'm committed to, but I can't concentrate. It's very much survival . . . I couldn't have gone on much longer – if the job hadn't come along I don't know what I would have done. But it has!'

She talked with passion about the plight of the disadvantaged. If as a single person with no other responsibilities she could not manage on social security, she despaired as to how families coped, and she reflected on widespread unawareness about the extent of poverty.[1] She avoided the consumerism she despised in shop window displays and spoke about the mixture of longing, anger and depression in young people, black and white, who with no hope of employment are constantly exposed to a battery of tantalising goods they will never be able to buy. She forecast more civil unrest after the recent trouble in Brixton, and a couple of months before the Toxteth riots of summer 1981 was saying that the frustration and violence could spread to the shopping areas rather than focus on destruction of property in streets where the young unemployed lived.

Liz sees no division between her political self and her personal life. She feels that a major strength is her capacity to make relationships easily with a whole range of people – men and women, black and white, young and old. After the break-up with Andrew she was initially more wary of a deep involvement with one person – indeed did not see an exclusive relationship as essential or desirable. She referred to some elderly people she had known who had invested everything – 'all your emotional, physical, mental, financial needs' – in 'the one other person', and who were still bereft, compared with a number of other single people, particularly women. 'They were just so lively, with so much interest in the world around them, with really bright, intelligent minds.' She also sees the possibility of becoming a single parent as a valid position for a feminist, though hazardous without a guaranteed income.

Since I last saw her Liz said she had learnt survival. She had become confident of her strength but was aware of intense feelings.

Liz: I think that was a thing with Andrew – I began to feel that I wasn't really expressing a lot of emotion with him. I express a lot more now, but it's dissipated between different people. I just sometimes feel that I've got so much emotion in me that if I lay it all on one person it would be too awful for them! That's what I'm saying about strength . . . it would have to be someone very strong.

P.M. To take all your loving.

Liz: Because I am very demanding. I know I'm demanding of friendship, probably laying much more on friendship than some other people would.

P.M. I suppose it's this thing about wanting to make up time, isn't it? To make up for things that you didn't have?

Liz: I don't know – not consciously, because I think I've done better out of relationships in the general term than most people have. I feel I've been lucky in that respect.

On the question of education she felt schools could do much more in preparation for university. No one had discussed it and she did not know what to expect. She had coincided with the student political unrest of the late 1960s. She became a socialist, made many friends, and was part of the 'sex, drugs, rock 'n roll' generation, moving away ideologically and rapidly from the constraints of her foster home. She failed her first year examinations and had to argue her case for repeating the year. That was the only time she had calculatedly used the argument of having grown up in care – painting a telling picture of herself as lost, on her own and unprepared for university life. She received her grant but it was only at the end of her degree course that she realised herself as probably an intellectual, wanting to pursue an academic career. Even then, her second year as a postgraduate student on a social work course was dislocated by the realisation that she did not really want to do social work and by the end of her relationship with Andrew. She had a continuing urge to do research and felt she might yet pursue a higher degree course.

Liz talked enthusiastically about her new job. She saw it as tailor-made because it would capitalise on her interest in race relations, her expertise in welfare rights, her degree in politics and her social work background. Earlier she had been released from her Probation sponsorship because no jobs were available locally. She then found working in a social services department very unsatisfying to a radical social worker.[2] To her it was depressing (for instance, meeting elderly people whose lives appeared empty) and frustrating because of lack of resources. Mainly she considered all her people were living in poverty beyond her means to help. She had learnt more from her own recent experience about some of the difficulties. 'I used to say to people who had a debt, say, of £20, which didn't seem too much, "Well, isn't there someone you could borrow it from?" I know now how difficult it can be to borrow, or that there just isn't anyone to borrow from.' She found much of the work boring, also 'limiting, tiring, badly paid (at the time) for the strains involved, and unstimulating intellectually'. She wrote to me then that she would wake at night shaking with worry over some of the problems with which she had to deal, but eventually left because the job became politically unacceptable to her. I was naturally interested in the relation between Liz as a social worker and herself as an ex-foster-child. However, she was in an intake team and although she received children into care, there was less scope for the relevance of her own care experiences than there might have been in a long-term team.

My coming prompted recollections of care which were mostly infrequent now. These had been more in the foreground during her social work course when there seemed to be 'endless talk about families'. Such discussion, though necessary, can be disturbing for any student – none of us has perfectly happy memories of family life – but more painful for someone whose own parents had barely figured and whose substitute care had left her without a real sense of family.

Liz: Obviously there wasn't really all that much about families – I just felt there was! I got so tuned in to every little thing there was about families . . . And even people I knew who seemed quite independent people – it would come to Christmas or Easter and everybody would go home. That first Christmas I just thought, 'Where do I go?'

She sometimes went to the Forrests' daughter, Jean, and she was on better terms now with her former foster-parents. She had, however, perceived her eight years with them much more negatively than we had realised. She felt Mrs Forrest took her out of duty – as something she could do for her sister Rose rather than through affection for Liz herself. (She was very shocked when she realised that her foster-parents received an allowance towards her keep when she thought they were doing it for love.) They had often seemed hostile to her – she felt unable to do anything right and learned to hold her peace rather than risk censure. She did not feel part of the family. 'I couldn't leave anything downstairs – I had to keep everything in my room. I had the sense that I didn't exist downstairs.' There was no physical affection – no kissing.

This bleak picture had softened now and she felt they had mellowed. 'I'm much fonder of Auntie Vi and Uncle Bob than ever I was, now. I don't see them very often, but I know they're there and I'm fond of them.' I was glad about this as I too had been fond of them, but I was left with a troubling picture of these well-intentioned foster-parents: correct, undemonstrative, providing a rather rigid, unstimulating environment for this intelligent foster-child with her unformulated longings for affection and the more interesting life emerging at school. School was one place where she could achieve, and a lot of her energies were invested in being a success educationally. Her happiest memory was of her short time with M.R.V. where she would have loved to stay. Sadly, she had virtually no memories of the two foster-mothers who died, both of whom had loved her and hoped to bring her up. She could only remember Auntie Rose being ill.

Lurking fears about her mother's illness were not helped by her father's insinuations when on an outing with him, aged 17.

Liz: We were on the train from Paxton and he leant across and said, 'By the way, did you know that your mother and I were first cousins?' He made it sound very sinister somehow, leant really close to me . . . I think it must have been this country thing about inter-breeding – and he went on to say, 'But Miss V. says you're very clever' – linking these two.

The implications had only gradually dawned on her. 'But it's something that registered – well, the fact that I'm telling you now,' and her fear had been heightened by her studies at the time.

> *Liz:* All that incest which led to the degeneration of Rome! (Laughed.) No, seriously, just thinking along those lines of the way he said it, and the fact that my mother was schizophrenic made me feel fairly definite that I was heading for a mental breakdown.

This conviction grew during her social work course and she felt she was almost deliberately submitting herself to self-fulfilling prophecies.

> *Liz:* I think I did feel then this whole inevitability about the fact that I had to crack at some point – I felt it was in my stars – I *had* to freak . . . I think I was playing a part of disintegration – and yet you can't act feeling as bad as I did; but I felt I was wilfully heading myself towards a particular thing.

The implications of her parents' brother and sister relationship were unlikely ever to worry Deborah (chapter 10) because of her mental retardation; but Liz's quick mind had tormented her with possibilities. She had not been told when in care of the slight doubt over her father's paternity because he had accepted the responsibility of the role, at least financially, and in my time was wanting to meet her and offer her a new home after his father's death. I had tried to clarify the question with him but he evaded a straight answer – and, indeed, perhaps could not be sure himself. I thought that Liz and I had talked about this earlier when she said how angry she had been with me about him, and I raised it now because of the worries she was expressing. It was, however, news to her and I told her as much as I knew.

> *Liz:* I really wish I knew my mother – what I've got I've got from her, not from him . . . I don't think I'm likely to find that out now – secrets from the grave!
>
> *P.M.* He was wanting to take an interest in you – he used to come in faithfully with his contribution.
>
> *Liz:* I've never really understood why he stayed in the background for so long . . . If he was prepared to make his contribution to the social services department and acknowledge his responsibility, why stay so far away from me?
>
> *P.M.* I don't think I know the answer to that. Whether he wanted to keep it secret, or didn't know how to cope with it. And then perhaps when you were growing up, whether he felt it would be nice to have a daughter in his life –

Liz could not contemplate sharing a house with him, a stranger with whom she felt no affinity – she wanted her own life.

P.M. And your mother – how do you picture her? It's impossible to in a way –

Liz: Well, I wouldn't know, would I? What sort of a person she was.

P.M. I tried to describe her to you, I think, didn't I, when I went to see her.

Liz: But when someone's been in an institution that long . . . I'd like to have known the person she might have been rather than an institutionalised, drugged-up body. I don't know – I feel very sad about my mother really. I remember getting a telegram that my father sent me – a telegram to the university and it came to my house, saying when she'd died and when the funeral was.

Her father had not long before asked if she would like to visit her mother with him (he visited her himself periodically). She had refused, wanting to face this ordeal alone, and was almost ready to meet her mother when the telegram came. She was angry that her father had given her no warning of so little time left. She did not go to the funeral. 'What's the point of going to the funeral of someone I didn't know?'

P.M. It's sad about your mother – that you'd just got to the point of thinking you might meet her.

Liz: Well, that's right, yes. I think I was building up – getting myself in the right frame of mind.

P.M. To make the effort.

Liz: And doing it alone . . . And sometimes – it's silly really – sometimes when I am very low, I just think . . . it sounds a bit ridiculous, but I just think my mother didn't have a life and in some ways I owe as much to her as to me to try and not be a failure in my life. It's silly, but it's something to fall back on – I suppose everyone has things like that. (Pause.) I do feel sad just talking about her now, actually. It's all there but I just don't talk about her – I think about her, I suppose, but I never talk about her – not to anyone – I never did with Andrew.

P.M. Didn't you?

Liz: No. I've always, I suppose, acted as though I never had a mother.

P.M. Well, that's what it felt like.

Liz: Yes, I think that's probably a real lack in me – lacking a mother.

P.M. It must feel a big lack. (Pause.) And does it make you feel, have ideas about what you'd want for your own children?

Liz: No, I mean as far as I was concerned I didn't get any love, and I think it's very important to show love . . . I think that's why I get so confused about the whole thing really; love became the be-all and end-all for me.

P.M. It seems extra important to find it.

Liz talked enviously of a woman friend who took for granted her relationship with her mother.

> *Liz:* She'll just sit and chatter on the phone, and it's just so easy – I've never had that – there's no need for explanations or excuses or justifications, it's just communication in a very easy way. Whereas with friends, well up to a certain point, like when you've established yourself, but that only happens with very close friends, always you have to be – I don't know – treading gently. It's not the same thing as a family should be ideally, in which any action, any behaviour is accepted, not necessarily acceptable, but accepted. It's that.
>
> *P.M.* And you had that long time of feeling you weren't accepted.
>
> *Liz:* It wasn't my feeling – I just wasn't.

I recognised that I had not helped her to tell me how things really were with her at the Forrests, and suggested that she was in a particularly strong position to influence my teaching now.

> *Liz:* I think not to pull any punches. Don't think it's in their best interests to hold things back when it's not . . . I think back on, say, my relationship with you as a social worker – yes, I think there must have been lots I could have told you, and that's maybe just coming out now – but why didn't I? Part of that was the physical restriction, the fact of not being alone long enough or feeling secure enough, and because I didn't really know what your role was.
>
> *P.M.* I should have made that clearer.
>
> *Liz:* Yes. I began to see you as an ally in the sense that you were sort of like a mentor – but you were still, I suppose, authority – a nice authority, but I suppose I never knew how far I could go with you. I never knew just what your interest was really. Yes, it's clarification, isn't it? This is all very obvious. Just don't accept things for what they are on the surface. Lots of kids are very good at survival – at showing they're O.K.
>
> *P.M.* Things were much worse for you than I was realising.
>
> *Liz:* Yes. (Pause.) I never cried very much you see. I was scared of crying – I still am – I'm scared of crying by myself. As soon as I stop talking I cry very easily . . . So I wouldn't cry when I was upset so much as – always when I went to bed for two years when I was about 12 or 13, I always had the same fantasy – planning running away. I planned it for two years! But I never did. (Laughed.) I kept planning it – that was survival tactics.
>
> *P.M.* I'm sorry it was so bad you felt you had to.
>
> *Liz:* But then I think I was fortunate in as much as school was quite a good escape really. I got away with murder. I expressed things there that I just felt incapable of expressing at home, I suppose. So I was very rowdy and cheeky – quite rude in fact. But I suppose I carried it off because they made a lot of excuses for me, and the fact that I was quite bright, and I got away with it.

Liz's advice not to accept things as they are on the surface was corrective, because some of her adolescent conversation had *seemed* superficial, but apparently I had not helped her feel safe enough to be herself. This could only be partly due to her perception of our not talking together enough. I used to talk with Mrs Forrest on her own; she would then bring in a tea tray when Liz came home from school and leave us to talk. It was no doubt inhibiting with Auntie Vi in the kitchen next door, but my memory was of our talking often on our own – and in my car on various expeditions. However, Liz's memory of the restriction had been strong enough to ensure that as a social worker herself she saw children alone whenever possible.

There was, however, an additional, crucial constraint – Liz said she did not feel sure I could do anything about her unhappiness then. This is a perennial problem for many foster-children – their uncertain status in someone else's family, and the fear that if they complain to their social worker as a potential ally, the latter might prove either impotent or over-active. Recognition and awareness of this fear can help, but for the social worker there is also the dilemma of trying to ally herself and empathise with both foster-parents and child, when they may be at odds. Where should the primacy of her work lie? There are practice and policy issues here which will be pursued in Chapter 12.

Liz said that I had one influence on her of which I was perhaps unaware: she was already an avid reader but I had helped to broaden her horizons in relation to certain books (poetry for instance) and had apparently introduced her to *The Manchester Guardian* (sic)!

Leaving care had not in itself been important. When she left the Forrests to go to university she was very conscious 'that that was that'. She returned a couple of times but did not feel they were offering a permanent base. The situation she encountered at university was similar to that of many other young people from a working-class background. However, there were particular ways in which she felt ill-prepared for leaving care. Surprisingly for a young person who had grown up in foster-care, she could not cook (Auntie Vi had not welcomed her in the kitchen) and she had little idea about money or paying bills. She had tried once, unsuccessfully, to get financial help from the social services department; when I mentioned their discretionary powers[3] she was aware that if she had had more information it would have been easier to quote the section number and to make a case for herself.

Liz was exhilarated now and a little apprehensive at the prospect of a new life in London. At this turning point she appeared to enjoy what she called 'this really luxurious thing of talking about myself'. The sense of being different, which can bedevil many young people in care and after, had developed a more positive meaning for Liz. From any viewpoint her achievements and the qualities of warmth, humour, lack of self-pity, intellectual rigour and political passion which make up the person she is now are remarkable in the context of her earlier life. With my long-term lens I see her emergence from a confused, sparse working-class background; her mother's illness and frightening disappearance, the death of two foster-mothers and the inability of her last foster-home to provide either the love or the stimulation she needed, and I wonder what so many and varied losses may have represented in her internal world.

In contrast, Liz sees her present strength, life style and political stance as a socialist feminist as having grown from a positive ability to build on her life chances. 'I basically perceived people as failing me and this led me to look outwards for explanations in societal terms – which led to politics and hence socialism.' She suggested that in one sense being in care had ironically provided her with an almost privileged opportunity to develop her acute sense of widespread disadvantage and inequality, later heightened at university by political consciousness (and the attainment of a university place is relatively rare for someone who has grown up in care). Her venture into social work she sees as largely accidental.

There is no need to polarise the personalist and political viewpoints, though Halmos[4] warns against a false synthesis, and urges a sensitive 'equilibration' of the tension between the two. The complex reality of Liz's life (or anyone else's) certainly demands a broader explanation than can be provided by one theoretical framework.

> Don't be afraid to ask!
> Don't do as you're told,
> work it out for yourself!
> If you don't find out yourself,
> you'll never know.
> Figure it out. It's your life.
> Look around; take it all in,
> ask: how did this get here?
> You must be ready to take
> the lead.
>
> Bertolt Brecht[5]

12

Sequel and implications for practice

Isn't it funny how we learn things. Ever since we spoke from the first about your book I feel as though I learn more about life, and my ideas and attitudes have changed.

I had revisited the young people (and some of their care-givers) to see how they were faring, to elicit their consumer opinions, to examine their possible continuing need to be known by at least one constant person, and to provide an opportunity to discuss again any hurts or misunderstandings arising from their care experiences. In this there had also been the more explicit therapeutic purpose of trying to enhance their present sense of identity.

Participant discussion of their chapters

A development of the original plan was a second return or contact to discuss their individual chapters. Two or three people asked to read what I wrote about them before publication and it was evident that I should offer this to everyone in the project. Because some of the material could make distressing reading for the participants, I tried to ensure that I saw or telephoned them to discuss their chapter a few days after they received it. These encounters provided an unexpected bonus in the shape of another chance to see how they were two years on, and also to reflect again with them about their lives in the light of their reading their own stories.

Most were moved by this experience. 'I cried when I read some of it'; 'I felt choked'; 'I had a lump in my throat'; 'I sat there with tears running down my face'. Only Maxine (chapter 2) said she would rather not have read it, because of the impact of seeing her earlier unhappiness written down. Her sister Paula initially disagreed with some of the more painful incidents, perhaps wishing they had not happened, but was more philosophical after talking to Meg Plover. 'Auntie says "That is *your life*"' (emphatically). Meg herself was on the point of retiring when she read the Waldo chapter, and it marked the end of an era for her and all the young people who still looked to her. Paula was now ensconced with her small daughter in a council flat in Paxton. She and Maxine and I were at Meg's retirement party, as was Elaine, their eldest sister. The latter, regarded as unfeeling by the others, said that tears had come into her eyes when Meg referred to Charlie's death in her speech, and I tried to help them to see beyond their stereotypes of each other. I could not see Wally, who was still pursuing his adventures in India and Europe but using Meg as his post box and tenuous anchor.

Nor, sadly, did I see Mark (chapter 3) again. He moved and my efforts to find him were unrewarded.

Jane Ryder and Celia Stone (chapter 4) were interested in the congruence of each other's understanding of Ralph. They both wrote after I saw them – Celia that she had wanted to live up to my standard (not expectations) for her charge, 'to enjoy making his life good. It was more than a desire to write a good essay for a favourite teacher – deeper than that'. Jane had been 'profoundly moved' by the care her children were given, and 'to relive the whole episode again through someone else's eyes'. Ralph had read the chapter, and went with Jane on a reunion visit to Celia.

Lorraine (chapter 5) had earlier written about the book, 'I agree with all my heart. I've always wanted to write a book about my childhood but if I did I would never finish it because there are many memories I don't want to go through again. But good luck with yours.' She and Helen and their grandmother all said, 'But it's true, isn't it?' when I saw them. Helen took trouble over the draft and had written down her thoughts for me. She later wrote excitedly when she and her husband moved to their own house. Her words, which started this chapter, illustrate the way in which many of the young people used our discussions to rethink some of the hurts of the past and their present feelings. She had come to realise how much she loved and owed her grandparents, and it did seem that a number of people in the project had clarified or enhanced their relationships in the course of it. In reading their chapter they were seeing my perceptions of other people in their lives for the first time. They did not always agree with me but more often there seemed to be movements closer.

Almost inevitably I had an unofficial adoption counselling role in the group of people who had sought or been brought together by adoption as in three instances an 18th birthday was near at hand. Michelle (chapter 6) was still inwardly grieving for Adrian, the more so because she had miscarried yet again. She knew what she would do if in time her daughter Sharon ever told her of premature pregnancy. 'What would you do?' 'Stand by her,' she said, and wept. Her son Adrian would be nearly 18 and we talked more of the possibility that he might try to see her. Steven, too, (chapter 7) was in his 18th year, and was more actively interested in learning about his first parents and the procedure for obtaining his original birth certificate. Surprisingly, he only learned his first surname from Mrs Scott while I was there, and he tried it out with quizzical enjoyment. Timms and Haimes[1] in their report to the DHSS on the working of Section 26 of the Children Act, 1975 conclude that 'telling' is best seen as a *process* which is also *two-way*. They make the point that 'disclosure' – a term they prefer – 'has as it were to be allowed by both parties and there is evidence that the adoptee resists this as much or even more than the adopter'.

Louise (chapter 8) came to see me soon after her 18th birthday. She had completed an application for her original birth certificate but was wanting to think with me how far she would 'quest' down this particular road. Her adoptive mother was sympathetic but said to me that she and her husband would also benefit from a group for adoptive parents in a similar position.

There had been a mixture of advances and setbacks in the intervening two years. When I saw Georgie and Mrs Cox (chapter 9) he had just been accepted by the prison service. He seemed less suspicious of me and showed me his service medal and his papers in which his army conduct was assessed as 'Exemplary'. He had built a porch for his mother and takes an interest in the garden. Mrs Cox saw a real change in him. He still mostly hides his feelings, but when she was ill in the night he had brought her a hot drink and sat on her bed and talked.

Deborah (chapter 10) also seems to be in a happier position. She is living semi-independently in a training flat with three others, and may move to a council flat. Although her capacity for lasting relationships is said to be in doubt, she is engaged. She also telephones the Murrays occasionally, so there is some slight contact again. Diana Murray thought that the 'hopelessness' which I had sensed had always been there, but now the picture seems less bleak.

On the dark side there was another tragedy in the Waldo family. Not long after I saw Maxine again her husband Paul was killed in a car accident. This seemed a devastating blow when she had at last attained happiness and was now left with two young children. The Plovers and I travelled to be with her for the funeral (which had inevitable echoes of Charlie's, and I tried to comfort Kathleen who was also there). Meg was, I think, a particular source of comfort to Maxine then and in the

167

following months. Maxine was very open in her distress – when I first telephoned she said, 'Keep in touch so I can talk.' She has shown a remarkable and thoughtful capacity for survival, practically and emotionally, and an ability to help others who are bereaved.

Liz (now doing a part-time MA) was upset in a different way by her chapter. She was angry and disappointed at my initial failure to understand or to represent her as she sees herself, and that I had put undue emphasis on aspects of her life which were untrue or irrelevant to her. She vehemently repudiated any suggestion that I had come back to help because for her this implied inequality. It may also have been painful for her that someone she was fond of entertained ideas which were ideologically alien, and she related to me with a mixture of withering scorn and strong affection. It was important to both of us to find a resolution and to safeguard our relationship.

Liz's anger and the tears of others on reading their chapters may cause some readers to see my re-entry into these lives as an intrusion, and to feel angered or upset themselves by the sadness revealed. Other readers may recognise that it can be a relief to shed tears which belong to the past or indeed to find a safe target for anger. However, Liz's accusation that on a return visit of a couple of hours or so I could only catch 'a shimmer of a person' was salutary. I have been conscious, too, of the difficulty of doing justice to each young person or family within the confines of a chapter, and this has limited the role of biographer which I assumed in some of their eyes.

Liz's reaction also raises all sorts of questions about the 'right' interpretation of any reality. There are so many possible ways of understanding any situation and no one perspective completely embraces 'the truth'. Social workers will not need reminding that another person's perception of reality *is* truth to them, nor that an essential part of any intervention is the attempt to understand the reality of other people. It is arrogant to assume that we can ever fully succeed, but it is incumbent on us to persevere, drawing on a range of knowledge and experience. In this connection Curnock and Hardiker[2] make a helpful distinction between explicit 'theories of practice', that is the underlying theoretical frameworks which are borrowed from the social sciences and taught to social work students, and the more implicit 'practice theories' which they learn from their own and others' experience, and which the authors attempt to make more explicit and accessible.

The young people's reactions to their chapters may have implications for open records. These may be desirable in principle, but it is naive to imagine that people will not have strong feelings at what they read about themselves. So the actual reading is rarely an end in itself. However, no one in the project dared not look at their chapter and most appeared to see it as a positive event in their lives.

How they were faring

The young people are now aged between 17 and 32. Their chapters have shown how each has fared individually and overcome to a greater or lesser degree the disadvantage of being in care. Their lives have, of course, been formed by the prevailing attitudes, pressures and inequalities of the society in which they have grown up as well as by their personal histories, though only Liz was fully aware of the interaction between these elements. They have also been subject to the ordinary ups and downs of fortune as well as to the risks attached to being dependent on the decisions and plans made for them by a public service.

With hindsight some of the decisions were debatable. Would Mark have been more advantageously placed in a permanent family at four years (while maintaining contact with his sisters)? Similarly, might Sally Waldo have emerged less fearful if she had been adopted at two instead of growing up in residential care, watching each of her older brothers and sisters leave Mulberry Close in turn at a vulnerable age? All the Waldos suffered hardship, insecurity and loneliness in their first years out of care, and this is perhaps the major drawback to residential care as a long-term plan. However, although scattered and only spasmodically in touch, as adults they do feel for one another and exist in each other's minds. Their story illustrates the complexities of trying to predict an outcome. They all had early fragmented experiences, and some of their short-term care would have been better then others; but although they all shared life at Mulberry Close, each gained something different from Meg Plover at different ages and related to her in different ways, and the outcome was different for each of them. Fuller and Stevenson[3] found in their survey of research into the literature on disadvantage that they could not as hoped 'identify crucial levers of change which would have "multiplier effects" in enabling people to escape from depriving life patterns'. Individual resilience, perhaps fortunately, remains unpredictable.

Several of the young women in the project were confident as

mothers, whereas the young men in the same age bracket were slower to commit themselves to one partner. In this connection Fuller and Stevenson look thoroughly at Rutter and Quinton[4] who in pursuing intergenerational continuity and discontinuities, examine the longer-term effects of being in care in two projects, one looking backwards, the other forwards. The latter is a follow-up investigation of 'approximately 220 young people who were in care during their childhoods and are now aged between 22 and 28'. In an interim report to the DHSS the authors write encouragingly about the adjustment of the 'in care' women, particularly their functioning as mothers, in spite of current problems. They also suggest tentatively at this stage that 'the adverse effects of childhood experiences are strongly affecting the current adjustment of men in both the in care and control groups'.

In my project it was important to virtually all the young people of both sexes to give their children (born and unborn) more love and stability than they had experienced with their natural parents (or for Liz with her last foster-parents). The determination to do 'better' as parents does, of course, put them under a considerable strain, and one which some still hesitate to risk.

The children adopted from infancy had come through with least hurt, but Lorraine and Helen (chapter 5) had been supported through their hurt within the extended family by their grandparents and are now happily settled in their own homes. Their success is in line with Rowe et al.'s[5] very positive findings in *Long-term Foster Care*, that the children fostered by relatives were performing better on most counts than the children in the main sample. This is reassuring to social workers considering this type of placement, though they would perhaps do well to bear in mind the kind of mixed feelings a grandmother in Mrs Moon's position expressed.

Any assessment is likely to be partial, containing dangers of selectivity, subjectivity and ideological bias, and above all needs to be dynamic rather than static. I have been concerned that the young people should not feel encapsulated for evermore in my description of them at a particular moment in time, like a fading snapshot in a family album. I was meeting them at different stages in their development. Louise and Steven who had experienced affectionate and constant parenting from infancy were sailing through their adolescence with few apparent problems and were satisfyingly employed. But whether they were doing well or less well none of them was frozen at this one point. For instance, Mark who felt unwanted at 21, still had strengths which would allow him to respond to positive later events. By chance I saw Liz at a moment of triumph and at 30 she was grasping it eagerly. But at Mark's age she still had much to work out. Kathleen and Maxine Waldo (at 29 and 24) were thriving as mothers and showing a sensitivity to their children's needs, but at Mark's age Maxine had been disturbed and suicidal.

Two years on Georgie appears to be kinder and in a more settled phase, and even Deborah is fulfilling more of her potential than had seemed remotely possible. Paula and Wally are living precariously – but adventurously. In a time of economic crisis, none of them is unemployed against their will, which is a mark of their achievement as 'care' has seldom been seen as the best qualification for the employment market. It is therefore possible to feel hopeful for all of them. Smayle,[6] citing evidence of self-fulfilling prophecies, argues the need for social workers to believe in the people with whom they work and to convey hope to them. It seems to me that a mixture is needed of empathy for a child's present predicament and distress, coupled with a belief in his or her capacity for resilience.

Consumer opinions of the service received

The number of consumer studies is growing, but as far as I can discover no one else has revisited part of their own child care caseload and faced the consequences of some of their own work. It will I hope be apparent that I tried whenever appropriate to invite criticism from the young people and care-givers (and was not always successful in overcoming their reluctance to complain). To balance these invitations I have also included some of their more appreciative comments at the risk of appearing immodest.

They did not always find it easy to conceptualise their reaction to the social work intervention but one or two themes emerged. The care-givers were on the whole very positive, but some of the young people were uncertain about my role and my purpose in visiting. When responsibility for a child is transferred to a new social worker it is easy perhaps to assume that the explanations have been made, whereas it is important each time to discuss one's role within the new relationship and to discover the child's hopes. It is, of course, naive to assume that children (or adults) see us as well disposed. It is not enough to know in oneself that one's intentions are benign and I was surprised to find that I had not given enough weight to how they saw me. They also have to

171

discover the truth about us for themselves – mere reassurance or explanation will not necessarily convince a child whose experience of adults has not engendered trust.

It was noticeable that the young people were able to talk with me much more easily than they had as children, and that there were things which both they and the care-givers were telling me now of which I had not been sufficiently aware at the time – nor of the strength of some of their feelings. This could be that I was no longer in a position of authority, or that the children had grown up, or that my skills in helping people feel safe to talk had improved, or a mixture of these. I certainly learned that I for one need to try harder to help people feel able to talk about the negative side of their ambivalence, and to be more aware of the feelings that are difficult to express to someone in authority or just in a helping role.[7] But of course decreasing people's fear is an essential part of helping (and often the most difficult).

Mark and Liz's chapters suggest that we should not underestimate how hard it is for children in care to confide their fears or dislikes, and how uncertain they can be of our ability to intervene effectively, indeed whether speaking-out might make matters worse. Seeing children on their own is only a partial solution if they are not sure where the social worker's allegiance lies. And for many social workers it is still an unresolved dilemma as to whether the primacy of their support should be given to the foster-parents or the children.

The DHSS working party on fostering practice firmly held that where there is conflict between the interests of parents, foster-parents and the child, 'the primary professional responsibility of the social worker is towards the child',[8] and this view reflects the 'welfare of the child' principle in the Children Act, 1975. (Fuller and Stevenson[9] discuss the dangers of subjectivity and bias in this debate.) However, although the social worker often has to act as conciliator and mediator, working for the child's interests does not always mean working primarily *with* the child. In general I tend to agree with those who advocate the greater efficiency of supporting the surrogate parents, as their friendliness or otherwise is often the most crucial variable in the child's environment. Woodmansey's work in particular confirms that parent figures generally have a profound influence on the emotional state of their children, for better or worse, and that where relationships between them are hostile rather than friendly, parents need help rather than exhortation or blame.[10]

And yet if things are not going well, a child separated from natural parents does particularly and urgently need to have someone seen as an effective ally. Possibly those authorities who appoint a separate worker to service the well-being of the foster-parents as well as providing one for the individual child(ren) may have found the best solution. The case for this arrangement in residential care was argued in chapter 2. Another answer may be to set up special groups for foster children or those in residential care, as is happening within the Who Cares? and NAYPIC movements.

The young people expressed mixed feelings about the social workers they had known; some had been very much appreciated if they cared and took an interest, listened and *stayed*, but it was evident that the people of primary importance to them, again for better or worse, were the care-givers.

Following from this was the importance they attached to open expression of feelings, and some young people showed a real hunger for more outward affectionate caring. In the recruitment of substitute parents more consideration should perhaps be given to their attitudes to and enjoyment of physical contact and comfort. I remember a foster-mother who told me that three short-stay children were easy to comfort because she could see they were used to being cuddled – a comment which was also a comfort to their mother. The same foster-mother mentioned casually that a more disturbed small boy had been smearing his faeces – 'It's just his way of expressing himself.' This kind of warmth and tolerance can perhaps only be discovered fully once foster-parents are actually caring for a child. However, applicants who appear to take an undue pride in cleanliness or who strongly disapprove of sexual adventures may not let themselves enjoy much bodily touch – a possibility which could be explored in discussion.

As children the young people had sometimes turned to me for holding or cuddling, and in my revisiting I hugged or kissed most of them and on occasion comforted distress. Social workers are often made fearful of touching their 'clients' by respected pundits as well as by their own doubts, or realistic worries about allegations of sexual misconduct. And yet as Clare Winnicott[11] says, 'In times of acute distress the actual physical holding of a child is likely to be the only means of bringing any relief.' Crompton[12] too devotes a chapter to touch as a means of communicating with children. As Helen said, 'It is surprising how valuable a cuddle can be.'

The historical and subjective nature of the experiences of this small sample of young people and care-givers means that one has to be cautious in relating it to present circumstances and the task of social workers now. However, the aim was more to provide a consumer perspective of what it is like to need care from people other than one's original parents, and what it is like to try to provide that care – perspectives which may be an aid to empathy for practitioners now. If the book serves no other purpose I hope it will demonstrate that people in the sort of circumstances described have much stronger feelings than may be apparent.

Continuity and opportunities for further discussion

No very clear reasons emerged as to why this group of people had kept in touch with me. The care-givers had, it seemed, valued my continuing interest in their charges and in different degrees had found some sort of reassurance that I was still there in the background.

The young people had either turned to me for specific help in crises or from a more general wish to see if I was still interested and thinking about them – a friend they could rely on. Young people who have grown up in residential care are the least likely to have a sense of being known long-term by many people in their adult life. The Waldos were perhaps untypical in having such a constant person as Meg Plover (and her family) and I played second fiddle.

James[13] describes how her long-term care group aimed to identify at least one 'reliable caring adult' for each child for whom, exceptionally, family placement or rehabilitation was not possible. Kahan's[14] group agreed that every child in care should have 'someone who was able to act as an encouraging and special person to confide in and give comfort in distress'. It seems important that this kind of personal interest should continue after care, so that no young person is left without someone to whom he matters. This does not imply the inequality which Liz repudiated. There is no shame in using a secure base as conceived by Bowlby. With the assurance of a trustworthy person who can be held as an inner experience as well as an external reality, it is then more possible to act as a safe base for others.

Because I had no control group I can only speculate about the young people from my caseload who did not keep in touch. Some may have found their continuity in their substitute family or their own extended family. Some may have turned their back on social workers with relief. My project people were in a sense a self-selecting sample. None of the young people had come into care through the courts.

Some of them obviously had a more secure continuing base than others, but they were virtually all wanting uncertainties clarified. Movements such as NAYPIC and The Voice of the Child in Care are urging the child's right to know about his circumstances, and with the current move towards openness it is more likely that this principle (not a new one) will be emphasised. But children may still find it hard to hear painful information and may well need opportunities as young adults to question and discuss the meaning and implications of past events.

Whether or not it is theoretically fashionable to attach much weight to past misfortune, it seems clear that this often remains important to those directly concerned. Also, although past history cannot be changed, its meaning for the central characters *can* change over time, in the light of new experience and understanding. Therefore, just as follow-up is available for some adopted young people, an opportunity for retrospective discussion may be a valuable, economical exercise which could appropriately be offered to a wider range of adults formerly in care.

As well as uncertainties for the project group, there were also hurts still about some of the disadvantage, loss or gaps in their lives. Years ago Clare Winnicott[15] emphasised the value of looking at the overwhelming gaps in a child's life with him. It remains true for those grown up as well, that acknowledging a gap makes it more livable with – it becomes more possible to leave the hurt behind and to move on. In practice, an acknowledged 'gap' becomes positive 'space', no longer an intolerable void. It seems more effective simply to recognise such gaps, when both parties have sufficient courage to do so, rather than seek to fill them with irrelevant substitutes for what is felt to be missing. This involves meeting feelings at a level that can be painful for both parties – what Jordan[16] calls communication between the 'middle' of one person and the 'middle' of another.

If we seem to take over children's lives when we receive them into care then it is especially important to give them back their lives – whether it be at 18 or earlier – in a positive way which enhances their identity and self-esteem. There is a whole range of literature now on identity and how a sense of it develops or can be impaired. Berry[17] writes helpfully about self-image in relation to children in special circumstances. She uses Argyll's distinction between self-image or ego-identity (how one perceives oneself) and self-esteem (involving self-evaluation), and makes the point that 'there is no incentive to

175

picture oneself unless something pleasant can be seen'. I was trying to mirror back to the young people my recognition of their earlier gaps, my recollection of positive factors in their lives then, and my appreciation and affection for them now as young adults with a sense of future. I was also hoping to give them more sense of control over circumstances than they had had as children – not least by giving them a power of veto over the contents of their chapters in whole or part.

I was enlisting their help with students and practitioners in mind. They talked generously and agreed to publication in the hope that other children might be helped. That is my hope too.

The road from knowledge to love is far longer and less pleasant to travel than is the road from love to knowledge.

Thomas Bodkin[18]

References and notes

Chapter 1

1 Lomax-Simpson, J., 'Practical Ways of Fulfilling the Needs of the Child in Care', *Case Conference*, vol. 10, no. 7, 1964, and 'Further Ideas on Ways of Sharing One's Life with the Child in Care', *Case Conference*, vol. 12, no. 10, 1966.
James, G., 'The Child-centred Approach to Children in Care', in Brandon, D., and Jordan, B., eds., *Creative Social Work*, Blackwell, 1979.
2 Lomax-Simpson, J., 1966, *op. cit.*
3 For instance, Timms, N., ed., *The Receiving End: Consumer accounts of social help for children*, Routledge and Kegan Paul, 1973; Sainsbury, E., *Social Work with Families*, Routledge and Kegan Paul, 1975.
4 Kahan, B., *Growing up in Care*, Blackwell, 1980.
5 Page, R., and Clark, G., eds., *Who Cares? Young People in Care Speak Out*, National Children's Bureau, 1977. The Who Cares? groups, sponsored initially by the National Children's Bureau, was a pioneer movement which gave a voice to young people in care. Out of it grew their own organisation, NAYPIC (National Association of Young People in Care).
6 For discussion and practical guidance on life-story books see, for instance, Berry, J., 'Notes on Making a Photograph Album for a Child in Care', in *Planning for Children in Long-term Care*, ABAFA, 1976; Ryan, T., and Walker, R., *Making Life Story Books*, Barnardo's Homefinding Project, Leeds, 1982; Sawbridge, P., 'Putting it down on Paper', *Community Care*, February 12, 1982. In this book see chapters 3 (Mark) and 11 (Liz).
7 O'Neil, T., *A Place Called Hope*, Blackwell, 1981.
8 Kahan, *op. cit.*
9 Berry, J., review of Kahan, ibid., *British Journal of Social Work*, vol. 10, no. 3, 1981.
10 Kahan, *op. cit.*, p. 132.
11 Winnicott, D.W., 'Mirror-role of Mother and Family in Child Development', in *Playing and Reality*, Penguin Books, 1974.
12 Winnicott, ibid., p. 117.
13 Tonnesmann, M., 'The Human Encounter in the Caring Professions' (Fourth Winnicott Conference, 'Containing Stress in Professional Work'), *Social Work Service*, no. 21, DHSS, 1979.
14 Rogers, C., *On Becoming a Person*, Constable, 1961.
15 Rogers, C., *Client Centred Therapy*, Constable, 1951.
16 Woodmansey, A.C., 'The Internalisation of External Conflict', *International Journal of Psycho-analysis*, 47, pp. 349–55, 1966a, and 'Transmission of Problems from Parents to Children', in *Mental Illness in the Family: Its effect*

on the child, NAMH, 1966b; also 'The Unity of Casework', *Social Work Today*, vol. 2, no. 19, 1972.

17 Care for the care-givers. The idea that workers in any of the caring professions need replenishment for themselves if they are to give of their best is argued by Berry, J., in relation to residential social work in *Daily Experience in Residential Life*, Routledge and Kegan Paul, 1975, ch. 4. Woodmansey, A.C., postulates a model of support for doctors, psychiatrists, social workers and health visitors in practice and training in 'First Things First: A blueprint for mental health', *Public Health*, vol. 93, 1979a, pp. 131–9.

18 Lishman, J., 'A Clash in Perspective? A Study of Worker and Client Perceptions of Social Work', *British Journal of Social Work*, vol. 8, no. 3, 1978, pp. 301–11.

19 *Report of the Care of Children Committee* (Curtis Report), Cmnd. 6922, HMSO, 1946.

20 Pugh, E., *Social Work in Child Care*, Routledge and Kegan Paul, 1968.

21 Packman, J., *The Child's Generation, Child Care Policy in Britain*, second edition, 1975/81.

22 Bowlby, J., *Separation, Anxiety and Anger*, vol. 2 of *Attachment and Loss*, The Hogarth Press, 1973, and *Loss*, vol. 3, 1980.

23 Bowlby, J., 'Self-reliance and some Conditions that Promote it', in *The Making and Breaking of Affectional Bonds*, Tavistock Publications, 1979.

24 Robertson, J., and Robertson, J., *Young Children in Brief Separation: A guide to the film series*, The Robertson Centre, London, 1976.

25 Clarke, A.M., and Clarke, A.D.B., *Early Experience, Myth and Evidence*, Open Books, 1976.

26 Rutter, M., *Maternal Deprivation Reassessed*, second edition, Penguin Books, 1972/81.

27 Gill, O., and Jackson, B., *Adoption and Race: Black, Asian and mixed race children in white families*, Batsford Academic and BAAF, 1983.

28 Younghusband, E., Foreword to Kahan, *op. cit.*

Chapter 2

1 Tolstoy, L.N., *Anna Karenina*, 1878.

2 Child Care Act, 1980, s. 2 replaces s.1 of the Children Act, 1948 as the voluntary route into care.

3 The 'time limits' in the Children Act, 1975 were designed to prevent precipitous removal of children from care and to enable planning. Under the first of these, now s. 13(2) of the Child Care Act, 1980, it is an offence for parents to remove a child who has been in voluntary care for six months without giving 28 days' notice.

4 The medical profession was curiously slow to acknowledge that a proportion of injuries to children were non-accidental; social workers were also reluctant to believe that parents could intentionally injure their own children. C.H. Kempe was one of the first writers to recognise the cluster of factors which can act together to constitute a syndrome of likely abuse, and later to plan programmes of help. Kempe, C.H., and Helfer, R.E., *Helping*

the Battered Child and his Family, Lippincott, Philadelphia and Toronto, 1972. See also Carver, V., *Child Abuse: A study text*, and Lee, C.M., ed., *Child Abuse: a reader and sourcebook*, both Open University Press, 1978.

5 S. 1 of the Children and Young Persons Act, 1963 conferred on local authorities their main preventive powers. Freeman, M.D.A. points out that it is psychologically and symbolically important that this section now becomes s. 1 of the Child Care Act, 1980. Freeman, M.D.A., *The Child Care and Foster Care Acts*, Sweet and Maxwell, 1980.

6 *Training in Child Care*, Interim Report of the Care of Children Committee, Cmnd. 6760, HMSO, 1945, para. 10, and *Report of the Care of Children Committee* (Curtis Report), Cmnd. 6922, HMSO, 1946, para. 478.

7 Berry, 1975, *op. cit.*

8 Kaye, A., and Matchan, D.C., *Reflexology*, Thorsons Publishers, Wellingborough, 1979.

9 For instance, Caplan, G., *An Approach to Community Mental Health*, ('grief work', pp. 43, 58–63, 219–22), Tavistock, 1961; Lindemann, E., 'Symptomatology and Management of Acute Grief', in Parad, H., ed., *Crisis Intervention*, Family Service Assoc. of America, New York, 1965; Miller, D., *The Age Between*, (adolescent mourning, ch. 9), Cornmarket/Hutchinson, 1969; Parkes, C.M., *Bereavement; Studies of grief in adult life*, Penguin Books, 1972/75; Marris, P., *Loss and Change*, Routledge and Kegan Paul, 1974; Pincus, L., *Death and the Family: The importance of mourning*, Faber, ch. 10, 1976; Bowlby, 1979, *op. cit.* and Bowlby, 1980, *op. cit.* Most writers agree that the process of grief which any loss sets in motion contains recognisable stages, and that there is a need to mourn, to express grief, to come healthily through the experience.

10 Caplan, *op. cit.*, and Parad, *op. cit.* Crisis intervention has been reassessed by Butrym, Z., *The Nature of Social Work*, Macmillan, 1976.

11 Page and Clark, *op. cit.*, p. 16.

12 Page and Clark, *ibid.*, p. 51.

13 For instance, Holman, R., *Unsupported Mothers and the Care of their Children*, Mothers in Action, London, 1970; Crellin, E., Kellmer-Pringle, M.L., and West, P., *Born Illegitimate*, National Foundation for Educational Research, Windsor, 1971; Streather, J., and Weir, S., *Social Insecurity: Single mothers on benefit*, Poverty Pamphlet 16, CPAG, 1974; Lambert L., and Streather J., *Children in Changing Families*, Macmillan, 1980.

14 Pincus, *op. cit.*; Pincus, L., and Dare, C., *Secrets in the Family*, Faber, 1978.

15 Woodmansey, 1966b, *op. cit.*

16 Bowlby, J., 'Psycho-analysis and Child Care', in Sutherland, J.D., ed., *Psychoanalysis and Contemporary Thought*, Hogarth Press, 1958, reprinted in Bowlby, 1979, *op. cit.*, p. 14.

17 Winnicott, D.W. (ref. not traced).

18 Parkes, *op. cit.*, pp. 212–20.

19 Caplan, *op. cit.*, p. 59.

20 Rogers, 1951, *op. cit.*, pp. 483, 494.

21 Local Authority Social Services Act, 1971.

22 Child Care Act, 1980, s. 27 (also ss. 28–9) This provision may be familiar as

'Section 20 powers' (Children Act, 1948).

23 Stewart, J., and Stewart, G., eds, *Social Work and Homelessness*, Social Work and Homelessness Group, University of Lancaster, 1982.

24 Ricketts, A., 'Surviving after Care', in Stewart and Stewart, *ibid*.

25 Parker, R.A., ed., *Caring for Separated Children: Plans, procedures and priorities*, Macmillan, 1980.

26 Sawbridge, P., 'Seeking New Parents: A decade of development', in Triseliotis, J., ed., *New Developments in Foster Care and Adoption*, Routledge and Kegan Paul, 1980.

27 Erikson, E.H., *Childhood and Society*, Hogarth Press and Penguin Books, 1950.

28 DHSS, *Report of the Committee of Inquiry into the Care and Supervision Provided in Relation to Maria Colwell*, HMSO, 1974, p. 49.

29 Pick, P., *Children at Treetops: An example of creative residential care*, Residential Care Association, London, 1981.

30 Berry, 1975, *op. cit.*, translates into local authority residential social work the ideas about milieu therapy first illustrated by Bettelheim, B., in *Love is Not Enough*, Collier Macmillan/Avon, 1950/71.

31 Winter, A., 'Only People Cry', in *Working with Children who are Joining New Families*, ABAFA, 1977.

32 Brearley, P. *et al.*, *Admission to Residential Care*, Tavistock Publications, 1980, suggest five possible perspectives in admission: provision of a resource (with the social worker as gate-keeper), a crisis experience, separation, emergency, and compulsion.

33 Holden, A.S., *Children in Care*, The Association of Directors of Social Services Guide to Personal Social Services Legislation, Comyn Books, 1980, p. 95.

34 Mann, P., *A Secure Base: Experiences of social work education and practice*, in preparation; Berry, 1975, *op. cit.*, pp. 16–17 and pp. 134–44; Tonnesmann, *op. cit.*, describes the effectiveness of support to nurses in a hospital setting, as does Parker, G., in relation to senior staff, *Social Work Service*, 21, 1979.

35 Bowlby, 1973, *op. cit.*, p. 359, and 1979, *op. cit.*, pp. 103–25.

36 Gutteridge, P., in Brearley, P. *et al.*, *Leaving Residential Care*, Tavistock Publications, 1982, p. 88.

37 Child Care Act, 1980, ss. 28 and 29. Holden, *op. cit.*, p. 96, suggests that there is some overlap between these two sections, but with the person's increasing age (from 16–21) 'the onus passes from the area authority's satisfying itself that the child is not in need of help to the person himself seeking help when he requires it'.

38 Woodmansey, A.C. and Chapman, M.G.T., *Policy in Child Abuse*, Soc. of Clinical Psychiatrists, Derby, in preparation. Berry, 1975, *op. cit.*; Mann, P., 'A fragment of research', Reflections on the Auckland Inquiry, *Social Work Today*, vol. 6, no. 18, 1975.

39 Berry, 1975, *op. cit.*, pp. 10–17.

40 Righton, P., 'Parental and Other Roles in Residential Care', in *The Parental Role*, Conference Papers, National Children's Bureau, 1972.

41 Beedell, C., *Residential Life with Children*, Routledge and Kegan Paul, 1970, pp. 17–18.

42 Newson, E., 'Towards an Understanding of the Parental Role', in *The Parental Role*, Conference Papers, National Children's Bureau, 1972, p. 34.
43 Brearley, *et al.*, 1982, *op. cit.*
44 Winnicott, D.W., *The Child, The Family and the Outside World*, Penguin Books, 1957/64.
45 Reid, A., 'Growing, Flying, Happening', in *Weathering*, Canongate, Edinburgh, 1978, p. 3.

Chapter 3

1 Shaw, M., and Hipgrave, T., *Specialist Fostering*, Batsford Academic and BAAF, 1983, pp. 8–9 on assessment fostering.
2 For instance, Kadushin, A., *Adopting Older Children*, Columbia University Press, 1970; and Tizard, B., *Adoption: A second chance*, Open Books, 1977. For other references see 'Knowledge from research' in *Child Adoption*, ABAFA, 1977.
3 Mann, P., 'Working with Children Towards Placement', in *Working with Children who are Joining New Families*, ABAFA, 1977.
4 Dickens, C., *Dombey and Son*, 1848.
5 Winnicott, C., 'Communicating with Children', in Tod, R.J.N., ed., *Disturbed Children*, Longman, 1968, pp. 70–1. Clare Winnicott's concept of 'a third thing' or shared experience (such as a game, a drawing, a story, a song, a car-ride, feeding the ducks) must have provided many a social worker and uncommunicative child with a safe neutral environment in which to lay the basis for talking about more painful feelings. Crompton, M., in *Respecting Children*, Arnold, 1980, offers further imaginative means of communication.
6 See ch.1 note 6, also Greenwood, A., 'Garry and Darren – their story. The Making of a Life-story Book for Children in Care', *Social Work Today*, vol. 9, no. 34, 1978. The Milestones staff and senior management in County Hall liked the idea of the Drummonds' life-story book, and subsequently all children who passed through Milestones were equipped with a photograph album. The Drummonds' book therefore made history (as well as their own).
7 Gillian was then six and a half. Downes, C., provides useful notes on children's typical reactions to separation at different ages and how the distress can be eased in foster care in DHSS, *Foster Care, A Guide to Practice*, HMSO, 1976, Appendix I.
8 Looking back I wonder why I did not ask Mr Land to come with us, at least for a short time. Presumably he was on duty, and division of roles between field and residential workers was sharper then. Fitzgerald, J., Murcer, B., and Murcer, B., in *Building New Families*, Blackwell, 1982, illustrate how to time the move in relation to the pace the individual child can tolerate and to the personal circumstances of the new family.
9 The 'time limits' (see ch. 2, note 3) now act as a spur to social workers to plan more decisively with parents, and to help them to be more aware of what the passage of time can mean to a child; also that children need continuity of care and a sense of belonging – now, not in some hoped for

future. The other 'time limits' are what is now s. 3(d) of the Child Care Act, 1980, and s.29 of the Children Act, 1975.

10 D. W. Winnicott wrote about transitional objects on many levels – for the 'ordinary good mother' in *The Child and the Family*, Tavistock, 1957; more theoretically in *Collected Papers: Through paediatrics to psycho-analysis*, Tavistock, 1958, and extended his theme further in *Playing and Reality*, Tavistock, 1974. 'Candy Floss' had lived in my car in the four and a half years I had known Mark in Ringshire. It had been one of the comforting objects which he had clutched tearfully that hot summer day – and played with subsequently.

11 Children Act, 1975, s. 12, 2(b). For discussion on dispensing with parental agreement to adoption see McClean, J.D., *The Legal Context of Social Work*, second edition, Butterworth, 1980, pp. 171–7. Also Hoggett, B., *Parents and Children*, second edition, Sweet and Maxwell, 1981, pp. 212–7. 'The majority of adoptions will have parental agreement, but an increasing proportion do not, and one of the most difficult legal problems is how far it is proper to deprive parents of their right to decide' (p. 212). Elsewhere, p. 114, Hoggett expresses the lawyer's view that 'social workers cannot and should not be sure that the courts will support them if the parents . . . oppose an adoption'.

12 In adoption applications 'The child's welfare is now the *first consideration* before the court (Children Act, 1975, s.3) but it is not the *paramount* consideration', Hoggett, *op. cit.*, p. 212. See also Freeman, M.D.A., *The Children Act, 1975*, commentary on s. 3. Only in custody and wardship proceedings is the child's welfare paramount. Much of the 1975 Act was a compromise between the views of the 'psychological' and 'biological parent' lobbies. There was a delicate system of checks and balances in the Act, which veered towards protecting the child's interests, but which also provided appeal procedures and access to legal aid to safeguard parents' rights (when fully implemented). The welfare section respecting children in care is now s. 18 of the Child Care Act, 1980.

13 Rowe, J., and Lambert, L., *Children Who Wait*, ABAA, 1973. 'The work done in the first 6–12 months after admission is crucial in determining whether the child will ever get home again.' And 'The stark reality disclosed by this study is that if a pre-school or primary school age child has been in care for as long as six months, his chances of returning to his parents are slim' (p. 37).

14 Adcock, M., 'The Right of a Child to a Permanent Placement', Rawstron, D., ed., *Rights of Children*, BAAF, 1981. 'It is not possible to say with certainty to the child in local authority care, "This is your home and you will stay here until you are grown up"' (p. 22).

15 Parker, *op. cit.*, is particularly helpful in examining the problems in planning for children and how these may be tackled. See also Parker, R., *Planning for Deprived Children*, National Children's Home, 1971.

16 Mackay, M., 'Planning for Permanent Placement', *Adoption and Fostering*, no. 99, 1980.

17 Hussell, C., and Monaghan, B., 'Child Care Planning in Lambeth', *Adoption and Fostering*, vol. 6, no. 2, 1982.

18 For instance, Holman, R., *Inequality in Child Care*, CPAG, 1976; and Jordan, B., 'Prevention in Achieving Permanence', *Adoption and Fostering*, no. 105, 1981.
19 BAAF evidence to Select Committee, *Adoption and Fostering*, vol. 7, no. 1, 1983.
20 Rowe and Lambert, *op. cit.*
21 Hardy, T., (1840–1928), 'Midnight on the Great Western', *Selected Shorter Poems*, Macmillan, 1966.

Chapter 4

1 Parker, R.A., *Decision in Child Care: A study of prediction in fostering*, Allen and Unwin, 1966, suggested that placement of a foster child too near in age to a child of the family was not a good predictor for success. A pink memo, reminding me of this, arrived from County Hall! Not all Parker's predictions have been validated, partly because social workers took extra care as a result of them. Ralph and Rupert did in fact enjoy each other, and kept in touch for a number of years.
2 'Landmark in Medicine – New "Sterile Ward" Unit', *International Nursing Review*, vol. 11, no. 2, 1964; 'Cancer: New frontiers of diagnosis and treatment', *The Sunday Times*, 6 December, 1964.
3 See ch. 2, note 2.
4 Presented by Jenkins, S., and Norman, E., *Filial Deprivation and Foster Care*, Columbia University Press, 1972; and Davison, R.F., 'Restoring Children to their Families', in Triseliotis, *op. cit.*
5 Mapstone, E., 'Social work with the parents of children in foster care', in Tod, R.J.N., ed., *Social Work in Foster Care*, Longman, 1971a, p. 99.
6 Mapstone, *ibid*, p. 99.
7 Shakespeare, W., *Henry V*, Chorus.
8 Woolf, Virginia, *Mrs Dalloway*, Hogarth Press, 1925, Granada, 1976, p. 6.
9 Downes, *op. cit.*
10 Robertson and Robertson, *op. cit.*, *John, 17 Months, for 9 Days in a Residential Nursery*.
11 For instance, two training packages, *Parenting Plus* and *Added to Adolescence*, National Foster Care Association. A well documented model of foster-parent group support is found in Hazel, N., *A Bridge to Independence*, Blackwell, 1981. See also, Shaw and Hipgrave, *op. cit.*, ch. 6.
12 BASW, *Guidelines for Practice in Family Placement*, 1982.
13 Holman, R., 'The Place of Fostering in Social Work', *British Journal of Social Work*, vol. 5, no. 1, 1975, pp. 3–29, and 'Exclusive and Inclusive Concepts of Fostering', in Triseliotis, *op. cit.* Rowe, J., argues in Triseliotis, *op. cit.*, pp. 63–4, that 'the attributes of both concepts are needed, but in differing mixtures according to the particular child's situation'. And Fuller, R., and Stevenson, O., *Policies, Programmes and Disadvantage*, Heinemann, 1983, pp. 103–4, take a critical look at the status of Holman's contribution.
14 Aldgate, J., 'Factors Influencing Children's Stay in Care', in Triseliotis, *op. cit.*, pp. 22–40.

15 Fanshel, D., 'Parental Visiting of Children in Foster Care: Key to discharge?', *Social Services Review*, vol. 49, no. 4, 1975.
16 Josselyn, I.M., 'Evaluating Motives of Foster Parents', in Tod, 1971a, *op. cit.*
17 Towle, C., Discussion of Josselyn's paper, *ibid.*, pp. 31–7.
18 Kay, N.V., 'Foster Parents as Resources', in Tod, 1971a, *op. cit.*

Chapter 5

1 Young, M., and Willmott, P., *Family and Kinship in East London*, Routledge and Kegan Paul, 1957, Penguin Books, 1962.
2 Gorky, M., *Childhood*, Oxford University Press, 1913, revised English translation, 1961.
3 S. 1 of the Child Care Act, 1980, previously s. 1 of the Children and Young Persons Act, 1963. See ch. 2, note 5.
4 Stevenson, O., Minority Report in DHSS, *Report of the Committee of Inquiry into the Care and Supervision Provided in Relation to Maria Colwell*, HMSO, 1974.
5 Rowe, J. *et al.*, *Long-term Foster Care*, Batsford Academic and BAAF, 1984.
6 Houghton Report, *Report of the Departmental Committee on the Adoption of Children*, HMSO, Cmnd. 5107, 1972, pp. 27–31.
7 Children Act, 1975, Part II, Custodianship Orders, s. 37.
8 Shakespeare, W., *Macbeth*, Act IV, Scene 2.
9 DHSS, *Foster Care: A guide to practice*, HMSO, 1976, ch. 16, 'Relatives as Foster Parents'.
10 Rowe *et al.*, 1984, *op. cit.*
11 Suttie, I.D., *The Origins of Love and Hate*, Kegan Paul, 1935, Penguin Books, 1960, ch. 6.
12 Suttie, *ibid.*

Chapter 6

1 Rowe, J., *Yours By Choice: A guide for adoptive parents*, second edition, Routledge and Kegan Paul, 1982, p. 64.
2 *Report of the Committee on One-parent Families*, HMSO, Cmnd. 5629, 1974.
3 Children and Young Persons Act, 1933, Schedule 1 lists offences against children, including sexual offences. The Children Act, 1975 later inserted as an additional primary condition for the making of a Care Order the presence or likely presence, in the same household as a child, of a person who has been convicted of a Schedule 1 offence. This becomes s. 1 2(bb) of the Children and Young Persons Act, 1969.
4 'Dorset County Council Child Care Service', Report to the Secretary of State for the Home Department by the Chief Inspector, Children's Department, Home Office, HMSO, 1966.
5 Master of Foxhounds. As these two later jobs were in the next county we could have asked that local authority to supervise for us, but as I had known Michelle through various vicissitudes it was agreed that I could continue the supervision.

6 The previous system under which a parent's written consent to adoption was witnessed by a single justice or court officer is now replaced under s. 20 of the Children Act 1975 (implemented May '84). This provides for the appointment of a reporting officer who will witness agreements to adoption and be specially qualified to discuss the decision with the parent. The reporting officer will also investigate and report on Freeing for Adoption applications (s.14). See Houghton Report, *op. cit.*, paras 174–81 and 187, and M.D.A. Freeman's commentary on s.20.
7 Raynor, L., *Giving up a Baby for Adoption*, ABAA, 1971.
8 Packman, *op. cit.*, p. 101.
9 Crellin, Kellmer-Pringle and West, *op. cit.*; and Seglow, J., Kellmer-Pringle, M.L., and Wedge, P., *Growing up Adopted*, NFER, 1972; both of these contrasting studies were part of the national longitudinal study of a cohort of all children born in one week in March 1958.
10 Lambert and Streather, *op. cit.*
11 See ch. 3 note 2. Raynor, L., has added to this encouraging evidence in *The Adopted Child Comes of Age*, Allen and Unwin, 1980.
12 Rowe and Lambert, *op. cit.*
13 Packman, J., *Child Care: Needs and Numbers*, Allen and Unwin, 1968.
14 Rowe, J., *Parents, Children and Adoption, A handbook for adoption workers*, Routledge and Kegan Paul, 1966. The law, and indeed the whole adoption scene as well as attitudes to illegitimacy, have changed since this book was written, but there is still much in it that is helpful to practitioners about casework with natural parents.
15 Timms, *op. cit.*, p. 26.
16 Hill, S., *The Magic Apple Tree: A country year*, Hamish Hamilton, 1982, p. 13.
17 Children Act, 1975, s. 26; for discussion see Houghton Report, pp. 83–7.
18 Children Act, 1975, First Report to Parliament, HMSO, 1979.
19 Leeding, A., 'Access to Birth Records', *Adoption and Fostering*, no. 89, 1977; and Day, C., 'Access to birth Records, General Register Office Study', *Adoption and Fostering*, no. 98, 1979. Both these studies are now available in Hall, T., ed., *Access to Birth Records: The impact of s.26 of the Children Act, 1975*, BAAF, 1980.
20 Triseliotis, J., *In Search of Origins: The experiences of adopted people*, Routledge and Kegan Paul, 1973.
21 Day, C. in Hall, *op. cit.*, p. 32.
22 Smith, Stevie, *Selected Poems*, ed. MacGibbon, J., Penguin Books, 1975/78, 'Human affection', p. 92.

Chapter 7

1 Houghton Report, *op. cit.*, p. 4.
2 *ibid.*, pp. 5 and 59–62, and see ch. 3 note 12.
3 Children Act, 1975, s.3. See ch. 3 note 12.
4 Summarised by Rowe, J., in 'Adoption in the 70s', in *Planning for Children in Long-term Care*, ABAFA, 1976; and by Packman, 1975/81, *op. cit.*, pp. 86–101.

5 See ch. 3 note 2, and ch. 6 note 11; also Maas, H., ed., 'Child Welfare', in *Research in the Social Services: A five year review*, Nat. Assoc. of Social Workers, 1971. Subsequently, Jewett, C.L., *Adopting the Older Child*, Harvard Common Press, 1978, and Churchill, S.R., Carlson, B., and Nibel, L., *No Child is Unadoptable*, Sage Publications, Beverley Hills and London, 1979, have also been influential.

6 Adoption Act, 1958, s. 37(1).

7 Goodacre, I., *Adoption Policy and Practice*, Allen and Unwin, 1966, pp. 121–8.

8 Houghton Report, *op. cit.*, pp. 23–5; Children Act, 1975, s. 28(a) amends s. 29 of the Adoption Act, 1958. In future those who arrange private placements and those who benefit from them will be liable to prosecution, except where the placement is with a relative (narrowly defined as the child's grandparent, brother, sister, uncle or aunt). See also BAAF practice notes, 1, *Private Placements*, 1982.

9 Adoption Act, 1958, s. 38.

10 Goodacre, *op. cit.*, p. 84.

11 Children Act, 1975, s. 22(3). Implemented May '84. See Houghton Report, *op. cit.*, paras 237–40; and Packman 1975/81, *op. cit.*, pp. 93–4 and 98.

12 *A Service of Blessing upon the Adoption of a Child*, Church Information Office, Church House, Westminster, London.

13 S.20 of the Children Act 1975 (implemented May '84) now amends s.9 of the Adoption Act 1958. The appointment of a guardian *ad litem* will in future be made at the discretion of the court, rather than mandatory in all applications. See Houghton Report, *op. cit.*, paras 244–56 and recommendations 61–3.

14 Children Act 1975, s.14. Implemented May '84. See Freeman, M.D.A. commentary on s.14 for the thinking behind the new 'freeing' procedure. 75% of mothers in Raynor's 1971 study, *op. cit.*, thought that consent once given should be final and irrevocable; 80% said that the finalising of consent was too slow.

15 This was a needless fear. Agencies then and now have different eligibility criteria.

16 Kirk, D., *Shared Fate*, The Free Press, New York, Collier-Macmillan, London, 1964.

17 For instance, Rowe, J., 'The Reality of the Adoptive Family', in Tod, R., ed., *Social Work and Adoption*, Longman, 1971b; Berry, J., 'The Authenticity of Parenthood by Adoption', in *Child Adoption*, ABAFA, 1977; Triseliotis, 1973, *op. cit.*; McWhinnie, A., *Adopted Children: How they grow up*, Routledge and Kegan Paul, 1967; Raynor, L., 'Twenty-One Plus and Adopted', *Adoption and Fostering*, no. 87, 1977; and Raynor, 1980, *op. cit.*

18 For instance, Althea, *Jane is Adopted*, Souvenir Press, 1980; Lapsley, S., *I am Adopted*, Bodley Head, 1974; Livingstone, C., *Why was I Adopted?*, Angus and Robertson, 1978.

19 Goodacre, *op. cit.*

20 Triseliotis, J., 'Identity and Security in Adoption and Long-term fostering', *Adoption and Fostering*, vol. 7, no. 1, 1983.

21 Raynor, 1980, *op. cit.*
22 Lee, J., 'A sense of belonging', *Adoption and Fostering*, no. 97, 1979.
23 Triseliotis, 1973, *op. cit.*
24 McWhinnie, *op. cit.*; Triseliotis, *ibid.*; and Raynor, 1980, *op. cit.*
25 Triseliotis, 1983, *op. cit.*

Chapter 8

1 Child Care Act, 1980, s.18.
2 Freeman, 1980, *op. cit.*, commentary on s.18.
3 Parsloe, P., 'How Training May "Unfit" People', *Social Work Today*, vol. 9, no. 4, 1977.
4 Goldstein, J., Freud, A., and Solnit, A.J., *Beyond the Best Interests of the Child*, Free Press, New York, 1973; and Robertson, J., and Robertson, J., 'The Psychological Parent', *Adoption and Fostering*, no. 87, 1977.
5 Goldstein, Freud and Solnit, *op. cit.*
6 Solnit, A.J., 'Least Harmful to Children', *Adoption and Fostering*, no. 87, 1977.
7 Much has been written about bonding and about attachment and separation. Fahlberg, V., *Attachment and Separation*, BAAF, 1981; *Helping children when they must move*, BAAF, 1981; and *Child Development*, BAAF, 1982, are helpful on a practical level.
8 Triseliotis, 1973, *op. cit.*, p. 84.
9 Smith, C.L., 'The New Families Project', in Triseliotis, 1980, *op. cit.*, p. 205.
10 'Talking about origins' – one of three leaflets produced by BAAF for all parties affected by s. 26 of the Children Act, 1975 – this one for adopters; the other two are for people who are adopted and for parents who placed a child for adoption years ago.

Chapter 9

1 Robertson and Robertson, 1976, *op. cit.*
2 Kerrane, A., 'Timing the Introduction', *Adoption and Fostering*, no. 96, 1979.
3 Katz, L., 'Older Child Adoptive Placement: A time of family crisis', *Child Welfare*, vol. LVI, no. 3, 1977.
4 Bowlby, J., 'Psychoanalysis and Child Care', in 1979, *op. cit.*, pp. 9–12.
5 Tizard, *op. cit.*
6 Rowe, 1966, *op. cit.*, pp. 255–6; and Jewett, *op. cit.*, pp. 160 and 173–6.
7 Day Lewis, C., 'Walking away', *Selected Poems*, Penguin Books, 1951/69, p. 35.
8 Now s. 3 resolution, Child Care Act, 1980, previously s.2, Children Act, 1948.
9 Bowlby, 1979, *op. cit.*, p. 12.
10 Woodmansey, 1966b, *op. cit.*
11 Berry, J., *Social Work with Children*, Routledge and Kegan Paul, 1972, discusses defences in terms of 'reappraisal' of information for internal and

external publication, pp. 49–50.
12 Kay, in Tod, 1971a, *op. cit.*
13 Berry, 1972, *op. cit.*
14 Raynor, 1980, *op. cit.*, found that her study tended 'to confirm that for certain adoptive parents something much less than an ideal or problem-free situation can prove satisfying over the years if the difficulties have some compensations' pp. 34–5.
15 Abelard, P., *Medieval Latin Lyrics*, 'Good Friday: The Third Nocturne', trs. Waddell, H., Penguin Classics, 1953, pp. 178–9.
16 It was not particularly relevant to Georgie to make the point that the new legislation which allows access to birth records for adopted people over 18 does not accord a parallel right to natural parents to have access to their grown-up (adopted) children. The initiative rests with the person adopted. The BAAF leaflet 'A child from the past' gives advice to natural parents.
17 Tizard, *op. cit.*
18 Miller, *op. cit.*
19 Day Lewis, *op. cit.*, p. 35.

Chapter 10

1 Younghusband, E., Birchall, D., Davie, R., Kellmer-Pringle, M.L., eds, *Living with Handicap*, National Bureau for Co-operation in Child Care, 1970, p. 211.
2 Parkes, *op. cit.*, ch. 11.
3 Fried, M., 'Grieving for a Lost Home', in Duhl, L.J., ed., *The Environment of the Metropolis*, Basic Books, New York, 1962.
4 Marris, *op. cit.*
5 *ibid.*, p. 44.
6 Bayley, M.J., *Mental Handicap and Community Care*, Routledge and Kegan Paul, 1973.
7 CCETSW, *People with Handicaps Need Better Trained Workers*, 1974.
8 Stevenson, O., and Parsloe, P., *Social Service Teams, The Practitioner's View*, HMSO, 1978, pp. 335, 304.
9 Stevenson, O., *Specialisation in Social Service Teams*, Allen and Unwin, 1981.
10 Anderson, D., *Social Work and Mental Handicap*, Macmillan, 1982.
11 DHSS, *Fit for the Future – The Report of the Committee on Child Health Services* (Court Report), HMSO, 1976.
12 *Better Services for the Mentally Handicapped*, HMSO, 1971.
13 For instance, Cole, R., Greatorex, D., and Preston, N., 'Stretching out a Hand to Those Facing an Uncertain Future', *Social Work Today*, vol. 11, no. 47, 1980.
14 Schaefer, N., *Does She Know She's There?*, Harper and Row, 1978, Futura Publications, 1979.
15 Olshanski, S., 'Chronic Sorrow: A response to having a mentally handicapped child', in Younghusband, E., ed., *Social Work with Families*, Allen and Unwin, 1965.
16 Ballard, R., 'The missing milestones', *Community Care*, 4 February, 1982;

and in Lonsdale, G., Elfer, P., and Ballard, R., *Children, Grief and Social Work*, Blackwell, 1979.

17 Turvill, P., 'Incest', *Adoption and Fostering*, no. 104, 1981.
18 *Genetics in Adoption and Fostering*, Practice Series: 8, BAAF, 1982.
19 Wolkind, S.N., *Medical Aspects of Adoption and Foster Care*, Heinemann, 1979.
20 Private communication from Tony Hall, BAAF.
21 Heron, A., *Mentally Handicapped School Leavers: A follow-up study*, E.R.G. Reports, no. 13, Evaluation Research Group, University of Sheffield, 1981, p. 25.
22 Hill, S., *The Albatross and Other Stories*, Hamish Hamilton, 1971, Penguin Books, 1974, pp. 24, 34.
23 Oppenheimer, H., *The Hope of Happiness: A sketch for a Christian humanism*, SCM Press, 1983.

Chapter 11

1 Townsend, P., *Poverty in the United Kingdom*, Penguin, 1979, gives evidence of public unawareness of poverty. Quoted by Fuller and Stevenson, *op. cit.*, p. 197.
2 In *Radical Social Work and Practice*, Brake, M., and Bailey, R., eds, Arnold, 1980, argue that 'social workers, *like other workers*, are trapped in a structure which severely delimits their power and hence their ability to initiate significant change. Social workers, *unlike other workers*, confront daily, as their job, the victims of an economic and political structure that creates poverty and humiliation' pp. 7–8. Examples are given of ways in which social workers may attempt to tackle some of the inherent frustrations. Statham, D., in *Radicals in Social Work*, Routledge and Kegan Paul, 1978, also writes from a feminist viewpoint.
3 Now Child Care Act, 1980, s.27, also ss. 28, 29; see ch. 2, notes 22, 37. Holden, *op. cit.*, adds, 'It is vitally important that children are informed of their right to seek help in later years when they go out of care' p. 96.
4 Halmos, P., *The Personal and the Political: Social work and political action*, Hutchinson, 1978.
5 This adaptation from the revolutionary song 'Praise of Learning' – which conveys that learning is a weapon that leads to power – was chosen by Liz. From the play, Brecht, B., *The Mother* (based on the novel by Maxim Gorky); published in exile in *Lieder, Gedichte, Chöre (Songs, Poems and Chorus)*, Editions du Carrefour, Paris, 1934.

Chapter 12

1 Timms, N., and Haimes, E., *Access to Birth Records and Counselling of Adopted Persons under Section 26 of the Children Act, 1975*, Report to the DHSS, 1983.
2 Curnock, K., and Hardiker, P., *Towards Practice Theory: Skills and methods in social assessments*, Routledge and Kegan Paul, 1979.
3 Fuller and Stevenson, *op. cit.*, p. 193.

4 Rutter, M., and Quinton, D., 'Childhood Experiences and Parenting Behaviour', reports to the DHSS/SSRC, 1979 and 1980.

5 Rowe *et al.*, 1984, *op. cit.*

6 Smayle, G.G., *Prophecy, Behaviour and Change: An examination of self-fulfilling prophecies in helping relationships*, Routledge and Kegan Paul, 1977.

7 In the context of group teaching for medical students, Woodmansey illustrates the kinds of fears which can prevent people from being helped, and demonstrates how these fears may be met. Woodmansey, A.C., 'The Nurturing of Medical Students: A psychotherapeutic approach to psychiatric education', *American Journal of Psychotherapy*, vol. 33, no. 4, 1979b, pp. 592–602.

8 DHSS, *Foster Care – A Guide to Practice*, HMSO, 1976, p. 133.

9 Fuller and Stevenson, *op. cit.*, pp. 56–61.

10 For instance Berry, 1972, *op. cit.* and 1975, *op. cit.*; and Woodmansey, 1966b, *op. cit.*, and 'The Common Factor in Problems of Adolescence', *Br. J. Med. Psychol.*, vol. 42, 1969, pp. 353–70.

11 Winnicott, C., 'Face to Face with Children', *Social Work Today*, vol. 8, 26, 1977.

12 Crompton, *op. cit.*

13 James, in Brandon and Jordan, *op. cit.*

14 Younghusband, Foreword to Kahan, *op. cit.*

15 Winnicott, C., *Social Work in Child Care*, Bookstall Publications, 1964, p. 43.

16 Jordan, B., *Helping in Social Work*, Routledge and Kegan Paul, 1979.

17 Berry, 1972, *op. cit.*, pp. 77–81.

18 Bodkin, T., *The Approach to Painting*, Collins, 1945.

Select Bibliography

ADAMSON, G., *The Care-takers*, Bookstall Publications, 1973.

BARCLAY, P., *Social Workers: Their roles and tasks*, Report of the Barclay Committee, NCVO, Bedford Square Press, 1982.

BEEDELL, C., *Residential Life with Children*, Routledge and Kegan Paul, 1970.

BERRY, J., *Social Work with Children*, Routledge and Kegan Paul, 1972.

BERRY, J., *Daily Experience in Residential Life: A study of children and their care-givers*, Routledge and Kegan Paul, 1975.

BOWLBY, J., *Separation, Anxiety and Anger*, vol. 2 of *Attachment and Loss*, The Hogarth Press, 1973.

BOWLBY, J., *The Making and Breaking of Affectional Bonds*, Tavistock Publications, 1979.

BRAKE, M., and BAILEY, R., eds, *Radical Social Work and Practice*, Arnold, 1980.

BRANDON, D., and JORDAN, B., eds, *Creative Social Work*, Blackwell, 1979.

BREARLEY, P. *et al.*, *Admission to Residential Care*, Tavistock Publications, 1980.

BREARLEY, P. *et al.*, *Leaving Residential Care*, Tavistock Publications, 1982.

Central Council for Education and Training in Social Work, *Good Enough Parenting*, 1978.

COOPER, J., *Patterns of Family Placement*, National Children's Bureau, 1978.

CROMPTON, M., *Respecting Children*, Arnold, 1980.

CURNOCK, K., and HARDIKER, P., *Towards Practice Theory: Skills and methods in social assessments*, Routledge and Kegan Paul, 1979.

Curtis Report, *Report of the Care of Children Committee*, Cmnd. 6922, HMSO, 1946.

DHSS, *Foster Care: A guide to practice*, HMSO, 1976.

DHSS (Social Work Service), *Study of the Boarding Out of Children*, 1981.

FAHLBERG, V., *Attachment and Separation*, BAAF, 1981.

FAHLBERG, V., *Helping Children When They Must Move*, BAAF, 1981.

FAHLBERG, V., *Child Development*, BAAF, 1982.

FERGUSON, T., *Children in Care – and After*, Oxford University Press, 1966.

FESTINGER, T., *No One Ever Asked Us . . . A postscript to foster care*, Columbia University Press, 1983.

Finer Report, DHSS, *Report of the Committee on One-parent Families*, Cmnd. 5629, HMSO, 1974.

FITZGERALD, J., MURCER, B., and MURCER, B., *Building New Families*, Blackwell, 1982.

FITZGERALD, J., *Understanding Disruption*, BAAF, 1983.

FORD, J., *Human Behaviour: Towards a practical understanding*, Routledge and Kegan Paul, 1982.

FREEMAN, M.D.A., *The Child Care and Foster Care Acts, 1980*, Sweet and Maxwell, 1980.

FULLER, R., and STEVENSON, O., *Policies, Programmes and Disadvantage: A review of the literature*, Heinemann, 1983.

GEORGE, V., *Foster Care*, Routledge and Kegan Paul, 1970.

GILL, O., and JACKSON, B., *Adoption and Race: Black, Asian and mixed race children in white families*, Batsford Academic and BAAF, 1983.

GOLDSTEIN, J., FREUD, A., and SOLNIT, A.J., *Beyond the Best Interests of the Child*, Free Press, New York 1973.

HALL, T., ed., *Access to Birth Records: The impact of Section 26 of the Children Act, 1975*, BAAF, 1980.

HEYWOOD, J., *Children in Care*, second edition, Routledge and Kegan Paul, 1965.

HITCHMAN, J., *The King of the Barbareens*, Penguin Books, 1960.

HOGGETT, B., *Parents and Children*, second edition, Sweet and Maxwell, 1981.

HOLDEN, A.S., *Children in Care: The Association of Directors of Social Services guide to personal social services legislation*, Comyn Books, 1980.

HOLMAN, R., *Inequality in Child Care*, CPAG, 1976.

Houghton Report, *Report of the Departmental Committee on the Adoption of Children*, Cmnd. 5107, HMSO, 1972.

JEWETT, C.L., *Adopting the Older Child*, Harvard Common Press, 1978.

JORDAN, B., *Helping in Social Work*, Routledge and Kegan Paul, 1979.

KADUSHIN, A., *Adopting Older Children*, Columbia University Press, 1970.

KAHAN, B., *Growing Up in Care*, Blackwell, 1980.

LAMBERT, L., and STREATHER, J., *Children in Changing Families*, Macmillan, 1980.

LONSDALE, G., ELFER, P., and BALLARD, R., *Children, Grief and Social Work*, Blackwell, 1979.

MANN, P., 'Working with Children', in *Working with Children who are Joining New Families*, ABAFA, 1977.

MARRIS, P., *Loss and Change*, Routledge and Kegan Paul, 1974.

MAYER, J.E. and TIMMS, N., *The Client Speaks*, Routledge and Kegan Paul, 1970.

MCCLEAN, J.D., *The Legal Context of Social Work*, second edition, Butterworth, 1980.

MCWHINNIE, A., *Adopted children: How they grow up*, Routledge and Kegan Paul, 1967.

NEWSON, E., 'Towards an Understanding of the Parental Role', in *The Parental Role*, Conference Papers, National Children's Bureau, 1972.

PACKMAN, J., *Child Care: Needs and numbers*, Allen and Unwin, 1968.

PACKMAN, J., *The Child's Generation: Child care policy in Britain*, second edition, Blackwell and Martin Robertson, 1981.

PAGE, R., and CLARK, G., eds, *Who Cares? Young People in Care Speak Out*, National Children's Bureau, 1977.

PARKER, R., ed., *Caring for Separated Children*, Macmillan, 1980.

PARKES, C.M., *Bereavement: Studies of grief in adult life*, Penguin Books, 1972/75.

PICK, P., *Children at Treetops*, Residential Care Association, 1981.

PUCH, E., *Social Work in Child Care*, Routledge and Kegan Paul, 1968.

O'NEIL, T., *A Place Called Hope*, Blackwell, 1981.

RAWSTRON, D., ed., *Rights of Children*, BAAF, 1981.

RAYNOR, L., *Giving up a Baby for Adoption*, ABAA, 1971.

RAYNOR, L., *The Adopted Child Comes of Age*, Allen and Unwin, 1980.

RICKETTS, A., 'Surviving after Care', in STEWART, J., and STEWART, G., eds, *Social Work and Homelessness*, University of Lancaster, 1982.

ROBERTSON, J., and ROBERTSON, J., *Young Children in Brief Separation: A guide to the film series*, The Robertson Centre, London, 1976.

ROGERS, C., *On Becoming a Person*, Constable, 1961.

ROWE, J., *Yours By Choice: A guide for adoptive parents*, second edition, Routledge and Kegan Paul, 1982.

ROWE, J. et al., *Long-term Foster Care*, Batsford Academic and BAAF, 1984.

ROWE, J., and LAMBERT, L., *Children Who Wait*, ABAA, 1973.

RUTTER, M., and QUINTON, D., 'Childhood Experiences and Parenting Behaviour', reports to the DHSS/SSRC, 1979 and 1980.

SAINSBURY, E., *Social Work with Families*, Routledge and Kegan Paul, 1975.

SAINSBURY, E., and NIXON, S., *Social Work in Focus*, Routledge and Kegan Paul, 1982.

SCHAFFER, H.R., *Mothering*, Fontana, 1977.

SEGLOW, J., KELLMER-PRINGLE, M.L. and WEDGE, P., *Growing up Adopted*, National Foundation for Educational Research, 1972.

SHAW, M., and HIPGRAVE, T., *Specialist Fostering*, Batsford Academic and BAAF, 1983.

SHEFFIELD UNIVERSITY, *In and Out of Care* – Research under the auspices of SSRC, 1984.

STEVENSON, O., and PARSLOE, P., *Social Service Teams: The practitioner's view*, HMSO, 1978.

STEVENSON, O., *Specialisation in Social Service Teams*, Allen and Unwin, 1981.

TIMMS, N., ed., *The Receiving End: Consumer accounts of social help for children*, Routledge and Kegan Paul, 1973.

TIMMS, N., and HAIMES, E., *Access to Birth Records and Counselling of Adopted Persons under Section 26 of the Children Act, 1975*, Report to the DHSS, 1983.

TIZARD, B., *Adoption: A second chance*, Open Books, 1977.

TOD, R., ed., *Social Work in Foster Care*, Longman, 1971a.

TOD, R., ed., *Social Work in Adoption*, Longman, 1971b.

TOWNSEND, P., *Poverty in the United Kingdom*, Penguin Books, 1979.

TRISELIOTIS, J., *In Search of Origins: The experiences of adopted people*, Routledge and Kegan Paul, 1973.

TRISELIOTIS, J., ed., *New Developments in Foster Care and Adoption*, Routledge and Kegan Paul, 1980.

TRISELIOTIS, J., 'Identity and Security in Adoption and Long-term Fostering', *Adoption and Fostering*, vol. 7, no. 1, 1983.

WEINSTEIN, E., *The Self-image of the Foster Child*, Russell Sage Foundation, 1966.

WINNICOTT, C., *Social Work in Child Care*, Bookstall Publications, 1964/70.

WINNICOTT, D.W., *Playing and Reality*, Penguin Books, 1974.

WOLKIND, S.N., *Medical Aspects of Adoption and Foster Care*, Heinemann, 1979.

WOLKIND, S.N., and RUTTER, M., 'Children Who have been "In Care": An epidemiological study', *Journal of Child Psychology and Psychiatry*, 14, 1973.

WOODMANSEY, A.C., 'Transmission of Problems from Parents to Children', in *Mental Illness in the Family: Its effect on the child*, NAMH, 1966.

WOODMANSEY, A.C., 'The Unity of Casework', *Social Work Today*, vol. 2, no. 19, 1972.

WOODMANSEY, A.C., 'First Things First: A blueprint for mental health', *Public Health*, vol. 93, 1979.

WOODMANSEY, A.C., and CHAPMAN, M.G.T., *Policy in Child Abuse*, Society of Clinical Psychiatrists, Derby, in preparation.

YOUNGHUSBAND, E., *Social Work in Britain, 1950–1975*, Allen and Unwin, 1978.

Index